Michael Barnett is a retired Civil Engineer from Wellington, New Zealand. Initially, he worked as a geotechnician before moving to Chicago in 1967 to undertake advanced studies in Civil Engineering. During a career spanning fifty years, he travelled extensively in the 1970s, working in countries as diverse as Samoa, Spain, Saudi Arabia, Nigeria, Indonesia, the UAE, the USA, Australia, and latterly in Chile, Peru, Columbia, and Southeast Asia.

Michael is a writer and a thinker with a special interest in national and international affairs. He reads extensively and writes about the political issues of the day, including their historical context.

To my parents Malcolm and Audrey, who gave me the freedom to explore my
world.

Michael Barnett

FINDING MICHAEL: A JOURNEY IN SEARCH OF MY SOUL

AUSTIN MACAULEY PUBLISHERS®

LONDON * CAMBRIDGE * NEW YORK * SHARJAH

A CIP catalogue record for this title is available from the British Library.

ISBN 9781035855209 (Paperback)
ISBN 9781035855216 (ePub e-book)

www.austinmacauley.com

First Published 2024
Austin Macauley Publishers Ltd®
1 Canada Square
Canary Wharf
London
E14 5AA

"If you don't know where you are going, how can you expect to get there?"

For as far back as I can remember I displayed an interest in the world around me and as my horizons expanded I set out to explore that world with all its wonder, contradictions and complexity. This took me on a journey from the close confines of the community into which I was born onto a much wider world and exposed me to the vagaries of life throughout my country of birth and on five continents around the world. Along the way I recorded details of my travels, initially through letters home and in more recent times compiling detailed journals of my travels. I have shared the tales of my adventures with family and friends and the positive feedback I received convinced me that I had a tale worth telling to a larger audience. This memoir is the result of what I call my bachelor days.

My thanks to the Editorial Board of Austin Macauley Publishers who accepted the raw manuscript that in their words "deserves to be published and given the opportunity to be launched for the reading public" and to the production and editorial team who have made it happen.

A special thanks to; David Hollands fellow engineer and an early mentor who picked me up and guided me during in the initial stages of my career when I risked losing my way, Professor Bob who imparted in me the intellectual stimulus to question the way the world works and enthusiastically commented on drafts of the manuscript, and Malcolm Wilson my mental coach and mentor who likewise read and commented on the draft manuscript and continues to encourage me in my endeavours.

Finally, I wish to acknowledge my family and friends whose interest and encouragement spurred me on to writing this book. These include my late my parents, Malcolm and Audrey, who gave me the freedom to develop and explore my world, my wife Sue, daughter Amy, siblings Philip, Catherine, Vivienne and Jenny, and all the members of my extended family. I say thank you for showing your interest and helping me navigate the various stages of my life journey.

Table of Contents

Prologue

I have often been called Mike, the Quiet One. During a visit to Cuzco, Peru, in 2009, my Spanish-speaking hosts dubbed me 'Mike Mysterioso'. I readily admit that I have my introspective side, but somewhere deep inside, there is another Michael, a soul mate who occasionally breaks out and fills my world with joy and laughter. This is a tale about my early years and search for this other Michael.

Introduction

During my early teenage years, I spent my summer vacations in my father's office at the Shaw Savill & Albion Line, a UK shipping company with an office in Wellington, where I worked as a mail delivery boy. My tasks included twice daily trips to the post office to collect mail, sorting and circulating it around the office, and delivering ship's mail when each ship came in. An additional duty was raising and lowering the company flag each day on the roof of the Tower Insurance building in Central Wellington. There was plenty of variety, I had a lot of fun and my coffers grew bigger from the money earned and saved.

However, observing the boredom and sadness on the faces of many of the older employees, and my dad's efforts to survive the petty politics that prevailed, I decided a career in shipping was definitely not for me.

During these years, I was encouraged to think about a career and life after my school days. I had a love of the outdoors and mathematics was my best subject at school. Placing a loose connection between the two led me to opt for civil engineering as a vocation. I cruised through my school days enjoying the sporting, social and recreational activities on offer and doing enough academically to persuade the teaching staff to accredit me with University Entrance, as was the custom in those days.

Somehow they got it wrong for I was far from ready for tertiary study, as the dismal results of two years of study at Victoria University of Wellington testify. At the end of the second year, my dream of being a civil engineer was slowly fading.

David, a tennis buddy and several years my senior, was a surveyor/engineer with a small consulting firm in Lower Hutt. One fine day, while playing tennis, he casually enquired about my progress. I told him of my miserable exam results and my despair of ever making the grade. Being older, wiser and perhaps recognising some latent talent, he invited me to apply for a job in a soil and concrete testing laboratory his employer had just set up. With nothing else on the horizon, I took up the offer and started my first career job, sans qualification.

The 1960s was a decade of economic prosperity in New Zealand and other parts of the so-called Western world. Jobs were plenty and if you didn't like the first one, there was always another just down the road. Here, in Wellington, there was an explosion in housing development and heavy earthwork machinery was to be seen everywhere carving off the hilltops and filling in the gullies to create building plots for new homeowners, many of whom financed their purchase through government housing loans paying 3 per cent per annum in interest. I was inducted into the art of soil testing and quickly became part of the action.

Commercial development was also booming and the second generation of high-rise buildings in Wellington were growing fast. I also had part of this action, being involved in the exploratory drilling and collection of core samples for testing the engineering quality for the design of foundations of these new and taller buildings. As I gained in confidence and experience, I was sent further afield and during the next four years, I travelled up and down the country performing these and other tasks assigned to me.

I enrolled in night classes and studied for the NZ Certificate of Engineering, the precursor of the diploma course that exists today. I was doing well in my studies and sometime along the way, I decided I should go on to university when I completed this course. By now, I was in my early twenties and itching to go abroad and explore the world. I started investigating opportunities to study in America and to cut a long story short, after four years of work and study, I completed my diploma and I was accepted at the Illinois Institute of Technology in Chicago commencing in the northern spring of 1967.

I packed my bags, said goodbye to family and friends, and set off on what turned out to be an amazing experience. Looking back, it was one of the more exciting times of my life.

The late 1960s was a fascinating time to be in America. Hippiedom was flowering and free love abounded. The Vietnam War was escalating and the cream of US youth was being sent off to fight a senseless war, resulting in growing protests and unrest on campuses across the nation. Martin Luther King was assassinated six months after I arrived, and four months later, Robert Kennedy, brother of JFK, suffered the same fate. Chicago erupted on both occasions and the National Guard was brought in to restore law and order.

As for me, I kept my head down, and focused on my studies and the social life around campus and in the city. I also took up opportunities to travel further afield, when the opportunity arose and I made many good friends, both American and students from around the globe.

My student visa gave me temporary residence status in the US, but there were rules attached and those relating to employment were quite explicit, restricting me to part-time work on campus and employment during summer vacation. This created a problem, for even with cross credits, I was faced with the prospect of two to three years of full-time study to complete my degree.

My meagre savings made even smaller by a 10 per cent devaluation of the New Zealand dollar in November 1967, had got me to Chicago and paid for my tuition, accommodation and basic living during my first year. Earnings from a job in the chemistry laboratory and a summer job in Portland, Oregon, carried me into my third semester, but the coffers were running low. Barring a miracle, my prospects for staying on beyond my third semester looked grim.

As I pondered my predicament, I noted an obscure clause relating to my visa, which effectively stated that if I faced unforeseen economic hardship during my stay, I could seek dispensation on the restricted work rule. Using the devaluation of the NZ dollar as justification, I applied to the authorities and was granted dispensation to seek part-time work while I continued my studies. Good fortune smiled upon me, for soon after, I landed a part-time job in the waterworks department of the city of Chicago. I soon found out this was not only a job but also an opportunity to study and get paid for my efforts at the same time.

I could report in any time during the normal working week and my official tasks were not that onerous. I came to refer to this as my Mayor Daley* scholarship. The $3 per hour I earned for my presence plus money from a real scholarship I secured six months later was sufficient to carry me through the rest of my studies and buy a beat-up car in the bargain.

I graduated in 1970 and through the next decade, I became a nomad travelling further afield practicing my chosen vocation. After a brief spell working in Boston and two years back in New Zealand, I made my way first to Samoa, then on to London where I joined a multinational American engineering consultancy. Still single and in search of adventure, I was willing to go anywhere and my employer was quick to oblige. Assignments in Spain, Saudi Arabia, Nigeria, Indonesia, the USA, and back to the Middle East came and went one after the other. My suitcase was always packed and a hotel room or construction camp was my home.

However, all good things come to an end and by the end of the decade, I had tired of the constant travel and returned home to New Zealand. I went through a lengthy unsettled period where I had a number of jobs none of which strongly appealed. Marriage, the arrival of my daughter, Amy, and the associated family responsibilities settled me down. Initially, I found employment with the government's Ministry of Works. Facing redundancy, there followed a stint in Melbourne Australia before returning to join the Wellington City Council, where I worked throughout the 1990s as a supervising engineer then manager of the Roading Design Unit.

I took charge of a business unit comprising nineteen technical staff, which I whittled down to thirteen, a manageable size to handle the work being undertaken by the unit. One of my significant tasks during the early 1990s was working as a liaison engineer to Tranzit NZ on the planning of the motorway extension between the Terrace Tunnel and the Basin Reserve. During this time, I undertook independent studies of transport planning in urban areas and compiled a paper entitled *Transport Policy in Wellington: A Report on Planning Issues,* which I presented at the 1992 Conference of New Zealand Institution of Professional Engineers.

During a round of restructuring in 1999, the Roading Design Unit was disbanded, I was made redundant for the second time and I set out on a new path and changed to a new vocation as a personal financial planner. I joined a small group of financial planners as a financial planning advisor and commenced part-time studies towards a Diploma in Personal Financial Planning at Massey University. I lasted three months with this group, during which, I attended several industry seminars and conferences run by major fund management organisations.

This exposure was sufficient to show me that the financial planning industry was commission-based and financial planners were nothing more than insurance salespeople dressed in new clothes, selling a new product. I quit my job and set about doing it my way by offering a fee-based service, placing emphasis on sound planning as the basis for achieving one's personal goals in life. I continued my studies, completed my diploma and continued to operate for several years, and published a book *Towards Financial Freedom* on personal financial planning.

However, my expenses had far outweighed my income and following a reality check early in 2007, I decided to seek a source of alternative income and I applied for and secured a position at the Porirua City Council as a project manager on infrastructure and transport-related projects.

During this time, I became involved in budgeting and mentoring low-income workers and beneficiaries; first, as a volunteer attached to the Wellington Citizens Advice Bureau, a stint with Refugee Services (now Red Cross) assisting refugees and migrants settle in and get established. In 1917, I was approached by the Strathmore Park Community Centre in Wellington to fill a position at the centre for which they had obtained government funding.

I resigned from the Porirua City Council in July 2014 as projects of interest had dried up and I was confined to working on matters which had little interest to me. I continued to take an active interest in Wellington' urban development and transport issues. At this time Wellington was undergoing extensive planning of its transport system and together with a group of semi-retired professionals I developed proposals for a transport system based upon light rail along key routes supported by a linking bus network, walking and cycling. Many of our ideas became incorporated into a program termed *Let's Get Wellington Moving (LGWM)*.

Chapter 1
Youth and Adolescence 1943–1967

Early Years in Days Bay

I was born on 22 July 1943, in Wellington, and spent the first seven years of my life in a small house at 27 Kotari Road, Days Bay. I was number four of five siblings in the family after Philip, Catherine and Vivienne. Jenny came along five years after me. Among my earliest memories is the time we four gathered at the bottom of Ferry Road sometime in 1947. The occasion was to welcome home our mum and dad in the brand new Hillman car they had brought with the legacy left them by one of our relatives. It was our first car and it was to become one of my favourite toys during my teenage years.

Our house was perched on the hillside above the road and to get to it, we had to cross a wooden footbridge that spanned a creek, then up a winding path through the trees to the house. Up at the house, there was a level lawn area at the front, a fence and a big drop below. There were also some creeping vines and during the summer, we would swing on those vines and eventually tear them down only to see them grow again during the winter for us to play on the following summer. On one side of the house was a large playhouse, which my dad Malcolm had built and in which I used to play a lot.

I remember one time I cut the index finger off (was it my left or right hand) which bled profusely. I also had these horrible-looking warts all over my fingers, which I used to get treated from time to time. They stayed with me for several years then one day—I don't recall when—they magically disappeared.

The house had three bedrooms, a lounge/living area and a kitchen. The main entrance was at the front of the house and led directly into the lounge. My bedroom, which I shared with Philip, was at the rear and was cold and damp. In the lounge, there was a large window with an equally large window ledge from which you could look out and see Days Bay beach below and further in the distance Rona Bay and Eastbourne Wharf. I was told sometime long ago that when I was a baby, Catherine left me on that ledge from which I duly fell onto the timber floor, landing on my head to much consternation of all who were present.

I survived to tell the story and maybe that explains why I have always had a fear of heights, unless there is something solid and secure between me and the drop below. Who knows? Then there was the fruiterer, Mr Muncton was his name, who arrived each week on Wednesday afternoons. His truck was full of fruit and vegetables and he would start peddling his wares at the top of the road and make his way slowly downhill with the street children following behind, occasionally hitching a ride, as the women folk would come out to buy. Fridges were a new commodity and supermarkets were unknown to us.

I mentioned a bridge over the creek below our house. One day, I was playing alone down at the water's edge below the bridge. I had a three-pence in my possession, a coin smaller than a five cent piece. I remember having it in my mouth and for a moment, it lodged in my throat. I bent forward and coughed it out. A small incident hardly worthy of note, but when recalling it as I have done several times over the years, I think how lucky I was that I did not panic, it did not block my breathing tubes and it came out so easily. With no one there to see me, mine could have been a short-lived life.

We still lived in Kotari Road, when I went to kindergarten in a large house on Muritai Road, then on to Muritai School. My best friend in those days was Clive Carpenter, who lived across the road from us. There were others in the street of various ages with whom we played, including Rolly Crone, Neville Price, Wendy Carpenter (Vivienne's best friend for many years), the Archer kids, the Browns, and Cliffy Hitchcock. We were all of middle-class stock except for Cliffy, whose Dad was a caretaker in the local park. Kids can be cruel and poor Cliffy used to come in for a lot of ribbing.

Other things I vaguely remember were the old Pavilion in Williams Park opposite Days Bay wharf and the corner store and dairy on the waterfront, where the Cobar Restaurant exists today. The pavilion was an old wooden building that was used for conferences, dances, and other adult events. It had a wide veranda and timber decking with narrow slits around three sides. It was a lucrative source of three and six pence coins for us enterprising kids, who with chewing gum on the end of sticks would poke through the slits and recover the coins that had been lost by drunken revellers.

Sadly, the pavilion burnt down in 1949, I think it was, the year that Jenny was born. The old Eastbourne pub also burnt to the ground around that time. It was a place that had no special meaning for me, but it did for my mother, Audrey. It was there that she spent her teenage years with her spinster aunts, Millie and Gertie, who took her in after her mother died when Audrey was twelve. She had already lost her father. He died when she was only three years old.

These are some of the things I remember in what I call my Days Bay years. They were happy times, life was just one big adventure and it was towards the end of this time when I was six or seven that I started to show an interest in sports, with tennis and rugby becoming major activities during my adolescent years ahead.

The Family Moves to Eastbourne

In 1951, we moved to a larger house at 26 Pukatea Street, a waterfront property located at the south end of Eastbourne This was to be our family home where I spent my teenage and early adult years, and where Audrey and Malcolm remained for all, but the last few years of their lives.

I remember my excitement when my mum and dad announced that we were moving to a new house in Eastbourne. "It has a T-shaped hall," said Audrey, and my fertile imagination dreamed up a giant teacup like that in Alice's Wonderland. The reality was nothing like that of course, but that did not dull my excitement about moving into our new home. I was seven years old and it was a time for making new friends and also a time for new adventures.

The first of my new acquaintances were the kids who lived in the neighbouring houses of our street. Across the road at number 27 were Brian and Denise (Tinker) McDavitt and immediately opposite at number 23 were the Mitchell brothers—Ian, Douglas, Robert, Bruce and Peter. At number 20 were the Coopers, along the road at number 30 were the Pickerel sisters, Diana and Wendy, and next door to them were Phil Bothamley, and across the road at number 33, the Lyons, whose names have long since deserted me.

In all, there was quite a gang and although we were of varying ages and classes in school, I can recall the many times we gathered in the street close to our homes to play hide and seek, kick the tin, and other kids' games that are possibly still played today, wherever young kids are given their freedom to indulge in such activities. A popular site for these games was the empty section with a tall macrocarpa tree next door to Phil Bothamley's place. Of this group, my best friends were Brian McDavitt and Nigel Cooper with whom I spent many a day playing table tennis in the small shed set up on the Cooper's property for this purpose.

We three became quite proficient at this game and went on to play in junior tournaments in Wellington and the Hutt Valley during our adolescent years. I also recall spending many a day in the McDavitt's house playing monopoly with Brian. Perhaps, this is where I learnt some of my property investment skills, although I have to admit that Brian seemed to play with more cunning than I and tended to win most of these and other board games we played.

As a kid, I seemed to have a natural aptitude for the various games and sports and this gave me my ticket into the circles in which I associated. I did not have any enemies to speak of, but within this group, there was one kid for whom I developed a secret dislike and that was Douglas from across the road. I had my own secret name for him, which I would keep as my secret. He was bigger although arguably no stronger than I, but for some reason, I could not understand at the time he seemed to hold me in disdain.

I recall two instances when he caught me by surprise and attacked me physically for no apparent reason. The first time was during one of our street games when he turned on me and punched me in the stomach, severely winding me and causing me much pain. The gang to their credit came to my aid to ensure he did not continue with the attack. The second and potentially more serious attack came when a group of us were swimming at the nearby beach. I was standing at the water's edge, when out of the blue he came alongside, pushed me over, and then held my head under the water for what seemed an interminable amount of time.

His hold over me was such that I could not escape and I was close to the point where I could no longer hold my breath, when he finally released me.

During my adolescent years, I continued to associate with Douglas, as he was in my class at school and part of the inner circle of friends I developed. We are encouraged to forget and forgive, but there were other instances in the years that followed that continued to reinforce my negative feelings towards him. As we grew older and our horizons expanded, I had less to do with him and thankfully our paths finally diverged completely, and I have not seen or heard of him for many years.

I have met many other people like him during my journey through life, but when they have appeared, I have given them a wide berth, preferring to associate with people who make me feel good.

During our first winter at Pukatea Street, a wild southerly storm hit Wellington. It must have been the cause of considerable distress to my mum and dad, although to me it was exciting to watch and just part of my life's big adventure at the time. Our house was located on a thin strip of land at the front of the section nearest the sea. On the south side boundary, there was a wide expanse of land that had been retained as a public right of way and has since become known as Heketara Street.

Along the seaward side, some 3 metres from our front boundary, was an old concrete slab retaining wall constructed I don't know how many years earlier. The fury of the storm was such that it completely demolished this wall along much of its length; north to the recreation ground and south to Makara Street. All the properties along this stretch of waterfront are situated on dune sand and during the few days of the storm, this sand was eroded to within metres of our house.

Recognising a significant threat to the local community, the Eastbourne Borough Council, of which my dad Malcolm was an elected member, commissioned Seaton Sladden and Pavitt, Engineers and Surveyors, to design and construct a new sea wall along the entire stretch from Muritai Road to the south to Karamu Street to the north. As time would demonstrate, this would take several years to be carried out and as a temporary measure, the council secured yards and yards of tank tracks from the New Zealand Army and proceeded to build a stepped wall by laboriously stacking these tracks one upon the other along the sections of waterfront most seriously threatened by future erosion.

Heketara Street became the storage area for these tank tracks, which arrived in their thousands. Labour for the task of building this temporary wall was provided by the local residents, my dad Malcolm included and the engineering expertise by Gordon Brickell of Days Bay, a friend of Malcolm's and who was to be my first employer, when I set out on a career in civil engineering. Though crude and ugly, this temporary wall was surprisingly effective in staving off further erosion and while they were there, the stacks of tank tracks on Heketara Street provided an additional feature and hiding place for the games we street kids played during this time of growing up.

Over the next ten years, there was continuing construction activity, with the dismantling of this temporary wall and the construction of a new seawall now largely redundant due to the accumulation of shingles and sand due to changed environmental factors at the harbour entrance and beyond.

These were my formative years. During the evenings, we would sit around the dining room table in the house at 26 Pukatea Street and have dinner, after my dad, Malcolm, arrived home from work at 7:15pm. There was no TV and for home entertainment, we would remain sitting around this table playing cards or a variety of board games and listening to the radio. My mum, Audrey, had a home job of sewing buttons on display cards for a Petone-based plastics factory. She did this work for many years, becoming very deft and proficient at her task and we kids would often help her in return for a bit of pocket money.

From early January to April, my dad would spend these evenings at the same table, laboriously writing the names on certificates for all the graduating students from the four universities at Auckland, Wellington, Christchurch and Dunedin. As a young man, he had trained himself in the art of calligraphy; copperplate writing was his forte and his services were in constant demand. All these activities going on in a tiny room, for me they were happy days indeed.

There were times of sadness too with my first experience of death in the family. We had these two widowed aunts, Millie and Gertie, who lived together in a house nearby on Muritai Road, across from the tennis club. Millie and Gertie had raised my mum during her teenage years after her mother died when she was only twelve (her father had died nine years earlier). Widowed aunts Millie and Gertie were heavy smokers and both died of cancer. Millie was the first to go, but the thing that has stuck in my mind all these years is Gertie and the kindness and devotion that my mother displayed in bringing her into our home and caring for her during her last days.

Today, given our busy lives and the fact that families are often spread out around the world, it is hard to take personal responsibility for the older generation. It is much easier to shunt us into retirement homes and the care of professional caregivers. Sadly, something seems to have been lost.

As I write this, there is more to tell, but I am starting to feel sleepy so I will finish this here with a favourite saying of my dad when he was angry.

Hells bells and buggy wells.

On the Tennis Court

In recent times, I have been enjoying chats with my daughter, Amy, on Skype, as we seem to talk longer and there is more intimacy. I also feel more inclined to become engaged than when on the telephone, which I have always tended to use as a means of passing on a message. An old flame, Margaret, once told me, that I always seemed to be in a hurry to finish the conversation when talking on the telephone. Margaret was one of the Queen Margaret girls we lads from Eastbourne used to chase during our teenage years. She ended up marrying Bill Oliver, who was one of our gang, but that's another story to be recounted later.

I have mentioned the Pukatea Street kids who I got to know and play with in the years after the family moved there in 1951. There were others and perhaps the best friendships that I made during these years were the boys and girls in my class at Muritai School, which I attended during the period 1948 to 1955. Being a July baby, I started school mid-year and during the next eighteen months, I attended the primer school across the road from the main school. Prior to this, I had attended the Eastbourne kindergarten further north along Muritai Road.

My memories of kindergarten are almost non-existent, although relatively recently I came across a photograph of the 1948 class and discovered that Phil Benge, who was to become a good friend later in my life, was there at the same time.

In those days, it was normal to spend two full years in the primers before going on to year one in the main school. However, in my case, I was advanced to main school at the beginning of 1950, which meant that for the rest of my school days, I was up to a year younger than the kids I went through school with. This did not seem to be any great handicap. Academically, I seemed to do better than most in exams and was generally near the top of my class. I was relatively small and light in stature and when it came to playing physical games like rugby, I might have been a bit disadvantaged, but I don't really think so.

I loved games and sports in general. I was always in the thick of these activities whatever they might be and I learnt to handle myself well. I was never the fastest runner among my peers, nor was I the best at any particular sport I took up, but I was up there somewhere. This seemed to make me popular with my classmates and I was usually one of the early ones called upon when making up teams for the various games and sports that we played.

It was around this time that I started playing tennis and rugby, which were to remain my main sporting interests throughout my school days and into early adulthood. During these years and into my teenage years, I would spend much of my spare time in summer on the tennis court. There I would regularly wear out three pairs of tennis shoes on the hard courts of the Muritai Tennis Club, much to the chagrin of Nana Audrey. With coaching from the senior players of the club, I became better than most of my age group in Eastbourne and I started entering and playing in junior tournaments in Wellington and the Hutt Valley.

My first tournament was a Hutt Valley primary school tourney held at Mitchell Park near the Hutt Hospital. I was selected to represent Muritai School in my age group singles and in the first round, I was drawn to play Derek Claxton from Dyer Street School. I started boldly, shot out to an 8-point lead and I recall thinking this is easy. However, Derek slowly clawed me back and eventually beat me 21–18. I was bitterly disappointed, but when Derek went on to win the title, I didn't feel quite so bad. He went on to become one of Hutt Valley's top tennis players for a period during the 1960s.

During the next ten years, I continued to play in tournaments around the Wellington region. I had my share of success winning the odd singles and doubles titles here and there and most importantly, having a lot of fun. I recall travelling to Masterton for several summers to play in an anniversary weekend tournament hosted by the Masterton Tennis Club. It was a well-run and popular tournament, to which the top NZ players of the day would turn up—Lew Gerrard, Ian Crookenden, Corbet Parker, Ruia Morrison to name a few.

I achieved one of my best results in 1958, being runner-up in the Under 15 boys singles, losing in the final to my doubles partner and tennis nemesis, Warwick Wyatt, who lived in Sunshine Bay and was one of my circle of friends at Wellington College.

As I got older, my game didn't improve and people I used to beat easily started beating me, which I found frustrating and somewhat disconcerting. In part, I think it was due to the fact that I was also playing in just about every other sporting activity that came along. In reality, I don't think my temperament was conducive to becoming a top-flight player myself. I seemed to lack the mental fortitude and killer instinct when playing competitive tennis. I stopped producing my best in competition and my dream of becoming a Wimbledon Champion slowly died.

I continued to play tennis into my sixties, but never with the same enthusiasm I had displayed as a youngster. By then, I was travelling the world and when I did play the game, it was a social activity as much as anything. Perhaps my best and most rewarding contribution to tennis and other sporting activities was my administrative and organisational skills. Over the years, I have usually involved myself in the management of the various clubs and organisations in which I have been involved. I made a good events manager and there are some stories to be told on this score, but they can wait until another day.

I continue to enjoy my chats with Amy on Skype. In a recent conversation, I mentioned I had just seen a very good movie, *Revolutionary Road* with Leonardo De Caprio and Kate Winslet. The setting was in the early 1950s, which I can relate to well and they played a suburban couple raising a young family somewhere in Connecticut. He hates his job working as a mid-level salesman in a large corporate organisation in New York City and she, once an aspiring actress, is equally disenchanted with her lot as a suburban housewife. One day, she suggests they sell up and move to Paris to rejuvenate their lives and initially, he is persuaded by the idea.

However, as weeks go by, he keeps putting off crucial decisions and as circumstances change, their relationship slowly falls apart. It is beautifully filmed and has a host of wonderful minor characters. What appealed to me about the film was its portrayal of how we tend to lose our youthful ideals as time goes by and become trapped in an existence of compromise and self-denial. Most of us lack the courage to break out and follow our hearts. Instead, we tend to let money and societal pressures dictate our actions and slowly something dies inside.

In this conversation, I said to Amy, "I admire what you have set out to achieve. It is not easy and far from conventional, but it beats working in office space and all that that entails."

On the Rugby Field

I have mentioned my exploits on the tennis court. Now it is time to tell you of my winter sporting passion. In Eastbourne, during the 1950s, it was rugby or nothing. After watching some of my schoolmates playing on Williams Park, Days Bay, during the winter of 1951, I was keen to be part of it. And so I did, initially being slotted into a team playing the position of lock forward, then in the next few years at tight head prop. I did not complain, I was just happy to be in a team with my mates and take part in the rough and tumble.

During the next four years, I played in a competition for Hutt Valley primary school teams and in a separate Saturday morning competition for boys representing the various Hutt Valley clubs. It was this Saturday morning rugby for which I have my most vivid memories. I just loved it and Saturdays could not come quickly enough.

We were put into teams based on weight and size. I was lightweight and relatively small in stature and during my first two years, I played for the Eastbourne midgets. By the time I reached standard 5 (year 5), I was moved up to the junior team to be with many of my classmates and others a year ahead. We had a very good team and after losing our first two games in the winter of 1954, we went unbeaten for the rest of that season and all the next. I remember the names of some of my teammates. There was our coach, Mr Cooney, and his son, Mich Cooney, who played on the side of the scrum and captained the team.

I played tight head prop alongside my nemesis, Doug Mitchell, at hooker. There was also Wal Louden, a tough and nuggety halfback, Greg Dellabarca outside him at fly-half and further out Mo Meo, who played on the wing. Greg was a stroppy fellow and both he and Mo were from the Catholic school down the road. All these characters have long since dropped off my radar, with the exception of Wal, who has remained a lifelong friend.

I have no clear recollection of the games we played, but I do recall one episode which is perhaps worth noting here. In 1955, I was selected to play in the Hutt Valley junior representative team against our counterparts from Wellington clubs. I wasn't an original selection but I was called up and told to report to training at the Hutt Marist School on the Wednesday before the game. I That morning, I wrapped up my boots, socks and shorts in my Eastbourne rugby jersey, which was how we carried our kit in those days and caught a bus to Randwick, then set off to walk to the school. I had a vague idea of where it was or I thought I did.

I walked for miles and miles, but I never did find the place. I was bitterly disappointed and gave up hopes of playing on Saturday. In fact, when Saturday morning came, I just lay in bed moping until my dad Malcolm hustled me out of bed and drove me to the game. Using his influence, he got me back in the team and onto the field of play.

After that, it was on to Wellington College, where I played my rugby for the next five years making my way up through the various grades. In my third form year (year 9), I fractured my left arm in a fall from a tree while at a scout camp in Wainuiomata. A bone was cracked rather than fully broken and I trialled for a team with my arm in a cast. That year, I was selected for the 4C team in my normal position as a prop forward and was joined by my good mate, Wal. It was a strong team, as were the other fourth grade teams, and if memory serves me correctly, none of these teams lost a game that year.

For me, the attraction of rugby was not so much the physicality of the game, but the idea of running with ball in hand and trying to beat your opposite number by skill and not brute force; I was never big enough to do the latter. While at primary school, I often hankered to play in the backs, but I never made this known to the team coach and simply went along and played in the position I was assigned to. Finally, in my fourth form year, I decided to assert myself and I moved out into the backs, initially playing at inside centre.

I developed the skills to beat my opposite and when the opportunity arose, I would run my centre and wing in for many a try, occasionally having the thrill of scoring myself. I also developed the skill of kicking goals. I did not have a powerful boot, but at close range, I was deadly accurate and for a while I became the team's goal kicker.

During the rest of my Wellington College days, I moved up through the grades, as I slowly put on weight. In my final year, in 1960, I trialled for the 1st fifteen and I was slotted in at the unfamiliar role of first five eight opposite the incumbent Keith Sturrock. I played a great game but not sufficient to convince the coach, Frank Crist, to include me in the team. I had got myself offside with him over an incident earlier in the year and I had to settle for playing in the seconds that year. At the time, it was a big disappointment for me, but as the years have rolled by, it has become rather insignificant in the overall scheme of things.

I recently mentioned this incident to an old schoolmate, Bob Gregory, who went on to play rugby for Wellington and pursue a distinguished academic career in public policy and these days spend a stimulating hour on Tuesday evenings at the Back Bencher pub opposite parliament talking rugby and politics. Bob knew Frank Crist very well and has assured me that it was not in his character to hold grudges. I now accept Bob's viewpoint for when I think about it, it was highly unlikely that I would displace the incumbent first five, who was also an outstanding sportsman and had the world at his feet.

Sadly, booze got to him early in life, he did not fulfil his potential and as Bob told me much later, Keith died many years ago a sad alcoholic. Another side story here, is a photo of me with a demure young girl on my wall of memories, which Amy has often commented on with wry amusement. Her name was Susan Uttley (my first date). Apparently, she married Keith Sturrock and from what Bob told me, hers was also a rather tragic life.

When I left school, my loyalties were with Eastbourne and I signed up to play for the local club playing at centre for the third grade team with many of my old pals from primary school days. We were a very good team and were encouraged to play open running rugby by our coach, Clarrie Gibbons, an Eastbourne stalwart and friend of my dad and a senior official in the NZ Rugby Football Union. There are a number of stories I could tell about this team but one will do here. Sometime mid-season, we travelled by bus to play a friendly match against a Masterton Club team.

An incident during the game keeps coming back to me from time to time. I was playing my normal position of centre outside my good mate, Wal Clementson. We were winning a lot of the ball and it was being passed quickly along the backline, as we had been trained to do. My opposite was a solidly built Maori fellow, with a mean tackle. He was marking me closely and the first time I received the ball, I was flat on the deck just as it came into my hands. This happened a second time, then a third, when finally I screamed at Wal, "For f…s sake, don't give me the ball."

Brian Lochore was in the opposition team that day. He was soon to become an All Black and went on to have a distinguished career as a player, coach and administrator. I don't recall whether we won or lost but I do remember having a great time. My dad, then president of the club, was in a generous mood dishing out cigars to all and sundry. I am also sure we must have gotten through a lot of beer.

I found the transition to club rugby difficult and I became prone to injury for the first time. At the end of my first season, I found myself resting up in Hutt Hospital for three weeks with a painful hematoma in my right thigh. It was potentially life-threatening and in the end, the surgeon attending me cut it out and the operation scar is still visible today. My leg was put in a plaster cast from hip to ankle and I hobbled around for the next six weeks until it was removed.

The following year, I was promoted to the Eastbourne senior team, where I had three glorious games at fullback before injury hit me and I was back in Hutt Hospital with another hematoma in the same right thigh. No operation was necessary but the leg was placed in a cast by the same nursing sister of the previous year, who chastised me for continuing to play 'such a stupid game'. This time, I listened to her and at the tender age of twenty, I decided to give playing the game away.

I took up coaching and had the satisfaction of steering an age-grade team to winning their competition in 1963 with an unbeaten record. However, perhaps my most satisfying coaching achievement was with a bantamweight team (first-timers age seven and eight). I recall in the early part of the season trying to teach them to run and pass the ball and perform other sophisticated manoeuvres. The opposition was beating the pants off us, then one day mid-season, one of the young lads stumbled onto a loose ball and kept kicking it ahead until it rolled over the opposition goal line, where he fell on it and scored the team's first try of the year.

I immediately realised that I was trying to get them to perform skills that they were not ready to absorb, so I changed my coaching strategy and focused on teaching them to just get the ball upfield by kicking it ahead. It seemed to work, for we started winning matches and by the end of the season were toting up big scores.

My love of the game was such that I also enjoyed just watching, particularly when it was played at the top level. I remember in 1953 at ten years of age going to several matches at Athletic Park to watch the Wellington provincial side play. Wellington held the Ranfurly Shield that year and the team had a backline full of All Blacks. More memorable still, was camping out overnight outside Athletic Park on three separate occasions in 1956, to get a seat on the Western bank to watch the touring Springboks play Wellington, the All Blacks and the NZ University team.

I was there to watch winger Ron Jarden, my idol at the time, score a famous try that wasn't. I continued to follow and watch rugby played, predominantly premier games involving the All Blacks and the Wellington provincial side. I was fanatical about my rugby and there was a time between 1953 and 1960 when I could recall the name of every All Black and the games they played and won or lost. Now years later, it hardly seems important.

Like anyone else, I like to support my local team. However, there have been a couple of occasions, where my sympathies have been with the opposition. In 1971, the British Lions toured NZ and cleaned up the All Blacks, playing a brand of running rugby I have seldom seen before or since. Again in 1983, when I was courting Sue, the Aussies played a test series against the All Blacks. They too played a spectacular brand of running rugby but lost a series of close games against an All Black side playing a dourest form of kick and chase rugby. To me, the way the game is played is important and I almost found myself cheering for the Aussies. Ask Sue!

Today, I still watch the Hurricanes and All Blacks when they play, but only from the comfort of our lounge. Can't say I like big crowds anymore and sometimes I wonder why I watch at all. I don't particularly like the way the game has evolved with the emphasis on power and brute force to break the opposition line and with the coaches calling the shots from the sideline. And the rules of the game are now so complicated, I sometimes wonder if the players themselves know what is going on. I miss the free-flowing running game and relatively simple rules of the game I used to play those many years ago.

Muritai School Days

I have been recounting stories about my early childhood in Days Bay and my exploits on the tennis court and rugby field during the years that followed. Let me return to those formative days, when from age seven to age twelve, I was expanding my world and exploring Eastbourne, the Hutt Valley, Wellington and beyond.

I attended Muritai Primary School, which is located near the hub of the community shopping centre on Rimu Street. It was there that I established my circle of friends and one or two have remained lifelong friends. First and foremost, there is Wal Louden. As you know, Wal along with Phil Benge are two of my mates with whom I have gone trapping possums at Butterfly Creek during the past decade. Wal tells me his family moved to Eastbourne in 1948 and I guess that is when our friendship started and has continued until this day.

Others in this group included John le Grove, a real speedster, Bill Oliver, tops at rugby, Bruce Walling, Doug Mitchell, Peter Hall, another speedster, and Jeavons Bailey, the brains of the class. Then there were the girls including Denise Mathews, on whom we all had a crush, Penny Smythe, Jackie Williams, Marie Hunt (my first kiss), Robin Target, and Shirley Sanson.

As a student, I was quiet, generally well behaved and I was quick to grasp an understanding of things. I was near the top of the class in most subjects, my writing was clear and legible, my spelling was very good and I seemed to excel in arithmetic. These were characteristics that seemed to endear me to the various teachers and earned me privileges that on occasion, I am sure I did not deserve.

Once a week during our form 1 and 2 years, the class would be bused to Petone to attend woodwork (boys) and cooking (girls) lessons, which were part of the curriculum of the time. I never was particularly good at creating things with my hands and during these two years, I developed some dubious skills making toy boats and other small objects, which I do not remember. Finally, during the course of the second year, our tutor, Pansy Millar, moved us on to a more ambitious task and each of us was given the option of making a four-tier stepladder or a sea-grass stool.

Jeavons and I opted for the stepladder and being the only ones to choose this option, Pansy made us work together. Laboriously over the final weeks of the year, we each made our own ladders. When it came to final marking of the finished product, we both scored a 10 out of 10. I recall observing the join of the treads and the legs were far from perfect and thinking at the time that I did not deserve such a high mark. However, that stepladder became well-used around our house and went on to serve my dad Malcolm very well.

It was still functioning many years later during the time when he was building windmills on the roof of the shed at the rear of the family home at Pukatea Street in the late 1980s. Perhaps, Pansy was a little wiser than the eccentric carpenter we all thought him to be.

Sports Day at the end of the year was one event I always enjoyed. Running, jumping, egg and spoon, and sack races—I entered them all. The sack race was one that I came to excel in, particularly after watching the technique of my good mate, Wal, who was and remained the champion. While most others would hop and jump down the track, Wal stuck his feet in the corners and ran as fast as he could without falling over. During that form 1 year, I spent many a day practicing this technique on our front lawn and when the sports day arrived, I was good enough to beat all but Wal, who turned up in a broad onion sack which enabled him to take longer strides than I.

However, my second place was good enough to get me on the team for the interschool sports the following February. In that event, I had my moment of glory winning my heat and being in with a chance in the final. However, the ultimate glory eluded me. My favourite sack was well worn in the corners and I had patched it up several times. It finally gave out as I raced down the track and I hobbled home a distant and disappointing last.

There are many other stories I could relate to of my days at Muritai School and I will make but a quick reference here. Swimming club on Friday nights at the rugby club gymnasium, where we would pair off in the dark and steal our first kisses. In my standard three years, I was moved up to a composite class of year three, four and five-year students. This was where I discovered my lack of aptitude for art. My teacher, Bill Renwick, also experimented in trying to get me to write right-handed, but to no avail. One day while playing bull rush, I was the last runner left and I outwitted them all by taking off early and getting to the other end of the playing field.

I was selected as head prefect in my final year—an unexpected honour considering Wal seemed the popular choice. Sometime that year, I was caught by a truant officer while at the movies in Wellington, although I had a valid reason and avoided censure. Daydreaming in class during a reading exercise, but surprising our teacher, Colin Dallas, and picking up at the right spot when called upon to take my turn, discussing the previous Saturday's first division rugby game refereed by the same Colin Dallas, and a certain pride on prize giving day in early December 1955, when I stepped up to receive my prize—a book entitled *Down in the Drink*, a collection of wartime stories of allied airmen who had been rescued after coming to grief in the ocean.

Over the years, sentiment has taken hold and I have retained the book to this day. It sits on my bookshelf above me with inscription and all, a reminder of a happy time in my life when I was starting to venture out and explore a wider world.

I end with this quotation, which picks up my mood and sentiments when I look back on my primary school days.

When I was in China on the All-American Ping Pong team, I just loved playing with my Flexolite ping pong paddle.

Forrest Gump

She'll be Right Sir

I attended Wellington College from 1956 to 1960. On the last weekend of March 2010, I attended a reunion of the Class of 1960 and what a memorable occasion it was. A variety of functions had been organised and for me perhaps the highlight came on the Friday morning meeting up with former classmates many of whom I and not seen since leaving Col, attendance at the morning assembly, which was followed by a tour of my old school conducted by the current headmaster, Roger Moses, and reunion organiser, Stephanie Kane.

Morning assembly had not changed much in fifty years. On this day, there was a spirited haka, as we were led into a hall somewhat smaller than the one I knew yesteryear. This was followed by a bible reading by the head prefect, a school hymn (on this occasion a spirited rendition of *Forty Years On*), notices and a warm welcome to me and my former classmates given by headmaster, Roger Moses, who allowed us to lead him out of the hall at the end of these formalities.

In my day, the head prefect, Peter Stokes, took up position stage left to read the bible lesson of the day, a duty prefect stood stage right to bring the assembled throng to order and the rest of us prefects or those that bothered to attend were seated to the rear right of the hall, where the teachers and finally Headmaster Heron 'Sir' filed into the assembly.

I was one of a small contingent of from Eastbourne, who attended Col during the late 1950s. Those were the days before zoning was brought in and all of us had chosen to attend, where brothers and fathers had trod before.

I cruised through the junior school in the upper stream, doing enough to squeeze through the school certificate at my first attempt, being accredited University Entrance in my lower sixth form year and staying on for the upper sixth for the sporting and social activity more than anything else. I loved my sport, played tennis in the summer, and rugby in winter and I tried my hand at anything else that was going on during the year—boxing, fives, athletics, table tennis and swimming to name a few.

I don't claim to have been a model student but my sporting exploits and studious nature must have been sufficient to bring me to the attention of the Headmaster (Fish) Heron and his staff, for in my final year, I was made school prefect along with eleven other of my classmates. However, during that final year, things came a bit unstuck and I seemed to earn the displeasure of the headmaster on more than one occasion.

She'll be right Sir: Heron, a dour individual and stern disciplinarian, was in the habit of carrying a hefty tome to assembly, which he would hand to the prefect sitting nearest the door as he entered the hall. On one occasion, early in the first term, I was sitting in the hot seat and as he went to hand me the book, it slipped from his hands and fell to the floor. "Sorry, Barnett," he said.

I bent down to pick it up, and then I replied in a cheerful voice, "She's right, Sir," in my broadest Kiwi accent. Nothing else was said and he proceeded to his customary position centre stage to conduct assembly.

It was Heron's practice to preach a short sermon on a topic of the day upon the completion of the other formalities. On this occasion, he dispensed with his prepared topic and proceeded to give the assembly a short lesson on the proper use of the English language. Come the end of the session, he came down the centre aisle, where I waited with a book in hand ready to return it to him. He paused, glared into my eyes as I handed over the book, then he strode off to his office to busy himself in affairs of the day. Not a word was spoken, but of course, the message was clear.

Rebel on the Eastbourne Bus: There was another incident later in the year stemming from his morning missive. Us Eastbourne boys travelled to and from Col by bus together with a small contingent of St Pats and Wellington High School students. There was an established order whereby senior boys occupied the rear seats of the bus with the juniors up front and woe and betide to any junior who broke the established order.

It so happened that sometime during the second term, some trouble had occurred on one of the Karori buses, which must have come to Heron's attention. One assembly, he decided to make it his topic of the day by admonishing the practice of ragging junior students and demanding that they be treated with due respect and courtesy. I thought little more of it until the end of the day when I happened to be running late for the Eastbourne bus and arrived just as it was due to leave.

It was almost completely full and as I made my way to the back of the bus, I found my seat occupied by this third or was he a fourth former staring up at me with a challenging look in his eyes. What was I to do? I couldn't just let him stay there, for it would be an affront to my status and mana.

Taking in a breath, I roared 'Out' in my deepest voice. Initially, there was no response. He just stared back at me with a challenging grin. *F...I thought to myself, what do I do now?* Fortunately, my senior colleagues seemed to sense a threat to the established order, for in the next instant there was a resounding chorus chanting 'OUT', to which the astounded junior jumped up like a startled rabbit and moved quickly to the front of the bus. Order was restored and we went on our merry way home.

Teachers Remembered: Only three buildings remain of those in which I spent my college days; the headmaster's residence, Firth Hall where we dined and reminisced on the Saturday evening, and the pavilion on the lower playing field. While the loss of the old school hall is a shame I could not but help think that the modern campus had a better feel to it and has certainly moved with the times. As we wandered around and came across the Robert (Horsey) Bradley memorial building, I thought of some of those teachers under whom I studied and who made an impression on me:

- Horsey Bradley of course, who taught me math in my fifth form year. He played upon his name and who could forget the 'Nei…gh boys Nei…gh' when one gave a wrong answer at question time.

- Inky Dighton with his thick silver hair not unlike mine. Inky taught me Latin in the third form. "Hic, Hik, Hoc, Huius, Horum, Harum," he would recite as he strode around the classroom. It was all too complicated for me and I switched to History the following year.

- Jerry Auton, my third-form master and teacher of English. He also taught me History in fourth form and wrote in my mid-year report—'6th in the class, fair effort but could do much better'. *I will show you, Jerry*, I thought to myself and putting my head to the grindstone, I studied hard and jumped to the top of the class at the end of the year, winning a History prize into the bargain. I did not appreciate it at the time, but maybe Jerry did me a favour.

- Over the years, I have come to enjoy reading and researching history and I have come to appreciate that without an understanding of the past, how can we ever make sense of the present?

- Mickey Michael who coached me in rugby and stayed on for many long years teaching new generations of students. I bumped into Mickey some thirty years later and he clearly recognised me and remembered the exploits of our team.

- Sam Meads and his memorable laws of the Medes and the Persians. For one brief term, he lifted my performance in Maths and Science with his enthusiastic teaching style and amusing stories of the Firth House borders and their escapades.

- Foxy Sutton under whom I studied three years of French. We would stalk him in the corridor and yell tallyho, when we saw him coming, then run for our lives for woe and betide if he ever caught you, it just wasn't worth imagining.

Finally, it was great to get together with former classmates, many of whom I had not seen since our last year in 1960. We may have aged a bit but the youthful exuberance was there, particularly when recalling escapades of the past. There was:

- My old tennis buddy, Warwick (Sharky) Wyatt, now of Peka Peka on the Kapiti Coast, reminded me that we won every tennis doubles championship in our grade each year except 1960 when for some reason, apparently we did not team up. Warwick also seemed particularly enthused that we had also taken out the Junior Table Tennis doubles in our fourth form year.
- Remnants of the Eastbourne contingent include Wal Louden and John Robinson. Wal is back living in Eastbourne. We have been mates for more than sixty years and I still see him occasionally. These days we go trapping possums in the hills of Eastbourne.
- Arthur McIntosh, one of those I had not seen since our school days and whom I found had followed a similar career path in civil engineering in remoter parts of the world. He is now a resident in the Gold Coast, Australia and I have a standing invitation to go visit any time.
- Brian (BJ) Kelly and Quentin Collier, we played in the 2B and 2A rugby teams in our latter years, coached by the illustrious Mickey Michael and Fanny Flaws.
- John Beatson and Robin Phillip, both of whom followed lifelong careers in the UK. Robin still lives and works there, while John told me he came home a few years ago and now spends half the year with his wife, Vicki, living in a magnificent eco-home near Greytown in the Wairarapa. For the remainder of the year, they live on Magnetic Island, Queensland, where they go to escape our winter. Seems like a good lifestyle choice to me.

Those were happy days indeed.

Other Sporting Activities

As mentioned earlier, during these years, I took part in almost every sporting activity including; the third-form boxing tournament where I hardly landed a punch and was completely exhausted after three minutes of sparring, swimming being selected for the school swimming team in my third-form year, athletics, cross-country, table tennis, fives—a handball game played within three walls with rules and scoring similar to squash, basketball and possibly other sports I have since forgotten. I was good at them all without being the champion but that did not matter I was having fun.

One such activity that I feel is worth recording during these years was gym and sundry activities at the Eastbourne branch of the YMCA. On Wednesday evenings, an instructor from Petone would come out to Eastbourne to take gym classes and other activities, which I attended along with many of my local friends. In 1958, several of us including myself, Wal, Bruce Walling, Brian McDavitt, and Rob Mitchell (brother of Douglas mentioned earlier) were selected to represent the Hutt Valley in an annual Older Boys Tournament, to be held that year in September in Invercargill.

It was a competition for teams of six and included numerous activities including gymnastics, volleyball, basketball, cross-country, table tennis, a synchronised dance routine and public speaking. We spent much of the early part of that year preparing for this event and when the due date of the completion was nearing, our small group plus coach, Peter McKnight, boarded an overnight ferry from Wellington to Lyttleton and then transferred to the daylight train for Christchurch to Invercargill.

The tournament ran over a period of six days and what fun we had getting there and performing in these various activities. We obviously had a broad range of talent in our team for we returned home triumphant having won the overall team prize in that year's contest. I returned the following year to take part in the same tournament held in Auckland. Unfortunately, we could not repeat the result and somehow given the big city atmosphere and with new faces in the team, for me, it did not generate the same feeling of camaraderie and excitement.

Whangamata

In my late teens (circa 1962), my Eastbourne pals and I discovered Whangamata in the Bay of Plenty on the east coast of New Zealand. In those days, it was little more than a beachside village with a post office, general store, fish & chip shop, a camping ground, a few batches and a pub three miles down the road. It was a wonderful place for a summer vacation and for several years at Xmas, we drove there in our Morris Minors, Model A Fords and other assortment of vehicles. We pitched our tents in the camping ground and spent two wonderful weeks basking in the sun, playing beach cricket, surfing and other erroneous activities.

During each successive summer, our group grew bigger in numbers and in the summer of 1966/67, we hired a marquee tent in which all forty of us slept. That was to be the last of these bachelor holidays, as many of my friends drifted into wedlock and others set out on their oversea experience, which had become a rite of passage for many and remains so to his day. As for me, wedding bells were out of the question. Travel was on the horizon and my plans for further study in the USA were coming to fruition. Before the year was out, I would find myself in Chicago enjoying all that exciting city has to offer.

During that same summer, I bought a section backing onto the river estuary at the south end of the village and for sixty pounds deposit and nine monthly instalments, the land was mine, all for the princely sum of six hundred pounds ($1200). I returned to Whangamata one last time in the summer of 1970/71 upon my return home from the USA. Together with Philip, Vivienne and Jenny, and Vivienne's friends, Judith Cornwall and Fergus Dick, we camped on my piece of real estate.

I noticed new houses had sprouted up around me and the village was certainly growing. However, I had moved on and the attraction of Whangamata was no longer the same. I sold that piece of land a year later for the significantly larger sum of $2600, not a bad profit for a bit of intuitive buying. This was my first venture into property investment and it took a long time for me to appreciate that holding on would have been a better option.

I recall visiting Whangamata in 2010 with Sue and Amy. It had changed completely from the town I knew in my youth. Development over succeeding decades including holiday homes, condominiums, supermarkets and shopping malls had turned it into a mini-metropolis making it completely unrecognisable to me. I made inquiries and sought out my former plot of land, which had a modest bungalow on it and was surrounded everywhere by similar housing developments. Upon further investigation, I found this property had a valuation of $800,000.

Do I regret selling the land? A little perhaps but I don't dwell on it. Over the ensuing years, I have come to appreciate the things that make me happy and being super rich is not one of them. The Whangamata of today is not a place that I would want to go back to. Much better that I have a loving family, good friends, a roof over my head, food, clothing, and sufficient funds to meet all our needs, which we have and I am happy with that.

Chapter 2
A Chequered Start 1960–1967

Holiday Jobs

In mid-December 1960, at the spritely age of seventeen and five months, my schooldays came to an end. Three years earlier, I had decided on civil engineering as the career I wanted to pursue and I now set about preparing to go to university and study for the degree of Bachelor of Civil Engineering. In those days, the course comprised an intermediate year studying mathematics, applied mathematics, chemistry and physics, which could be at any of the four major universities in Auckland, Wellington, Christchurch and Dunedin, followed by a further three years of study at either Auckland or Canterbury University. This being the case, I opted to stay close to home and do my first year of study at Victoria University in Wellington.

During the 1950s and 60s, the cost of attending university was minimal and we could finance our tertiary education by working in one of the numerous and well-paid holiday jobs that were available and accumulating sufficient funds to see us through the university year. Sadly, during recent decades, things have changed dramatically and most students have to bear the full cost of their studies and in many, perhaps most, cases emerge with a huge debt before they get a start in the workforce. However, that is another story and back to mine.

That summer I secured a job working at the Gear Meat Works, which was situated along the Petone esplanade immediately west of the Petone wharf. I worked on one of the automated chains where sheep were slaughtered, skinned and gutted, then moved on to a freezer for later shipment to wherever. I was stationed near the head of the line, where the slaughtered sheep came up from the slaughterhouse below, throat slit, head hanging loose, dripping blood, and suspended from a hook around one of its hind legs.

I worked on a raised platform between two skilled knifemen, who would proceed to skin each free hind leg before the carcass moved on along the chain. My job was to transfer the hook from one leg to the other, a task that required a considerable amount of strength and agility. The pay was good but the conditions and the monotony of the work made this one of the most boring jobs I have ever had and I couldn't wait for the end of each day to arrive. I stuck it out for a month until I could bear it no longer and moved on.

The following summer, at the end of my first year at Victoria University, I secured work on the Wellington wharves unloading and loading cargo on the many ships that were coming and going. In contrast to the meat works, the work was varied and I had a lot of fun. These were the days before container shipping had arrived and radically transformed the shipping industry. Ships of all shapes and sizes would arrive in port and cargoes would be loaded directly into the ship's hull by wharf side cranes that looked like giant ants. The work available would vary from day to day depending on the number of ships in port.

Jobs were allocated on a daily basis and the labour force was strictly controlled by the waterside union delegate, who assigned jobs and tasks to registered union members, after which we casuals called seagulls were given the crumbs. These were prosperous times, there were plenty of ships coming and going through the port and I was kept gainfully employed throughout that entire summer. The pay was good and I saved heaps, earning more than sufficient to see myself through the university year.

Working alongside these tough, seasoned waterside workers was a far more pleasant experience than at the meat works and I also got an education into a slice of life in the company of these men during that memorable summer. A typical day would be to turn up outside the dispatcher's office near Queens Wharf and hang around until jobs were assigned for the day. This would take up to fifteen or twenty minutes, after which we would make our way on foot to the assigned ship, which would take up another ten to twenty minutes depending on where it was berthed, then a further five to ten minutes would pass as the union delegate would allocate specific tasks for the day.

Work got underway in earnest about 9am. Us seagulls were usually assigned the dirtiest jobs, often in the hull of the ship. It was hard physical work lifting and stacking cargo, but this did not phase me and I applied myself to whatever task I was assigned. We would work through the day taking regulation breaks; smoke mid-morning, an hour for lunch at noon, smoke once again in the mid-afternoon and finish up a 5pm. Overtime was frequently worked and after an hour's break, we would be called back to work on from 6pm until 9pm at night, being paid for an extra three hours at the overtime rate of time regardless of whether the full three hours were worked.

I recall one day, I was working in the hull of a ship berthed at Kings Wharf, when early in the afternoon the word came around from the union delegate, "Go slow, boys, this ship is due to go out this evening," he said in a threatening voice. Our gang duly obeyed this instruction and come 5pm, there was still a small amount of cargo still to be loaded. We took our tea break, then returned at 6. By half past the hour, loading was complete and we were all off home, much the richer with three hours extra pay to come. Such was the way of things and who was I to complain?

Everyone was happy except perhaps the ship owner, who had to foot the bill for our wages and the demurrage. As I have said, it was a fun job and I got a real education into the bargain.

During the summer of 1962, I took on a job close to home working as a labourer for the Eastbourne Borough Council in the days before local government reform and its absorption into the Hutt City Council. Sandwiched in between were two forgettable and dismal years of study attempting to complete the intermediate year of my engineering degree. I studied hard and managed to scrape through math and applied math with Cs in first my year, but chemistry and physics proved to be a mystery and after failing to pass these subjects a second time around, I began to despair of making the grade as a civil engineer.

Perhaps, immaturity had played a part. Certainly, some uninspiring teaching during my latter days at Wellington College left me wallowing in these subjects in which I showed little interest. Whatever it was, I was not ready for the transition to university and in hindsight, a gap year or two may have been beneficial.

I was nineteen years old and wondering what to do next. Looking through the job ads in the *Evening Post*, I noticed that Woolworths (in those days operating as a clothing and merchandise department store) was advertising vacancies for management trainees. I fired in an application and was invited in for an interview at its Cuba Street store. During the interview, which was conducted by the store manager, I was invited to view the shop floor from the mezzanine and immediately knew that retailing was not a career I wanted to pursue.

I was in a despondent mood for much of that summer, my job at the council gave me some respite and certainly lots of time to reflect upon my situation. The job was far from unpleasant for together with my mate, B Wal, I was given the task of scrub cutting and clearing the walking tracks to Butterfly Creek on the hills behind Eastbourne. We would clock in in the early morning, then pick up our gear and disappear into the hills to reappear again in the late afternoon and clock out at the end of the day. It was hard physical work but we set our own pace and took plenty of time out to rest and even swim in the creek on the far side of the hill.

In between work, I continued to socialise and play tennis and sometime during the latter part of that summer, David, a tennis buddy, enquired about my progress at university and I told him of my miserable exam results and my despair of ever making the grade. David, a few years my senior, was a civil engineer himself and he worked for a small consulting firm Brickell Moss and Partners in Lower Hutt. Apparently, recognising some latent talent within me, he invited me to apply for a job in a testing laboratory this firm, had just established.

I cannot recall my immediate reaction, but I do know I took up the offer and started my first civil engineering job in February 1963, and set off on a career that would extend over the next fifty-one years and carry me to many places around the world.

Soil Technician Supreme

The 1960s was a decade of economic prosperity and here in New Zealand, we were enjoying the benefits of a strong and growing economy on the back of our sheep meat and dairy industries. Jobs were plenty and if you didn't like the first one, there was always another just down the road. Here, in Wellington, there was an explosion in housing development and heavy earthwork machinery was to be seen everywhere carving off the hilltops and filling in the valleys to create building plots for new home owners, many of whom financed their purchase through government housing loans paying 3 per cent per annum in interest.

I was inducted into the art of soil testing and quickly became part of the action. I spent many a day dodging overloaded motor scrapers, which screamed down from hillsides above and onto the fill, where I would spread my tools, collect samples and perform the test to verify the stability of the compacted dirt. Occupational health and safety was not such a big deal in those days.

I recall on occasion during my first year, when I was inspecting and testing the construction of a small earth fill on the hill slopes above Taita College in the Hutt Valley, destined to be the site of a water storage tank to serve the valley below. This work was being undertaken by a contractor by the name of Graham (Shorty) Heberley. He was short and tubby in stature and he had an exuberant personality. I soon noticed that if I was at the site around 10 in the morning, Shorty would stop for smoko and invite me to join him and his men and proceed to fill me up with cream buns and sausage rolls.

For a short time thereafter, I planned my day to be at this site at 10 in the morning, blissfully ignorant of the possible expectation of a favour in return.

One day, I was called aside by my boss. "I have been hearing stories about you, Michael," he said in a stern voice, adding, "I was talking to Shorty yesterday and he tells me he has been feeding you cream buns and sausage rolls."

At this point, my boss broke out in a broad grin and went on to say, "He also tells me you still condemn his fill, tell him to dig things out and do it again, when tests show it to be unsatisfactory."

I went back into the laboratory a little bemused, not quite sure whether I had been reprimanded or commended for my actions. I can't remember exactly but I think the cream buns stopped coming and thereafter I decided that it was probably best that I vary the time of future site visits.

This work was a significant part of my job. The tools I used were relatively primitive and going by the book, it would take twenty-four hours to get a result. This was far too long when some earth fills could rise up eight to ten feet in that time. I developed techniques to get an answer within an hour when back in the lab, but even then the time lag between testing on site a getting a result in the lab was too long. Desirous of avoiding conflict and with experience, I started using my judgement on whether a fill was satisfactory or not and advising the contractor as such. I was usually right and developed the respect of the contractors I worked with over time.

Commercial development was also booming during this era and a second generation of high-rise buildings in Wellington was growing fast. I also had part of this action, being involved in exploratory drilling and the collection of core samples, to be tested for their engineering properties and derive data for the design of foundations for these new and taller buildings. As I gained confidence and experience, I was sent further afield and during the next four years, I travelled up and down the country performing these and other tasks at sites near

New Plymouth, Rotorua, Whangarei, Timaru, a radio mast in the hills west of Oamaru, and a hospital ward block in Dunedin to name a few.

This was a wonderful introduction to civil engineering, as I enjoyed the outdoors and the freedom for which I craved together with exposure to the world of construction and construction workers.

Encouraged by my mentor, David, I enrolled in night classes and commenced studies for he NZ Certificate of Engineering, the precursor of the diploma course that exists today. I was starting to find my way again; I was out and about most days, the job was fun and exciting, I was learning new skills and I started doing well in my studies. Sometime along the way, I decided that it might be a good idea to go back to university when I completed this course. However, I was now in my early twenties and itching to go abroad and explore the world.

I was keen to follow in Vivienne and Philip's footsteps, who had both been to Europe on their overseas experience rite of passage and returned home with tales of the fun times they had living and working in London and on excursions in Europe. Enthused by their stories, I decided that I could kill two birds with one stone and combine travel with study abroad. I started investigating opportunities to study in the UK, but it soon became apparent that the cost would be prohibitive and I switched my attention to the USA, where it seemed there would be greater opportunities for obtaining financial assistance.

My sister, Vivienne, was now back home and working for the US Information Service in Wellington and it was to her office that I headed and sought information on opportunities to study in America.

What followed was two years of exhaustive inquiries to various institutions, which might accept me into their undergraduate programme and were of sufficient standing that my degree would be recognised back here in New Zealand when I returned home. In this, I was given wonderful assistance by Joan Livingstone, a colleague of Vivienne, whose job was to assist with such inquiries as mine.

There followed two years of reading through tomes at USIS library in Warring Taylor Street identifying universities and the programmes they offered, narrowing my choice down to twelve and letters back and forth to each of these chosen twelve, which included Stanford University, California Institute of Technology, Massachusetts Institute of Technology, New York University, Illinois Institute of Technology, plus seven other universities which I have long since forgotten. My desire was to go and live in California and my preference was to attend either Stanford or Caltech, but both turned my application down, as did three other universities.

Finally, in April 1967, I received notice that I had been accepted in the Illinois Institute of Technology programme and invited to enrol in the autumn semester commencing the following September. This was no time for procrastination and I immediately accepted and made plans for my overseas adventure. However, I am getting ahead of myself. Now back to work and study.

In December 1964, I was sent north to Whangarei to supervise the exploratory test drilling for an oil-fired power station to be located near the harbour entrance, adjacent to the Marsden Point Oil Refinery. This location was subsequently discarded and we moved the drilling programme to the beach front near Ruakaka. Six months later, I returned to this site to supervise the earthworks and I took up residence in the single-man quarters, where I remained until August 1966 undertaking my work, while the power station structures arose around me.

This was my first experience encamped on a project of significant size and it was my first exposure to the life of construction workers and their families and I enjoyed every moment.

I had a small bungalow in a complex occupied by single management staff on the construction team and shared with them a common room where we relaxed in the evenings, watched TV and threw the occasional party. For our meals, we ate in a communal canteen nearby. At age twenty-two, I was considerably younger and far less experienced than these men, but I was accepted into their world as I was by many of the other construction workers I met most of whom lived a somewhat nomadic life moving from one construction job to another, never having a permanent place to call home.

Two of the single men who I got particularly friendly with were Bob, the senior site surveyor, and Graham, the chief mechanic, both Aussies who must have been in their mid to late thirties. In spite of the age gap, Bob and Graham had a common interest in stock cars and regularly drove down to Auckland on a Saturday night to attend the midget car races at Western Springs. I joined them for this excursion on several occasions and they seemed happy to have me along.

The construction hours were from 8am in the morning until 5pm in the afternoon, Monday to Friday and 8am until 3pm in the afternoon on Saturdays, with regular breaks statutory breaks for smoko and lunch. On Saturday when work had finished, we would shower and clean up and dress for our night out and set off in either Bob or Graham's car and drive to Auckland, where our initial destination was the Trioka Restaurant near Britomart. There we would have a good meal, before heading out to Western Springs and the midget car races.

Now before or since I have never been what is commonly described as a petrol head, but I must say I enjoyed these nights at these races and appreciated the skill of these racers and the motor cyclists on their brakeless bikes as they zoomed around the small oval track at hair raising speed and impossible angles with the occasional cartwheel thrown in. Perhaps it was the company I was with, for Bob and Graham were both warm and friendly characters and seemed only too glad to share their passion with me and listen as I spoke of my plans for the future.

My other memory of this experience was that I had a lot of downtime during the work day, as there was only so much testing that needed to be done and spent much of this time on my studies and keeping fit running back and forth along the broad expanse of the Ruakaka Beach, which extends for several kilometres from Waipu in the south to Whangarei Harbour entrance to the north. The beach, Whangarei Heads, the view of Bream Bay and the Hen and Chicken Islands further out to sea are magnificent.

I recall standing on the dunes above this same beach with German engineer Karl Schwinn some twenty years later, while working on the Marsden Point Refinery expansion project and part of Prime Minister Robert Muldoon's think big projects, Karl made the comment, "What a beautiful piece of real estate, such a pity that powers that be chose to build this ugly edifice in such a location."

This extended period away from Wellington had interrupted my night school study programme, but under a deal I had negotiated with my boss, John Moss, I returned home in August 1966 to attend a three-month block course to complete my diploma studies, while remaining on full pay. It was at this course that I met and became friendly with Dave Gamble, who was from Dunedin and attending the same block course. Dave was a traffic engineer with the Dunedin City Council. We soon became friends and early on during this course, he moved in and became with us at Pukatea Street as a boarder.

He was a gregarious kind of person and my mum and dad soon warmed to him. In the evenings, we would all play darts in the small kitchen while Nana Audrey was preparing our meal. We studied hard and for peace and quiet on Saturday mornings, we would go out to my work place, an old converted house in Pretoria Street, Lower Hutt to study through until mid-afternoon, when we would close our books, get into my Morris 1000 car and cruise out to the tavern that had recently opened in Cannons Creek, Porirua.

I don't recall why but at the time, it was the trendy place for all the young from around Wellington to congregate and enjoy a beer (young men) and a Pimms or sherry for the girls (sheilas or chicks we called them) during the late afternoon.

This was during the days of 6pm closing and licensing laws were rigorously enforced, but not so much the drink/driving laws. Pubs and hotels were they only places where liquor was served outside the home and this led to some interesting social behaviour. When drinking at a pub, it was cheapest to order on tap beer in a 32-ounce (1 litre) jug. Last orders were taken shortly before 6pm, when the taps were closed off and the barmen stopped serving. Then we had fifteen minutes to finish our drinks and be out of the pub and the doors were closed.

Naturally, a lot of drinking was done in those fifteen minutes in what was commonly known as the 'six o'clock swill'. From there, it was the long drive home to Eastbourne, somewhat inebriated I am now ashamed to say, but always without incident I am happy to report.

Come November 1966, with our course work completed and exams behind us, Dave returned to Dunedin and I spent the rest of the summer working on projects around Wellington and anxiously waiting for a response to my applications to study in the US. Slowly, the responses came back with rejections by Stanford, Caltech, University of New York, and two others. It was not looking good.

At the beginning of April 1967, I was asked to go to Dunedin to carry out foundation investigation for a six-storey ward block in central Dunedin for the Dunedin Hospital. I was happy to do this, for it took my mind off the disappointment of these rejections and it meant an opportunity to catch up with my new friend, Dave.

I was in Dunedin for almost a month and what fun I had thanks to Dave, his wife, Jeannette, and their circle of friends and perhaps best described in the letters I sent home at that time.

65 London Street, Dunedin

10 April 1967

Dear Family,

Well, I have been down here a week now and I guess it is about time I sat down and wrote to you. I arrived in the city at 9pm last Sunday and phoned Dave (Gamble) from the NAC terminal. He called around in his friend's Jaguar and took me first to the hotel to check in and then around to his flat. It was great to see him again and both he and Jeannette were pleased that I had come down. We sat and talked for quite a while that evening and at about 11pm, I returned to the hotel. On Monday, I moved out of the hotel and into their flat.

Most of the time during the first week, we spent the evenings at home talking, playing cards and watching TV. Progress on the job is slow as anticipated and I have a lot of spare time during the day. Most days I have lunch with Dave. On Thursday, I met Brian Teviotdale. We didn't talk for long as he was in rather a hurry, but he gave me his address and phone number and asked me to come up when I was free. Dave Hollands came down on Friday to check on work progress and flew back to Wellington that night.

On Friday night, Dave and I had a night in the town. I finished work at 5:30pm, went home and changed then met Dave at the European Hotel at 6:15pm. We stayed there until 8:30pm, then bought some fish and chips and went back to the flat. After tea, we went back downtown with a friend of Dave's and spent the rest of the evening in the first the European and then the Gresham hotel. I must admit I like the licensing laws in Dunedin. One goes to a hotel after 6pm and receives a meal ticket, which enables you to stay on the premises. It is not necessary to have a meal there.

At the Gresham, Dave introduced me to a very nice girl. Her name is Jenny. She made the evening all the more pleasant and we had an interesting talk.

Saturday night, Dave and Jeannette stayed home. I went out with Dave's friend, Brian, and we ended up at a party in south Dunedin. It was quite an enjoyable night once again. Sunday morning I slept in and in the afternoon, we went for a drive around the eastern bays of the harbour. I rang Jenny at lunchtime and she came with us. It was a pleasant afternoon.

We visited a place called Glenfalloch, you may have been there Mum. It is a privately owned place with beautiful native bushes and gardens. I would imagine that it is even more beautiful in the spring. That night, I cooked for Dave and Jeannette and we had a relatively early night.

One weekend we are planning to go up to Queenstown and Wanaka. I am looking forward to this very much. We shall probably go the weekend of 22 April and I will tell you more about this later. I will finish now and get this post.

26 April 1967

Dear Mum, Dad & family,

I really seem to be slipping when it comes to putting pen to paper, but now while I have some spare hour or two, I shall put you up to date with what has happened during the past week. From Monday through to Friday, we had a relatively quiet time. Most evenings, we spent at home watching TV with the occasional guest popping around. I took the opportunity of doing a bit of study on one or two evenings as I have also been doing at odd times during the day when I have plenty of time on my hands.

On Wednesday night, I went for a swim in the Moana pool, which you may have seen when you were down here last. It is at the top of London Street (almost). On Thursday, Dave, Jeanette and I went to the movies and saw Picnic, *a rather old movie with two of my film idols, Kim Novak and William Holden. I had seen it years ago and loved it, especially the come hither look dance scene in which the gorgeous Novak performed to the film's wonderful theme tune Moonglow.*

On Friday night, we got invited to a party where I got into a rather embarrassing situation. It all happened when I got introduced to a very nice girl whom I took an instant liking to. The feeling appeared mutual, but unknown to me, she had been invited along by the host who was a good friend of Dave's As it turned out, their relationship was one where he (the friend) was really keen on her but she only looked upon him as a good friend. The embarrassing moment came when in my usual friendly manner I started introducing her to a group including Dave, Jeanette, and the host.

Dave was busy tapping me on the shoulder putting me wise to the situation as I carried on only half believing him. However, things soon became apparent to me and to save Dave further embarrassment, I decided to take my leave from her (Jan) for the rest of the evening. If this last paragraph does not make much sense, I will explain it later.

The next day, we set off for Queenstown at about midday. The weather was pleasantly mild as we left Dunedin, but as we travelled through Central Otago, it gradually deteriorated and at 6pm when we arrived in Queenstown, it was raining quite heavily. On the way, we stopped at Roxburgh to look at the dam and at Alexandra where we ate a late lunch. The scenery up central is very beautiful as you probably know and especially so at this time of the year, when the trees are just about to lose their leaves and the colouring is just magnificent. That night, we wine and dined at the Frankton Hotel in Queenstown.

It was a delicious meal and we were all pretty bloated by the time we had finished. Consequently, we turned in very early that night.

The next morning, it was still raining and we went for a few scenic drives around the area. We went for about six miles along the road to Glenorgie on the east side of Lake Wakatipu. After returning to Queenstown, we set off on the road to Skippers. This took us towards Coronet Peak and at the turnoff to Skippers, we ran into a light fall of snow. We followed the road for about six or seven miles, then decided to turn back before reaching Skippers, as the road was very greasy and I was fearful of getting stranded. It was an exciting bit of road to traverse, very narrow and vertical drops of hundreds of feet in many places.

We then drove on to Arrowtown, through Cromwell and retraced our path back to Dunedin, arriving home at 6pm. It was a most enjoyable trip despite the weather. That night, I invited Jan around to the flat where we became better acquainted. Actually, tonight she is joining Dave, Jeanette and I at the Cherry Lodge restaurant. David Hollands told me to take Dave and Jeanette out to dine sometime at the firm's expense and I have just been waiting to meet the right girl to accompany me. She's arrived!

For my racing tips at Napier last Saturday, I chose the first selection of the local paper in each race. This gave me six points I think. I have enclosed the picks and perhaps you would like to check them, Mum, but only do this if you scored less. For next Saturday's meeting where ever it is take as my picks the Evening Post's first selection in each race and I will leave it to you to work out my score, Mum.

Well, that is about all for now. If work continues at the present rate, I should be returning home towards the end of next week. However, I shall write again next week and let you know for sure. Goodbye for now.

3 May 1967

Dear Mum, Dad and family,

Thanks for your letter yesterday, Mum. It was good to hear from you again. You will be glad to know that I finally made the effort and went and visited the Chapmans, and I am very glad I did. Actually, when I read your letter yesterday and for the second or third time you mentioned them, I decided to go there and then. I managed to duck away from work early at 4:30pm and went up. Mrs Chapman was in and I was invited in straight away. She is very friendly don't you think; reminds me in some ways of Aunty Wilma. We talked for some time about the family connections. The husband I didn't meet but I have been invited back for a meal sometime and I am looking forward to this.

My work here will soon be finished, but not before the weekend. At the present time, I would say we will finish sometime on Monday, in which case I will fly home on Tuesday. For more definite information on this score, I suggest you ring either John Moss or David Hollands on Sunday.

I am continuing to enjoy myself down here, but I am looking forward to getting home. Time is tending to drag during the day as I am not very busy.

Last Wednesday night, the four of us had a very pleasant night out dining at one of Dunedin's licensed restaurants. I fought desperately all day to fight off a bout of flu I felt coming on. I was moderately successful but it hit with a bang on Thursday. Unfortunately, I still had to work, but on Thursday night, I had a bath and went straight to bed. On Friday, I started coming right again. That night, I had been invited to a stag party for one of Dave's friends, who was soon to be married. However, I felt it wiser to stay at home with my condition the way it was.

As it was, I didn't get to bed until 2am next morning as I involved myself in a set of amusing circumstances and ended up chasing the express train north to Palmerston, some forty miles north of Dunedin. However, that is a long and complicated story and I shall leave the details until I get home. Apparently, the stag party was a great success. One of the local strip girls was hired to put on a show for the boys. I hope this doesn't shock you; actually, it was quite harmless fun from all accounts. Saturday night a group of us went out dancing and had a lot of fun.

Earlier in the evening, I had spent a couple of hours at the night trots. I didn't manage to win a fortune but quite enjoyed the night. I had the misfortune of seeing one of the horses I backed pulled up when running into a sure place. Just outside the furlong, a couple of horses were interfered with and the horse behind put a foot through the sulky of my horse. I see Trentham is on next Saturday. Perhaps we can go the following Saturday if there is a second meeting.

I shall finish now as there is no further news. Claire Chapman sends her love and says she was very glad to have met me.

I received the news of the acceptance of my application to study at the Illinois Institute of Technology in Chicago via a telegram from Philip, while on this assignment in Dunedin. My joy was immense and although it was not my preferred choice of either university or location, I was over the moon and could not wait to get back home to make preparations to get there.

During the six years since leaving Wellington College, my good mate Wal had been pursuing a parallel career as a land surveyor with a competing engineering consultancy Truebridge Callendar and Beach, which operated from an office in Central Wellington. In those days, surveyors studied for their qualification by correspondence and I recall spending many an evening with Wal at his office studying for our respective qualifications. We were both single and dreamed of travelling abroad.

As my plans for study in the US were coming to fruition, we spent some of these evenings plotting a sea journey on the Southern Cross or Northern Star across the Pacific to Acapulco, where we would alight and travel overland by bus or train to my destination, where Wal would leave me and travel on to London and meet up with other fellow travellers. Alas, that was not to be, for love and the charms of Bet won over Wal's heart. He put his plans for any overseas travel on hold and he marched down the aisle into wedlock in May 1967.

I was happy for Wal and did not let his change of plan upset me, for I knew it was coming and it was not as if he sprung it upon me. Besides, a sea and overland trip to Chicago would take precious time, which I did not have. The age of jet air travel was now taking over from leisurely ocean voyages as the means of travelling abroad, and I spent the next two months arranging to fly from Auckland to Chicago via Los Angeles, with a twenty-four-hour stopover in Tahiti en route to experience the charms of the south sea island paradise.

With a scheduled departure date in mid-September, this would see me arrive in Chicago a week before the fall (autumn) semester was due to start—time enough to get acclimatised and get over any jet lag that may eventuate. That was the plan. What actually eventuated was somewhat more dramatic, which almost scuttled my well-laid plans completely.

I have failed to mention a medical condition that has plagued me since I was a toddler and that is I suffer from eczema. It comes and goes and from time to time when it flared up, I sought specialist treatment from a certain Dr Eastcott, who had his clinic in Petone. The standard treatment was the application tar based products and sulphur creams, which had only marginal benefits, if any, and it seems to me that those of us who suffer from eczema learn to put up with the discomfort.

I recall Dr Eastcott once saying to me that eczema may be uncomfortable but it would not kill me. I have long since learnt to live with the condition and in my own case, I have concluded that it comes on as a result of my reaction to stress and in particular, major changes that are going on in my life, for there have been many long periods when it has not bothered me at all.

What did this have to do with my travel plans? A lot I was soon to learn and in a somewhat dramatic fashion. Smallpox is a disease that has since been eradicated but is still a problem in certain parts of the world. When undertaking international travel at this time, it was a requirement to be vaccinated to counter the risk of contracting the disease. When I approached our family GP, Doc Martin, with a request to vaccinate me he was initially reluctant to do so, for as he explained it, there was some connection between eczema and smallpox and a risk that I may overreact to the vaccination.

Dismayed that I may not be able to proceed with my plans, I implored him to give me the vaccination, which he did with a small pinprick in my upper right arm. Within a day, a large scab the size of the palm of my hand had appeared where he had administered the vaccination and soon similar scabs were breaking out on my face, arms, and over much of my upper body. This alarmed all and sundry and I was quickly rushed into Wellington Hospital and placed in an isolation unit, where I was to remain for almost three weeks before recovering and allowed to go home.

I never thought that perhaps I was on death's door, but maybe the family and others harboured such a thought, it was never discussed. What I do remember is that I was horribly sick, and itchy as hell, and the medication applied to counter my reaction to the vaccine was more than I could swallow. Large tablets that looked and tasted like clay, which I invariably threw up until my doctor, Ian Prior, prescribed a liquid form of the same medicine that was marginally more acceptable. I was allowed visitors who came and went wrapped in gowns and masks and to their credit a number of my friends as well as the family called by to give me encouragement.

My other memory of this incident was the interest in my case shown by the wider medical fraternity at the hospital and one day when I was well on the road to recovery, I was present at a seminar for doctors and nursing staff where my condition was discussed and debated.

I remember returning home towards the end of August, despondent and relatively weak from my ordeal. I considered delaying my departure until the end of the year and travelling to Chicago in January for the start of the northern spring semester. However, my brother Philip, who always supported and encouraged me in my endeavours, persuaded me to stick to my original travel plan and go now. I perked up and said, "Yes, perhaps I should not delay."

This left me a couple of weeks to pack my bags, say farewell to friends, and drive north to Auckland with Mum, Dad, Philip, Vivienne and Jenny, where we exchanged a teary farewell in the late evening of 14 September 1967 and I flew out at midnight on a UTA French Airways flight bound for Tahiti.

Chapter 3
Chicago and Boston 1967–1970

Detained in Tahiti

20 Sept 1967
Tahiti, 9am
Mailed from Chicago 22 Sept 1967

Dear Mum, Dad and family,

Well, here I am on my sixth day away from home and boy what a predicament I got myself into. I was detained by the police in Tahiti for the past three days and have only just this moment taken off from Faaa Airport to continue my journey to the US. I was involved in a motor accident on Friday night (I was not hurt) and I was detained while enquiries were being made. At any other time, I would have been delighted to be stranded there, but the circumstances were rather worrying and for this reason, I have refrained from writing before now.

I had a most frustrating time with the French police as there was no one who spoke English and my French is almost non-existent—bonjour, bon soir, merci, parlez vous Anglaise, etc. However, I spoke to an official at UTA Airlines on Saturday morning and he was most sympathetic and helpful. His name is Sydney Pollock and he arranged to get me on the first flight out of Tahiti after I had been cleared (at no extra cost) to leave, which was yesterday afternoon. Sydney also spoke to the police and was able to give me a full picture of my situation.

The flight from Auckland was pleasant but uneventful and I slept for most of the flight. No, I didn't get preferential treatment, but that did not matter. I woke just before we landed to see the sunrise far out to sea, arriving at Papeete at 6am, where the temperature was already 72 degrees F, and as I was driven to the Hotel Taone, where I had booked to stay for the next twenty-four hours, I noticed the Northern Star was just leaving the harbour. My hotel was just a little way out of town and consisted of a main building with office and single and double sleeping quarters, spacious grounds with a number of bungalows and right on the beachfront an exotic dining room bar and a swimming pool.

The beach was about the best I saw, for in general, the island does not appear to have good beaches. After settling in, together with another chap I met on the flight from Auckland, we hired a car and drove around the island. It was very pleasant, the vegetation was very rich but almost became monotonous as there was little variation in the scenery. We stopped several times for a closer look at the scenery, swim and sample the local ale at a country pub.

We arrived back at the hotel at 1pm for lunch, then proceeded to wander around Papeete in the afternoon. It is a city with lots of charm and fascination with sidewalk cafes and bars, quaint buildings and literally hundreds of men and women charging round on motor scooters, mopeds, etc. The latter part of the afternoon we went back to the hotel to swim both in the sea and in the hotel pool. Prior to the evening meal, we watched a group of Tahitian dancers practising for a concert later that evening.

I enjoyed this very much, all so casual and relaxed. After dinner, I went into Papeete and Quinns Bar for a few drinks with the small amount of Francs I had left. I got talking to a Tahitian chap who couldn't speak English and danced with some of the local girls. When I finally had enough, I got into the car to drive back to the hotel and it was then that I had the accident. A tendency to drive on the left-hand side of the road caused me to go into that lane, while making a left-hand turn. A scooter came round the bend and ahead and before I could take evasive action, he caught my front mudguard.

The driver of the motor scooter was taken to hospital and I felt very awful about this, for despite the unfamiliarity of driving on the RHS, I was still technically in the wrong. I spent an anxious night in the gendarmerie (language problem) and about 6am, finally realised I would not be able to catch my plane. By this stage, my passport had been taken from me and a case against me for negligent driving is to be heard on 7 November. However, according to Sydney, the UTA official, who spoke to the police on my behalf, both the police and the court's sympathy lies with me, as a blood test indicated that my blood contained no alcohol and also due to unfamiliarity with driving on the RHS.

I may possibly have to pay a fine of up to US$40. Details will probably arrive in NZ as I gave them that address. Please don't worry too much, I am now alright *and also very lucky I think. It was quite an experience for the first stage of my trip, one I never want to repeat. Oh to be able to speak French.*

On Saturday, I was forced to take a room in the town at the cheapest rate available to conserve my money, not being sure of when I could leave. I got a room for 300 Fr a night at the Hotel Stuart, which is about the tallest building on the Papeete waterfront. It was not very good but beggars can't be choosers. The best I can say about this hotel is that it has a very nice balcony overlooking the harbour and I spent many hours sitting there anxiously awaiting news from the police. My other main pre-occupation was swimming at the beach nearby and walking up and down the waterfront.

During the next three days, I got quite friendly with Madame Stuart, the hotel proprietor, a rather unusual person. She told me that she had travelled to various places around the world including New Zealand and I formed the impression that she was an ex-society woman of Tahiti (if they exist), who had slipped from grace to a lower level of living. Also living in the hotel was an English gent and I could never figure out why he was staying in such a rundown hotel as the Hotel Stuart.

Impressions of Tahiti—everyone is very casual particularly the French, the police infuriatingly so, though this may have been due to the language problem. The Tahitians appeared rather friendly but also rather dirty. Papeete has a lot of charm with streetside cafes and literally hundreds of girls and boys running round on motor scooters. The traffic is heavy all the time and where they are all going I could not guess.

I am now on a flight direct to LA and will fly on from there and arrive in Chicago early tomorrow morning. Vivienne, I apologise for all the arrangements you made for me in Honolulu, but as you see, the situation was beyond my control. There is a bit more to tell but I am running out of space. I made friends with a Japanese chap, Kiezo Ishida, who is en route to NZ. I swapped the NZ dollars I was carrying for US dollars. I'm glad I took that little bit of NZ money with me. He may be ringing you when he reaches Wellington (6 Oct) to pass on a friendly message. His English is quite good. Well, goodbye for now, I shall write again soon from Chicago.

Much love
Michael XXXXXXX

Fifty years on, as I look back on this incident, it is not something that I am proud of. I never did find out how badly the Tahitian was hurt for at the time my entire focus was on my personal predicament and the possible delay to the start of my studies. I can only hope that he recovered from his injuries to live a productive life.

Other memories of these three days in Tahiti were the multi-gender toilet shared with the Wahines at Quinns Post bar, and falling asleep on the beach for several hours one hot and sunny afternoon. Fortunately, I had covered my torso with a towel, but my face and arms were exposed to the hot tropical sun and in the days that followed, I suffered from severe sunburn and dry flaky skin, compounding the after effects of my recent smallpox scare and eczema. By the time I reached Chicago, large chunks of dry skin were falling off and after a night's sleep, my sheets would be covered in loose flaky pieces of skin.

Fortunately, there were no severe after effects to the sunburn and a month after settling into my new life in Chicago, miraculously my eczema disappeared completely.

On to Chicago

I have almost no recollection of the flight to Los Angeles except that on Wednesday morning 20 September 1967, I boarded a plane and eight hours later, we landed at Los Angeles International Airport. It was 8 o'clock local time. I was quite taken aback by the size of the airport, but I was in for something even more amazing, when I reached Chicago several hours later that night.

I cleared customs in less than thirty minutes, then I had to wait a further hour and a half for my connection to Chicago. On this flight to Chicago, I was seated beside a young marine who was returning home after three months of fighting in Vietnam. We chatted and he had some intriguing tales to tell. The time passed quickly and before I knew it, we were circling above the city of Chicago, awaiting our turn to land.

The lights of the city extended for miles in all directions and as we approached O'Hare International Airport, I was just overwhelmed at its size and the amount of air traffic that was coming and going in the early hours of the morning, as our plane prepared to touch down. It seemed an age before our plane arrived at a terminal building, and then another before I had recovered my checked-in baggage.

I should pause to mention here that Chicago was and still is the third most populous city in the United States and it is located on the southern shores of Lake Michigan. The Illinois Institute of Technology (IIT) is a relatively new university, having been formed by the merger of the Armour and Lewis Institutes in 1940 and is located in what is referred to as the near south side of Chicago. It has a modern campus that covers several city blocks between 31st street to 35th street going south and from South Michigan Avenue to South Federal Avenue and the Dan Ryan Expressway on its western perimeter.

To the north, east and west, the campus is surrounded on three sides by low-income Negro neighbourhoods. To the west of the Dan Ryan Expressway, there is a low-income ethnic neighbourhood of various cultural backgrounds. As I was to observe, the residents of these respective neighbourhoods did not mix.

It was 4am when I recovered my luggage and rather than hang around at the airport, I decided to catch a bus into downtown Chicago, thinking I could park myself in the lobby of the Palmer Hotel in State Street, wait for daylight then make my way to Illinois Institute of Technology, some thirty-two city blocks further south. It was not a good time to arrive, as there was little activity going on and I could not find a lounge or seat to rest upon, so I decided to move on to the IIT.

I found a friendly porter who hailed me a taxi and as I got aboard, I heard him say to the driver, "Now this boy is going to IIT along there on State Street. He's gonna college, so don't you over charge him." The taxi driver took me to the address I had given him and dropped me off on the road outside. It was now 5:30am, still dark and as was to be expected everything was closed down. Fortunately, I ran into some cleaners who were heading to work in the administration building on the far side of the campus and they took me to their small room, where I rested while until things started to open up.

It was Thursday morning, I was late to register and classes were due to start the following Monday. At 8:15am, I made my way to the admissions office and from there it was one continued rush, as I walked here and there to talk with faculty advisors, determine what courses to register on, fill in forms, doubling back when I was given misleading information, in my tired state it all seemed chaotic, and my first impressions were not good. Finally, by the early afternoon, I was at a stage where the courses I would take that semester were signed off by the respective department head and I made my way to the registration desk to complete and hand in the forms.

I had not slept for twenty-four hours and I was so tired that halfway through this final exercise, I nodded off and fell asleep at the desk. It was at this point that a kind and sympathetic administration official tapped me on the shoulder and told me to go and get some rest and come back tomorrow. "All will be well," he said. I picked myself up, found my way to the South Dormitory on Wabash Avenue, and collapsed in a heap on my bed in Room 314, which would be my home for the next nine months. However, my ordeal was far from over and there were still things to take care of before I could rest.

As part of a welcoming programme for foreign students, I had been assigned a buddy, who was to meet me and help me settle in, when I arrived in Chicago. His name was Ed Cook and when I finally met up with him in the late afternoon, he was a most welcome helpmate. Ed was a good fellow and he immediately invited me to dine with him in his fraternity, where I explained the reason behind my delayed arrival, my experiences on arrival at IIT and my need to return to O'Hare Airport to pick up a suitcase that I had sent as unaccompanied baggage. He was only too willing to help me and after we had finished eating, he drove me out to the airport.

As we drove to the airport, I made the following mental observations—one car in ten seemed to have a bashed-in fender or two, everyone seemed to drive as if they were half an hour late for wherever they were going and they travelled much too close to the vehicle in front. This trip to the airport turned to be a fruitless exercise for when we got there, it was nowhere to be found. We headed back to IIT and it was 8:15pm when Ed dropped me outside South Dormitory. I thanked Ed and I headed straight to bed and twelve hours much-needed sleep.

It had been a hectic and unsettling thirty hours since I had left Tahiti. I completed registration on Friday morning and then did little else but eat and sleep for most of the weekend. It was good to have Ed there to help me during this initial period, but as I became immersed in my studies and made new friends, we slowly lost contact.

Illinois Institute of Technology

I had arrived almost a week late, I was tired, my skin was in a mess and with only two days of rest, I was straight into class and course work. Perhaps this was not a bad thing, for I had no time to dwell on any misgivings I had about adjusting to life in the American university system, the structure of the civil engineering degree and the course work I would be required to study. Fortunately, I settled in quickly and soon found that the IIT semester system was much to my liking.

In contrast to the New Zealand university system at the time, where courses were studied over the entire university year and a pass or fail was largely determined by results in a final exam, courses at IIT were taken and completed in one semester and pass or fail was largely determined by the standard of course work presented throughout the semester with a final exam contributing only 20 per cent. This suited my study habits and I soon found that I was thriving in this system and achieving very good grades as the semester progressed.

Achieved a grade point average (GPA) of 3.4 (maximum 4.0), during my first semester, which turned out to be the highest I would achieve. I never slipped below 3.2 and in subsequent semesters, I maintained a similar high level of achievement without applying quite the same effort. Along the way, I won a scholarship from the American Society of Civil Engineers (one of four awarded nationwide) and a commendation from one of my professors, who ranked me among the top civil engineering students he had seen in recent years. I had adapted well.

I chose to live in a dormitory for undergraduate students during my first year at IIT. My reasoning is that it would be easier to assimilate with fellow students and make friends. This proved to be the case and I soon developed a good circle of friends, both American and foreign, or aliens (an ugly term), as the latter are referred to by government authorities. However, there was a downside to this accommodation arrangement, which I wrestled with until I moved off campus and into an apartment in nearby Bridgeport the following year.

I was twenty-four years old when I arrived at IIT and the students in my dorm including my roommate, Bernard Liller, were in their late teens and fresh out of high school. To put it mildly, there was a maturity gap and aside from Bernard, or Bernie as I would call him, the friendships I developed came from introductions to several Americans living in Chicago and from activities I became involved in on and off campus.

The Folks at Marina Towers

I was fortunate to be given an introduction to Jim and Sandy Marshall by one of Vivienne's colleagues at the US Embassy in Wellington. Jim and Sandy were a middle-aged couple, who lived in a luxurious apartment on the upper floors of Marina Towers overlooking the Chicago River in downtown Chicago. I made contact with the Marshalls during my first few weeks in Chicago and they were quick to invite me into their home and introduce me to their friends.

The highlight of my stay so far occurred last Saturday night. As I told you in my last letter, I was going out to dine with the Marshalls. What wonderful people. So friendly and informal and what an apartment. Right at the top of Marina Towers, you can see for miles when the haze lifts. I arrived at 6pm and introduced myself. In turn, I was introduced to three girls, nurses Marianne, Tina and Beth whom they had invited along to meet me. Apparently, they were expecting to hear from me, as they had been planning this before I had arrived in Chicago.

Also, in the party was the manager of the La Salle Hotel, a very good friend of theirs and he was just like the Marshalls. After a few drinks, we went down to the restaurant at the base of the Towers for dinner. And what a meal. We spent almost two hours there then returned to the apartment. More drinks followed; we got on marvellously.

Later in the evening, Marianne, Tina and Beth took me to a party. Here were more people to meet and I really had a good time. In fact, I was the last to leave and helped clean up the flat a bit.

I was invited back to the Marshall's apartment on several occasions over the next few months to socialise and relax in their company. They seemed to enjoy my visits and we took to making reel-to-reel tape recordings of events and discussions we were having. During the time I was in Chicago, postal mail was still the main form of communication with home. International telephone calls were prohibitively expensive and the age of the internet was still decades away. As well as frequent letters going back and forth, I made several other tape recordings with the Marshalls and my campus colleagues.

I still have those tapes, which I must get digitised. My letters suggest some were quite amusing and they fill in some of the gaps not recorded here.

Sadly, I slowly lost contact with the Marshalls due to a combination of factors including health problems on their part, the demands of my study programme and an expanding network of friends and activities on campus. For a while, Marianne, whom I had introduced to Bernie, became a romantic feature in his life, but all three girls soon disappeared almost as quickly as they came into my life.

The ROTC Kid

Bernie Liller: The first and one of my longer-lasting friendships was with my dormitory roommate Bernard. Much to his chagrin, I took to calling him Bernie, a shortening of his name he came to grudgingly accept from me, although he continued to refer to himself as Bernard with emphasis on the second syllable. Our friendship lasted well beyond my Chicago days, but for me, it was one fraught with contrasting emotions ranging from frustration and annoyance to periods of joy and laughter, as we each came to know the personality traits of the other.

When completing an application for residence in a dormitory, I requested an American roommate, but what I got in Bernie was a composite. Born in Maryland near Washington DC, Bernie was the only child, his father was American and a military attaché in the US forces stationed in Europe. His mother was French and Bernie had spent much of his life attending schools in France and Switzerland. From the beginning, his immaturity shone through. He presented a gung ho American military persona along with a fluency in the French language and he had two strong interests, girls and the US Navy.

He was attached to the IIT Reserve Officers Training Corp (ROTC), was highly impressionable and he latched onto me like a faithful lap dog. If I encouraged him, he would follow me everywhere.

I had a little laugh to myself last night. Bernie has just changed his brand of toothpaste. He's now using 'Ultra Bright' toothpaste with sex appeal. It's a new brand, which has been advertised on TV a lot lately.

Letter home 31 Dec 1967

As I mentioned above, he was the first friend I made and during our early exposure to our new environment, we explored the nightlife in Chicago together. One of our preferred haunts was in and around Rush Street on the near north side of Chicago, where we found countless nightclubs, strip joints, topless go-go dancers, and bars and restaurants, and of course the Chicago Playboy Club. Most were far too expensive for this poor student, but Bernie had already discovered credit and for him, this did not seem a problem.

Not far away on the northern fringe of downtown Chicago was an area called Old Town, which was more down market with numerous bars and entertainment facilities. In an early letter home, I referred to it as the hippy area of Chicago and we returned there many times to enjoy the nightlife it had to offer.

Although he was a good friend and I enjoyed his company, I found him impossible to live with and at the end of the semester, I moved down the hallway to share a room with Bill who was relatively stable and good company. Initially, this caused some tension between us but this was soon overcome and we remained good friends and shared many fun moments during the rest of the time at IIT.

You will hear more about Bernie in in the passages that follow, but there is one incident that occurred during this initial period of our friendship which I feel is worth recording here. Most of our meals were taken in a student cafeteria where there was usually a choice of two or three main courses on the menu. Given my broad Kiwi accent, communicating verbally with the serving staff was rather difficult, but usually, this was not a problem as I could point at what I wanted. However, there was one occasion when I opted for fish but I did not want the accompanying tartare sauce, so in my broad in Kiwi accent, I said to the cheerful coloured serving woman.

"Fish fingers, chips and no tartare sauce." She stared at me blankly, there was no response, so I politely repeated my request.

"Fish fingers, chips and no tartare sauce."

Again, there was the same blank look and it was at this point that Bernie, who was right behind me, came to my rescue and yelled, "He wants fish sticks, and fries with no tartar-are sauce." Thanks to Bernie, my message was finally understood and my order was cheerfully served.

This was by no means the first or last time it appeared to locals that I was speaking in a foreign language.

My Michigan Family

Two years before I left for Chicago, my sister Jenny had started up a pen pal relationship with Karlene, the eldest daughter of Betty and Spike Reynolds who lived in the small town of Clark Lake, Michigan, approximately two hundred miles by east of Chicago. Jenny had already informed Karlene of my study plans and upon making initial contact shortly after my arrival in Chicago, I was invited to spend the coming Thanksgiving holiday period with the Reynolds and their circle of friends.

There were no lectures during the week leading up to Thanksgiving day and I accepted the invitation. On the day before Thanksgiving, I packed a small travel bag, hopped on a Greyhound bus and made my way to Clark Lake on the Wednesday afternoon prior to Thanksgiving. Betty, Spike, Karlene and her sister, Lori, were there to meet me when I hopped off the bus in nearby Jackson and what a warm welcome I received. Back in Chicago a week later, this is what I wrote home:

What wonderful people they are. So friendly and in many ways so much like us back home. In fact, it was almost like being at home and I didn't want to leave on Sunday. By now, you will have played the tape and heard their voices. Betty and Spike are a young couple, about thirty-eight; Spike likes to hunt and fish and Betty, I guess I can say, she likes keeping house, cooking, etc., what a good wife should do. They are an average income family and I guess the best way I can describe how I felt in their company is the way Dave Gamble described our family if you remember that.

Karlene in many ways is a lot like you Jenny though she at least does the dishes without any pushing. They're all very anxious to meet you and you'll like them very much. Karlene thinks you should write longer letters though she is too polite to say so. I was surprised to find out what she didn't know about you. Actually, these are more my thoughts than hers. I like Karlene, she is a very nice girl.

Well, for a bit of what went on. Out with maps again. This time, I took off in a Greyhound bus south along the Dan Ryan Expressway and onto Motorway 94. The bus went non-stop to Battle Creek, where we stopped for refreshments, then onto Jackson. The Reynolds were there to meet me and we drove out to their home. It was now Wednesday evening at 7pm. We had supper and boy did they encourage me to eat. I later realised this was one way of being well received. What I mean is they appreciated my big appetite.

We sat around and talked till quite late and went to bed at 1am. Thursday, we had a late breakfast and then prepared for Thanksgiving dinner at a hotel in Jackson. About ten of us in all (in fact all those you heard on the tape) went to the Hoges Hotel at 3pm. I certainly knew I had eaten when I finished, boy what a meal. Chicken, duck, turkey, stuffing, vegetables, salad, etc., etc., etc. The Americans certainly turn it on. We left about 5pm. And went over to the Gibberds, who live at Liberty near Clark Lake.

There I played them our tape; they got a great kick out of it and everyone thinks you sound like a real character dad. I must say I always get a laugh out of that bit about the rubbish. After this, we made the tape for you and then I showed them the slides of NZ. We also sat around and recorded songs on the tape (us singing) and really had some fun.

Next day, we were up late again and after breakfast, we went for a drive around the nearby countryside. It's a real pretty spot and I liked it a lot. Clarke Lake reminded me a lot of Lake Taupo though it is much smaller and a lot prettier. The countryside is gently rolling with lots of wooded areas. It must be really beautiful at other times of the year. I can understand why Betty and Spike have always lived there, it is so peaceful. By the way, Jackson is about the size of Palmerston North.

That night, Karlene and I went to the basketball game. Loris' team won by the way. I must mention something that happened there, which was really funny. At half time, Karlene's friend, Vickie, who is the cheerleader, came dashing over with a couple of her good friends and introduced me to them. Well, one was really cute, so on the spur of the moment, I stooped and kissed her hand. Boy from her reaction you might have thought I was Ringo Starr. She stood there for a couple of seconds with the cutest grin you ever seen.

I was told the next day that I had really given her a big thrill. After the basketball, we returned home where a large group of people (about sixteen) had gathered to see my slides. They're certainly proving very popular.

On Saturday, we relaxed round the house for most of the day. They certainly have a lovely home, with a large section and not many other houses around. That evening, Karlene and I went to her Homecoming Dance and Concert. The Si Zentner Orchestra was playing and it was pretty good. Karlene and I danced and we had a great time. Vickie also came with her boyfriend and though to me they were perhaps a little young, they were refreshingly so and I enjoyed being in their company.

On Sunday, we spent most of the day relaxing around the house. Betty asked me if I would like to cook dinner to which I responded with a brown stew and vegetables. Actually, she ended up doing the cooking and I gave the directions. I tried to think how you went about cooking the stew, Mum, and I must say it turned out pretty good. It was a new idea to them and they all enjoyed it. After a short siesta, I made preparations to return to Chicago. I caught the bus at 8pm and was really sorry to be leaving. It took me several days to settle back into the routine of school.

A month later, I returned to spend Xmas with the Reynolds and I went back to Clark Lake on several more occasions during the time I was in Chicago and it was like I had been adopted into the family. We have remained lifelong friends and I continue to correspond with Betty and Spike to this day.

The Vicar and the Petrol Head

One evening shortly after my arrival in Chicago, I was invited to a social evening hosted by campus Chaplin and Episcopalian Priest. Father Lawrence in his nearby campus apartment. It was an enjoyable evening, during which we discussed topics of interest including campus life and America's racial problems amongst other things. He was a dynamic individual and so unlike some of the staid vicars of St Albans Church back home where I had been inducted into the Anglican fold. I enjoyed his company, he was a good listener at times when I was feeling low and I spent a lot of time with him and other students at his apartment and occasionally socialising out on the town.

It was through Father Lawrence that I met Dan Dickel, a student of about my own age, who was sharing the apartment with Father Lawrence. Dan had a passion for fixing and rebuilding cars and though this was of no interest to me, we became good friends. He took an interest in where I was from and what I was doing in Chicago. On one occasion mid-semester, he took me on a road trip out into the countryside in a little beat-up Volkswagen Beetle he was doing up. Here is my account of this road trip as recorded at the time:

Sunday morning, 19 Nov, I set off with Dan at 10:30am. Along the Eisenhower Expressway and out onto Highway 64. We made our way through various small towns and about 1pm we stopped for lunch just out of Rockford. Boy, it was great to get away from the city. I now fully appreciate how choked up with smog the city is. After lunch, we continued west as far as a place called Galena, in the NW corner of the state. This reminded me of an English town and although I've never actually seen one, it was really quite quaint. Dan has asked me to go skiing with him up here over the Xmas holiday period.

From Galena, we drove south to Savanna, where we had a view of the Mississippi. This is apparently the area that Mark Twain wrote about in his books. Boy, the river is certainly huge. We crossed the Toll Bridge just so that I could say I had been to Iowa. We drove onto Mt Carroll, where we stopped for tea and also at Shamir College to speak to one of Dan's former girlfriends. We were there for about two hours. It seemed that most of the students there were problem students of the Hippie Type. It was most interesting to learn about what went on there.

It was about 9pm so we departed and had a fairly rapid trip back to Chicago and arrived back to IIT at about 11:30pm. It was really a fabulous day. By the way, Dan is doing postgraduate study at IIT and works for an auto manufacturer. He lives on campus with the Vicar in Bailey Hall.

I saw quite a bit of Dan during this time; we went skiing together during the holiday breaks over the winter, then one day during the early spring Dan called me and said, "I have found this car for sale sitting in the campus parking lot. It's a little rusty and there is no back seat, but it goes. Only $25. Do you want to buy it?"

"Does it go?" I replied.

"You can buy some parts, I will rebuild the engine, and it will be as good as gold," said Dan.

"Let's do it," I replied and with that, I became the proud possessor of one Dodge automatic car.

Easter was upon us and Dan had a private workshop in a small warehouse somewhere on the near north side of Chicago. The car, now mine, we drove it to Dan's workshop, then we went off to Sears Roebuck to buy the necessary spare parts at a cost of $25 and together, we set about re-boring and rebuilding the engine, a task which took us three full days from memory. Dan obviously knew what he was doing for I didn't have a clue, but I made myself useful by passing spanners and lifting things when needed. At the end of the third day, we fired it up and after a little hesitation, the engine finally turned over and gave out a throaty roar. I was now mobile on my own set of wheels.

Looking back, that purchase had to be one of if not the best value purchases I have made in my life. Who cared that it was an ugly duckling, it ran like a charm. It took me four thousand miles across the country to Portland, Oregon, and back during the northern summer of 1968. My friends found it a novelty and loved riding in it, no back seat and all and served me for the rest of my days in Chicago, where I left it abandoned still in running condition. The only additional expense I can recall was the need to purchase a new set of tyres upon my return from the west coast of America. What a bargain and what fun I had with it.

I continued a loose friendship with both the Vicar and Dan during my time in Chicago and both of them came out to New Zealand for separate visits in 1971 (the Vicar) and in 1988 (Dan and his wife and two kids). Sadly, I have since lost contact, for both were good friends and helped me immensely during my days in Chicago.

International Club

My first effort at reaching out and making friends on campus was to join the International Club, which was promoted by the Intercultural Centre, which operated out of a small intimate building on the central part of the campus. I turned up one evening during the second week of the semester and before I had time to decline, I found myself elected to the position of club treasurer unopposed. I did not really mind as it was a role I was familiar with and I have always found an active involvement in the various clubs I have joined over the years has been a good way to make friends and influence events.

My involvement in the International Club was no different. It provided me with an immediate social outlet, introduction to a broad range of foreign nationals and the opportunity to be involved in the organisation of some interesting cultural events. IIT had a policy of encouraging foreign students of all nationalities to come and study and at this time there were more than sixty nationalities represented in the student role. Among them was a group of students from Eastern Nigeria, whom I recall referring to their home country as Biafra.

I was only vaguely aware of events on the African continent at the time and mostly my knowledge was confined to South Africa, its apartheid regime, and rugby, and the Mau uprisings in East Africa during the mid-1960s. I was totally unaware of the civil war raging in Nigeria at the time of my arrival in Chicago and despite meeting and socialising with these students, I remained rather ignorant about these events. It was only several years later when I found myself on assignment in Lagos, Nigeria, that I developed a better understanding of the cultural and religious divide among the three major tribal groups of that fascinating county.

I have since read accounts of the Biafran War including the novel *Half of a Yellow Sun* by Chamanda Ngosi Adichie which gives a compelling account of events leading up to and during this war. It was brutal.

I developed a good working relationship with the director of the Intercultural Centre Allan (Al) Leibowitz and two of the more interesting activities I was involved in was an on-campus forum discussing problems foreign students face in the USA in which I was a guest panellist, followed a few weeks later by a conference and dinner at the Palmer House in downtown Chicago hosted by prominent Chicago businessmen with special guest speaker, Lord Carrington, UK Ambassador to the United Nations.

However, apart from a photo which hangs on the wall in my study to remind me of these events, my most enduring memory of this aspect of my introduction to life at IIT was an international festival I organised during my second semester.

At the beginning of the second semester, I was elected president of the International Club and with it came the responsibility of organising an international festival, an annual event held on campus each May. With guidance from Al Leibowitz and with the support of a team of student volunteers, I set about planning this event to be held in the main auditorium of Herman Hall with a seating capacity of five hundred people. This turned out to be quite a time-consuming task that involved contacting various ethnic groups and amateur performers around Chicago and persuading them to participate.

There were times leading up to the concert when I questioned my commitment to the festival, but as it turned out, the festival was a great success and well worth the effort. The following is my recollection of the evening as recorded in a letter home.

I have been working pretty hard on putting on the international festival, which we had last Saturday evening. It was a resounding success and I guess it was worth all the trouble. I don't know how but it went off without a hitch except for one incident at the end, which actually involved me.

The program was as described in the program enclosed. As president, I made the opening speech, which was not too much trouble. Then during the intermission, the fellows decided that I should say a few words at the end. One of the Indian fellows involved wanted me to call the artist back on stage one at a time and after a small argument, we settled on bringing them all back on stage together. Al Leibowitz also told me I should announce the national anthem at that stage. Well, the end of the show came and I was called back on stage by the Emcee. I said another few words and I was really warming up to my role in front of the microphone.

Then it happened. I called for the artists to come back on stage, but they hadn't been informed. After a gap of five or ten seconds, they started coming on in dribs and drabs, and finally, after I didn't know how many seconds or minutes, the stage filled up. The silence. No national anthem. Somehow after what seemed an eternity the Stars & Stripes came on and I was rescued from a somewhat embarrassing situation. Still, it was all worthwhile. The words of praise that came my way were proof of that. According to some, I've got talent and should be on stage. I think I may pay a visit to Hollywood after all.

Festival over, it was time to concentrate on final exams, which were looming then prepare for a trip to Portland, Oregon, where I had secured a job for the summer. When I returned for the fall semester in 1968, I withdrew from the International Club, but I retained close contact with Al Leibowitz, who called me in to assist with aspects of the festival the following year.

Road Trip to Miami

My first semester came to an end in mid-January and this was followed by a two-week break before the start of the second semester. I had no special plans for amusing myself and it had been my intention to stay on campus put my feet up and relax. However, it was about to change. Students came from all over the country and it was common (probably still is) for many to hitch rides home during vacation time. One day, during the final week of exams, I noticed an advertisement on a student notice board from a girl requesting a ride to Fort Lauderdale Florida.

Her name was Pam Asgaard and she was not just another student, she was the IIT Homecoming (beauty) Queen for the current year and she was gorgeous, like one of those beauties in a James Bond movie. In the spur of the moment, I called and offered to take her there and to my delight, she accepted my offer. It did not matter that I did not have my own car. I knew of agencies that contracted drivers to deliver cars across the country and I contacted one and signed to deliver a car to Miami.

Unfortunately, for reasons only known to her, Pam changed her mind and had already signed a contract and a commitment to fill, I picked up the car and set off on my own. The following describes details of my journey south as recorded in a letter home:

Wednesday morning, 24 January, I set off alone. At first, I was a bit nervous at the thought of driving through the Chicago traffic (recalling the Tahiti incident), but once I got behind the wheel, my confidence came back almost immediately.

Heading south from Chicago, I found myself on the wrong road and realising this, I cut across a secondary road onto Route 41, which I was meant to take. It is interesting to note that this road goes right to the Keys in Florida, but it is not the main route all the way and I did not stay on it for long. My journey south took me through Indianapolis, Louisville Kentucky, Nashville Tennessee, Chattanooga (where I once again got on the wrong road south and covered a few extra miles to get back on the right road), then on to Atlanta Georgia, Macon and into Florida. I drove steadily all day stopping only for petrol and to eat a bag lunch I had brought along with me.

The countryside in Indianapolis was unspectacular, being mainly flat. About 8:30pm, I stopped at a roadside restaurant in a small town in Kentucky and received my first introduction to people of the Southern states. At first, I had difficulty understanding what the waitress was saying and I guess she had the same trouble with me and my Kiwi accent. After three attempts, we got our respective messages across and I received what I had ordered. After eating, I continued on my way intending to stop somewhere and sleep in the car.

About 11:30pm, I pulled up outside an all-night restaurant, locked the doors of the car, and then attempted to go to sleep in the car. Unfortunately, after about half an hour, the car lost all its heat and the cold tended to keep me awake. After bearing with this for a while, I decided to drive on for several miles, warm up the car, then stop and go to sleep again. I carried on with this procedure for two or three times, and then about 3am, I finally resolved to continue driving through the night and pull up during the day when it was warmer and sleep then.

I stopped for breakfast somewhere in Georgia and then continued on. At this stage, I was looking for somewhere to pull over and park and go to sleep, but nothing suitable appeared and I kept on going. Early in the afternoon, I picked up two hitchhikers: students from the University of Illinois, who were heading for Tampa on the west coast of Florida. After quickly summing them up, I allowed one of them to drive and I got in the back seat and I got some sleep. These fellows, Larry and Don, were going to spend that night with an aunt in Tampa and since I did not need to deliver the car until Sunday, I offered to take them there in exchange for a bed for the night. This seemed a good arrangement.

It was dark when we arrived in Tampa and we had a lot of difficulty finding Don's aunt. We almost gave up hope of finding her and I called into a motel to see about a room for the night. The cheapest was $8 and I tried to beat the price down, but to no avail. We didn't take the room and by a stroke of good luck, we spoke to someone who new Don's aunt and we found our place to sleep. And boy did I sleep. Actually, as it turned out, this was the only time I spent in bed during the duration of this trip.

The details of the rest of this trip are to be found somewhere on one of those tapes I mentioned earlier. For now, here are the highlights as best as I can remember them. After a hearty breakfast, I said farewell to Larry and Don and made my way across Florida, arriving in Miami in the early afternoon. I resolved to keep the car until my delivery deadline on Sunday and to amuse myself during the daylight hours, I roamed around Miami taking in some of the sights and loafed on the ocean beach among the many sun worshippers with their aluminium concentrating the sun's rays on their leathery skin.

I spent part of one night at a nightclub/bar sipping beer and chatting up girls and ended up sleeping on a beach under the stars until the cold sent me back to the relative warmth in the car. Finally, on Sunday morning, I delivered the car to the destination I had been given, nicely judged with the petrol gauge registering empty and set about planning to get back to Chicago.

In this, I was quite lucky in that I had met a group of students from the University of Notre Dame in South Bend Indiana, which is not that far from Chicago. They had travelled south by the same means as I had and had a car, large black Cadillac they were taking back to South Bend and offered me a ride, which I gratefully accepted. I had a few hours to fill in before we departed north and as I roamed around nearby streets I was accosted by a seedy character, whose name Jimmy Sales, has remained etched in my mind all these years. He was looking for some casual labour and leaning out of his car from across the road he shouted:

"Where are you from?"

To which I replied, "New Zealand."

"Where's that?" he said.

"South Pacific," I said, to which he gave me a blank look and following a pregnant pause, he offered me a job cleaning cars.

"Good wages," he said. "$5 an hour." And indeed it was a good offer.

At this point, I decided to discourage further conversation, said I was going back to college and I moved on.

My memory of the trip back to Chicago is a blur. There were six of us in the car, we shared the driving and it was a fast trip back to South Bend, from memory less than twenty-four hours. From there, I hopped on a Greyhound bus and arrived back in Chicago just in time for the start of the new semester.

Chicago Erupts

In the early evening of 4 April 1968, Martin Luther King was assassinated and rioting broke out in many cities around the US. My memory and impressions of this tragic event and the rioting that occurred in Chicago are sketchy but worth recording here. That night and during the days that followed, rioting broke out in the black ghetto area on the west side of the city and in some local areas on the north and south sides and the near north side. Reports of rioters braking windows, looting stores and setting buildings on fire were recorded and the evidence of the fires was there to be seen from my campus dwelling.

The following day, thousands of troops from the Illinois National Guard and the US army were brought into Chicago to restore order.

Initially, I stayed on campus and listened to radio and television reports of what was happening, which seemed the sensible thing to do. However, one evening a few days later, when some order appeared to have been restored I ventured out with a friend to visit my favourite haunts in Old Town. I don't know how we travelled—I think it was by car—but when we arrived, the sight that I saw and has remained imprinted on my mind was the sight of building after building barricaded with plywood hoardings and hundreds of armed troops roaming the up and down the street. It was an eerie sight and curiosity satisfied, we turned around and retraced our steps back to the safety of the IIT campus.

This was just one of a number of anti-establishment happenings in Chicago and around the US that year and in the years that followed. A few months later, Robert Kennedy, brother of JFK, was assassinated while campaigning for the presidency and more rioting broke out in Chicago during the Democratic convention later that summer. The war in Vietnam was escalating and was the cause of a lot of student unrest on many campuses around the country, culminating in the killing of four students by National Guard troops at Kent State University in the summer of 1970.

On the lighter side, there was the hippie movement of the mid to late 1960s, Woodstock and the Height Ashbury love-ins in San Francisco. It was a fascinating time to be in the US and to witness close up these extraordinary events. Looking back, my time as a student at IIT ranks among one of the most stimulating and exciting times I have experienced in my life.

What follows are some of the impressions recorded in a letter home:

I will mention here my impressions of the people and places I saw on my trip south. First and foremost, Miami. Boy, it's the phoniest place I have come across in my life, it's unbelievable. The people you see there are very hard to describe. I got the impression that the majority of the tourists were not extremely wealthy, but were trying to convey that impression by the mere fact that they were able to stay in Miami. They dress in the gordyest of colours and to me, it is quite pathetic. The large expanses of grassed areas, the waterways and the beach I liked, but the buildings in the main were another thing.

To me, many were ugly and of cheap construction, which is quite ironical in such a wealthy area. One thing that rather impressed me on this trip was the people of the south in Kentucky, Tennessee, and Georgia. Those I met serving in restaurants and gas stations gave a more genuine type of personal service than that you experience in Illinois and the north. For the first time, I felt that giving a tip was worthwhile.

Money Worries

I had come to Chicago on a wing and a prayer, planning to meet my initial study and living costs from my savings accumulated during the previous years. I had the support of Malcolm and Audrey, but they were not in a position to help me financially and it never occurred to me that I should ask them for such help. Given the estimate of costs provided by the university, it seemed I had enough to get me through two semesters and maybe three. Tuition for two semesters amounted to US$1,600 and with living costs of approximately $1,400, added together this represented approximately 70 per cent of my savings.

Surprisingly, this seemed sufficient to persuade the US Immigration Service to grant me a student visa. This visa gave me temporary residence status in the US but there were rules attached and those relating to employment were quite explicit, restricting me to part-time work on campus and employment during summer the vacation. This created a problem, for even with cross credits, I was faced with the prospect of two to three years of full-time study to complete my degree. While this did not stop me from setting out on this great adventure, it was constantly in the back of my mind.

In the worst-case scenario, I would just have to break off my studies and seek work elsewhere and my fallback position was to go to Canada and seek work there to raise more funds.

I am a firm believer that good fortune comes to those who maintain a positive frame of mind and are determined to achieve their goals. As I pondered my predicament, I noted an obscure clause relating to my visa, which effectively stated that if I faced unforeseen economic hardship during my stay, I could seek dispensation on the restricted work rule. It so happened that in November 1967, the New Zealand government devalued the NZ dollar and using this as justification, I applied to the authorities and was granted dispensation to seek part-time work while I continued my studies.

Good fortune smiled upon me for not only did I secure a well-paying holiday job in the northern summer of 1968, later that year after I landed a part-time job in the water works department of the city of Chicago, and in 1969, I won a substantial scholarship all of which helped me through to the end of my degree course.

Summer Love in Portland

The job in Portland was with environmental engineering firm, Dames & Moore, an international consultancy with offices spread throughout the US and the around the world. I had been given a letter of introduction to one of their senior engineers in the Chicago office, by my previous employer, John Moss, who had worked for the company prior to his return to New Zealand. I contacted Dames & Moore and presented my credentials with a request for a summer job shortly after my arrival in Chicago. Just prior to Christmas, I was pleasantly surprised to be offered a summer job in their Portland office on a salary of $700 per month.

On top of this, I was advised that they would pay my travel expenses to get there and back. Compared with the six pounds ($12) per week I had been on for much of the time back home, this seemed like a small fortune to me at the time and it was. I imagine it reflected the work experience I had and the generally higher salaries that were paid in the US at that time. It certainly relieved some of the money worries that surfaced during this early period in Chicago.

The three months I spent in Portland were memorable for a variety of reasons: a weekend away in Mexico, exploring parts of Oregon and the state of Washington with its mountainous and forested topography and rugged coastline not unlike parts of New Zealand visiting family friends and acquaintances in Lake Chelan and Spokane, a busy social life frequenting the local bars and cafes where I would listen to jazz to all hours of the night, back on the tennis court, the parties I hosted in my studio apartment, my several girlfriends and dare say it, falling madly in love with Ellen, the pick of them.

Portland is just over two thousand miles from Chicago and there are two overland route choices for getting there; a northern route on State Highway 84 via Wisconsin, Minnesota, North Dakota, Montana, Idaho, and Washington State and a more direct western route, on State Highway 80 across the central plains of Illinois, Iowa and Nebraska, then over the Rocky Mountain range via Wyoming and into Utah, where you turn and head north and drive through southern Idaho and eventually on into Oregon. For the journey out, I opted to take the southern route.

The first year over, I packed my meagre possessions in the back of my rusty old Dodge, said goodbye to a few friends and on a balmy summer morning in early June, I set off west along Interstate 80 on my long journey to Portland. I had estimated that it would take me four days to get there and averaging five hundred miles a day this turned out to be a very good guess. My memory of this journey has faded somewhat but what I do remember is mile after mile of flat plains with fields of corn and maize as I passed through Illinois, Iowa and Nebraska, a long slow climb over the Rock Mountains as I passed through Wyoming and down into Utah.

It was on the morning of the third day of my journey west that I have one clear memory of where I was and how far had come. As I passed through the town of Ogden, a small distance north of Salt Lake City, news came over the car radio (yes, I had one) that Senator Robert Kennedy, brother of former President John Kennedy, had been shot while passing through a crowded kitchen of the Ambassador Hotel in Los Angeles.

At Ogden, the highway turns north. I was now well past the halfway point on my way to Portland but there remained another two days before I would get there. I was hot and tired but my youthful energy spurred me on and in the late afternoon on 7 June, I arrived and settled into some temporary accommodation that had been arranged for me. Again, I have no recollection of what happened during the next couple of weeks except that I was welcomed into the Portland office off Dames & Moore and I found myself studio apartment in a three-storey apartment block at 751 South-West Vista Avenue on the west side of the city, which was to be my home for the next ten weeks and a happy home at that.

The Portland office of Dames and Moore had a staff of about twenty and I settled in quickly making friends with all the staff, and I must have impressed my boss, Ken Robbins, with my prior experience for I was soon assigned projects of my own on which to work. Aside from work, what occupied much of my time and thoughts during this period of settling in was making arrangements for my trip to Mexico to rendezvous with Audrey Malcolm, Philip and Jenny in Acapulco, who were aboard the Northern Star en route to Britain for an extended holiday abroad. I had been planning this trip for months and nothing was going to stop me, even a day off work which was necessary in order to get there in time.

Acapulco Bound: I had been planning a trip to Acapulco for many months following a message from home that my dad, Malcolm, had been granted a free passage to London on one of the company's ships, the Northern Star, as a reward for his long service accompanied by Audrey, Philip and Jenny. The age of air travel around the world was still in its infancy and a six-week passage by sea was still the norm for those wishing get from New Zealand to Britain and the ship would be sailing across the Pacific Ocean, through the Panama Canal and onto England. En route a twenty-four-hour stopover in Acapulco was scheduled and I was determined to be there to see them.

The ship was due to arrive in Acapulco early on the Saturday morning of 16 June 1968 and during the week prior to its arrival, I made arrangements through a local travel agent to fly to Los Angeles the prior Thursday morning, connect to a flight that would take me to Mexico City, where I had booked into a cheap hotel for an overnight stay then fly on to Acapulco the following day. I was given two days leave of absence from my new job and my plan was to return to Portland on the Sunday in time to report back to work on Monday.

It all seemed so relatively simple, but my best-laid plans almost came unstuck for when I arrived in Los Angeles and I went to check in on my flight to Mexico City, I was refused a boarding pass on account that I did not have a visa. I had not given any thought to this requirement nor had I been advised by my agent that I would need one.

Now I pride myself that I am not prone to panic and I explained the purpose of my visit and politely asked the airline official what should I do. He rebooked me on a later flight and directed me to go to the Mexican Embassy in downtown Los Angeles, where it would be a simple matter of filing out a form and my passport would be stamped. I duly rushed out of the terminal building, hailed a cab, and made a mad dash to the address I had been given. I have no recollection of the time taken to get to the embassy, a vague recollection of waiting in queue anxiously counting the minutes ticking by, eventually getting my passport stamped and an equally mad dash back to the airport.

What I do know is that I made it back in time to get on that afternoon flight, arriving in Mexico City in the late afternoon and finding my way to my hotel, where I put my feet up for the night. I have only a vague recollection of Mexico City itself and flying on to Acapulco the next day and I kept no record of where I stayed for the two nights I was in Acapulco, except that it was somewhere on the waterfront for I have a clear picture of waking up on the Saturday morning, looking out the window and seeing the Northern Star in the harbour manoeuvring towards a berth at the docks nearby.

Dare I say, I lost my virginity that night for as I woke up, I saw this petit Mexican chica lying beside me and I was quickly reminded of the drinking and dancing to the strains of Mexican music on the terraces outside the hotel. What followed was also an embarrassing moment as I hustled her out of the room, so that I could shower and shave and get down to the wharf before the ship docked.

What followed was a most memorable day starting with hugs and kisses all round as I went on board, shared breakfast with Mum, Dad, Philip, and Jenny and told them all my news. They showed me there spacious cabin then we went ashore and did all the things that tourists always do, visited the La Quebrada Cliff Divers. Where the fearless young men dive from an incredible height into the sea below, timing the waves to perfection to avoid killing themselves in the process.

We returned to the ship in the late afternoon and dined with them and stayed aboard until midnight when all the visitors were instructed to leave the ship. Sadly, I said my goodbyes to the family I loved. And my emotions were running high as expressed in a letter I wrote upon my return to Portland:

I guess I never fully realised how much I love you all until it came time to say goodbye and leave the ship. For me, it was worse than when I had to say goodbye in Auckland and as I walked down the gangway, I have to admit I was close to tears. That is why I couldn't say much as we parted on the wharf Dad.

Our time together was short but it was the happiest day I had experienced since our trip up to Auckland last September. I woke the next morning at 6:45am dashed down to the beach in time to see the ship out in the harbour and I waited on the beach until it was out of sight.

After all this excitement and joy, the trip home was rather uneventful. I checked out of my hotel and made my way to Acapulco airport, from where I flew direct to Los Angeles, where I connected to an internal flight with a brief stopover in San Francisco, then onto Portland where it touched down at 8:45pm. I made my way to my pad at SW Vista Avenue and had a good night's sleep before reporting back to work the next day. What a little adventure it had been.

Social Life: On reading the few letters home during my stay in Portland, it seems it took me a little while to settle in and enjoy my experiences. Initially, I expressed boredom with the work I was being assigned at Dames and Moore, doing mostly menial tasks for others. However, this soon changed as my bosses recognised my skills and experience and by the end of June, I was being assigned my own projects, which boosted my confidence and enthusiasm immensely.

I was eventually given full access to a rental car to carry out a field assignment that lasted for several weeks. I would use it to drive to and from work and leave it parked in the basement of the building when not in use.

Those of you who have read the earlier chapters of this journal will surely appreciate that sports has been one of my major interests and from a very young age, I have always participated in one sporting activity or another. However, since I had arrived in the US, I had not indulged in any physical activity and upon arriving in Portland, I realised that I had put on several kilos and was feeling just a little lethargic.

I decided it was time to get back on a tennis court, I joined up a nearby club, soon found my form and started playing some of the best tennis I had in years. Played in a couple of tournaments and best of all, it was an outlet for making new friends and acquaintances. One was an English girl, Carol, whom I met and started dating. One Sunday, towards the end of July after playing a set, we took off to a local tavern for a quick beer. She was quite a character and what started out as a quick drink before heading home, turned into an unplanned party that lasted into the early hours of the following day.

We called on a friend of Carol and ended up in another tavern drinking more beers and popcorn and having loads of laughs.

Before long, there were other girls I met and started dating. A kookie bird from Montana who was on a short visit to Portland that summer. One day, towards the end of June, we packed a picnic lunch and went on a day trip to the coast where we ate our waded in the surf on a long deserted beach, came across two model plane enthusiasts throwing gliders off a cliff and watching them catch the currents and drift out to sea. I have mentioned Carol, the tennis queen, and then there was Kathy, the bank teller I got friendly with and finally plucked up the courage to ask out on a date.

There was Maureen, the quirky one, who had a liking for spontaneity and doing the unusual, a quality I have always liked in a woman. There were others too many to name who lived in the apartment complex at 751 SW Vista and I partied with them from time to time. Finally, there was Ellen who really won my heart.

Ellen lived in the apartment immediately above mine. I first noticed her coming and going from the apartment block and walking down the road to where she worked in the same building as Dames and Moore. After several weeks of gazing at her delightful form from a distance, one day I bumped into her in a local supermarket. I introduced myself and asked her for a date and to my delight, she said yes. This was the start of a beautiful friendship, which lasted until I had to leave Portland and return to Chicago at the end of August. For a short period, we became an item and our romance blossomed.

We dated regularly, we celebrated my birthday in style together and I particularly remember a day trip to the wild Oregon coast and swimming in the cold waters of the sea. For Ellen that was her first sighting of ocean seas as she had grown up in a small town in Illinois about a hundred miles south of Chicago and had only recently moved west to Portland. It was a sad moment when I came to leave and I asked her to come back to Chicago with me so that we could continue the romance. However, in spite of my pleading, she declined, although not without some tears.

The day before I left, I called on Buster, the apartment complex custodian to say farewell and I recall him saying in a friendly tone, "What kind of a man are you? She has been crying her heart out to me." I did try hard to persuade her to come with me, even calling her several times from Chicago when I got back. However, she had her reasons and continued to say no, and eventually, I gave up trying. The new semester was about to start, I had to find accommodation and get back to focusing on my academic studies. It was a short-lived but wonderful love affair and my life could have turned out quite different had she said yes.

Return to Chicago: I had travelled out to Portland via the flat and boring mid-western states and I decided that on my return trip, I would take the northern route via Washington State, Idaho, Montana, North Dakota, Minnesota, and Wisconsin. This gave me the opportunity to visit Cy and Marie Severance, an elderly couple who lived in Lake Chelan in Washington State. Malcolm and Audrey had met Cy on the Milford track and befriended him in 1965. I also planned to call on Valerie (cousin of Judith Cornwell) and Bill Powell who lived in Spokane, near the border of Washington State and Idaho.

When it came time to leave Portland, I was extremely reluctant to pack up and go. I had made many good friends, the city and Pacific Northwest countryside reminded me of New Zealand and of course, there were my feelings for Ellen. During a hectic last week, I was never in bed before midnight and it was a never-ending whirl of farewells and partying, the following are some of the highlights as recorded in a letter home:

Wednesday night, I was out on the town with Kurt, a barman at the tavern on Vista Avenue that I often frequented. On Thursday, I went swimming with friends Cy and Marie Severance, who were staying in town. On Friday, what looked like being a quiet evening at Henry's Tavern turned out to be a 4am affair and I ended up down in a classy restaurant dressed in short pants and a T-shirt with friends of Kurt. On Saturday, I threw a party, which turned out a great success. All my newfound friends came along and the last guest did not leave until 5am.

Sunday night, I was invited out to dinner by one of my latest acquaintances, Skip, quite an attractive and charming girl (I preferred Ellen). On Monday, I was taken water skiing all day long on the Columbia River followed by an evening meal with Merle Ryder and her family. Tuesday night I spent with Ellen then on Wednesday night I was on my way back to Chicago.

I spent the next two days with Cy and Marie Severance, whom I had already met on an earlier visit in June and I had a wonderful time picking apples, juicing them and making cider. Then it was on to Spokane where I visited the Powells, staying another two days during which time I went water skiing once more and visited a number of derelict mines owned by Bill, who fancied himself as a gold prospector. Then it was on to Chicago, a drive of almost two thousand miles, which I covered in three days only stopping to rest and sleep in the car when I got tired. My rusty old Dodge went like a charm and many of my Chicago friends expressed their surprise at seeing it once again.

3309 South Lowe Avenue Chicago: It was mid-September when I arrived back in Chicago and with classes due to start the following week, I had to move quickly to select and register for courses, find accommodation, and settle back into a study routine. Courses were soon sorted and I set about making inquiries and finding a suitable apartment not too far from the campus. This led me to the old administration building on the west side of the campus and a chance meeting with Robert, who would turn out to be a lifelong friend.

While standing at the counter of the administration office, I chanced to hear the words New Zealand. Glancing to my right, I saw this person with a bushy beard in conversation with an administration officer and naturally, this sparked my interest. I moved along the counter and introduced myself. He told me that Asher was his name, he had recently completed a degree in anthropology at the University of Michigan, had relocated to his hometown and IIT, and he was contemplating a move to New Zealand for advanced anthropological studies at Otago University. He also said that he too was looking for an apartment near the IIT campus, so we decided to team up and search together.

As I have already mentioned, the IIT campus is surrounded on three sides by a Negro ghetto area, not the ideal place for two white youths. Our only option was the Bridgeport area, a working-class ethnic area west of the Dan Ryan Expressway. We sighted an advertisement on a noticeboard in the administration for a two-bedroom apartment for lease at 3309 South Lowe Avenue, which was located ten city blocks west of the campus. We immediately rushed over there in Robert's car, located the landlord (Austin Herschel by name), who lived on the basement apartment and signed a lease for the first-floor apartment immediately above for the princely sum of $125 per month in rent.

Being homeless, I moved in immediately as the previous tenants were moving out. The place was a mess but I was pleased to be settled in before classes started and that was the least of my concerns. Robert moved in a few days later and we soon found a third flatmate, Mike Mast, a fellow student at IIT who was studying electrical engineering.

Perhaps, a few words about the apartment and surrounding area would not go amiss here. The landlord, Austin, who lived in the basement immediately below us, was quite eccentric and one of his conditions for leasing the apartment was that we paint the kitchen and do various improvements. He was friendly enough and often when he was away, he would give us access to his apartment to watch TV. Our apartment occupied the entire first floor and comprised a large living area at the front leading to a kitchen and dining area at the rear which looked out onto a lawn area and a separate single-storey apartment complex at the rear.

The apartment was two-storey brick-clad building typical of all the houses in the vicinity. Most of the streets in the neighbourhood were drab and dreary lacking in trees and other softening features. However, the street outside our home was lined with trees for one block to the north and two blocks to the south and there appeared to be a reason for this, as one of our near neighbours was one Richard J Daley, Mayor of Chicago. One of my lasting impressions is that when I arrived on the street, every house along this section of Lowe Avenue had posters in the window expressing support for their mayor.

The front window of our apartment contained one such poster 'We Love Mayor Daley'. We left it on display for more than a year, only taking it down when we became aware that almost all of the others had been removed and we felt it was politic to do likewise. This apartment at 3309 South Lowe was to be my home for the remainder of my time at IIT and what a happy, stimulating and fun time I had while I lived there. It was here that I studied hard, played hard, cemented existing friendships, and made new friends along the way.

Why such an expression of devotion to the city's mayor you may ask? I suspect it was linked to events of the previous month. The Democratic National Convention to elect the party's candidate for the November Presidential election had just been held in Chicago, rallies, demonstrations and marches had taken place on the city streets and lakefront parks prior to and during the convention. These activities were primarily in protest of the Vietnam War policies of President Johnson. Daley, who was influential in Democrat party policy, took a strong stand and throughout the convention, the city streets were awash with violence and the police response was brutal and vicious.

Many arrests were made and eight high-profile civil rights protestors referred to as the Chicago Seven (Eight) were charged and tried for various crimes against the State.

Roommates: Initially, there were three of us, Robert, Mike Mast and I, then Paul Wurtzebach, a friend of Robert, joined us in the summer of 1969. Before going further, let me tell you a bit about them.

First, Robert who was born and grew up in Chicago. When we met, I was twenty-five years old, Robert was two or three years younger and he had just returned from Juneau Alaska, where he had spent the summer months as part of a group of scientists doing research on the glaciers north of Juneau. With his scruffy beard and casual clothes, he certainly looked the part. Robert's father was the senior partner in a successful legal practice, Asher, Asher and Asher, the other partners being his elder brothers, Gilbert and Donald. From what Robert told me, I gathered it to be a practice that specialised in administering the estates and investments of its many clients.

I met Robert's family on several occasions during my student days and later visits to Chicago. My initial impressions were that here was a family with unbelievable wealth that I had never encountered before, but at the same time, extremely warm and welcoming to this strange character from the southern reaches of the globe. To me, Robert, with his physical appearance and interests, didn't seem to quite fit the mould. However, looks can sometimes deceive. Many years later, Robert took charge of the practice and although we have never discussed his business affairs, it was apparent to me that he was very astute and diligent in carrying out this task.

Robert and I have become lifetime friends. What I admire about Robert is the fact that he does not flaunt his wealth and he has been totally honest in his dealings with me.

Mike Mast was from the midwest state of Kansas and I dubbed him the Kansas Kid. Mike was in his second year of study, a little younger than Robert and I, but he fitted in well. We three often studied together in the evenings, threw lots of parties and enjoyed a good social time befitting of an active student life. Regrettably, like many of the friends I made while at IIT, I lost contact with Mike after I graduated and left Chicago for a job in Boston.

Paul, the fourth member of this quartet, was studying at the University of Illinois, Chicago Campus. What he was studying I can't remember, but what I do remember is he was a gun sailor and together with Robert, introduced me to sailing on Lake Michigan, where Paul was campaigning a Shields class yacht, out of the Columbia Yacht Club on Lake Shore Drive. I remember Paul as a good solid roommate, who also fitted in well and I have several photos of Paul, Mike and friend, Bernie, in Austin's beer garden during the summer months.

Paul liked to talk about sailing and I was happy to listen. Sailing was to become my sporting passion during much of my adult life. I lost touch with Paul when I left Chicago, but we were reacquainted when I visited Chicago and stayed Robert for a week during the spring of 1982.

Student Life: As the semester progressed, my life soon fell into a routine of attending classes during the morning plus the occasional evening class, participating in sporting and recreational activities during the afternoon, home in the early evening for a meal with Robert and Mike. Initially, we shared the cooking duties and once a week, we would go together to purchase supplies for the coming week. However, I seemed to be the most talented when it came to preparing meals and cooking food and I eventually took over this task leaving the cleaning up to Robert and Mike, which often became an early morning chore the following day.

In a recent message conveyed to me by Robert, Paul writes:

I do remember the good days at 3309 South Lowe. We ate a lot of tuna or sardines because someone liked it or it was on sale at the butcher shop so we bought every can on the shelf. The apartment had the old fashion pantry with lots of shelves, so storing a lot of tuna or beef stew cans was no problem. KP's duty for washing dishes was a little lacking. When all the dishes and silverware were dirty, we all pitched in with a washing party to clean everything. You two (Robert and I) had some funny IIT friends.

Asher had a friend who needed his car started once a month, and I remember going to a gas station with Robert to fill up with diesel. Back then, the attendant pumped the petrol, however, this poor guy pumped regular and not diesel which the car was diesel. My friend, Robert, insisted he remove the diesel which he did with a syphon tube. I'm sure it wasn't very tasty. At least we got an education!

Night time was study time and we would often sit together around a large table we set up in the living area for this purpose. During the week and sometimes on weekends, I would studiously get out my books and lecture notes and work away at my studies until close to midnight, then I would close the books and either retire for the night or adjourn to a neighbourhood tavern/bar around the corner I had discovered that remained open until 2am.

This bar became a regular haunt for me where I would go and relax after a long day, appearing soon after midnight and often staying on until it closed at 2am in the morning. I was an oddity among the local clientele, the more so for having a strange accent and coming from a part of the world they had never heard of. However, this seemed to appeal to their sense of what the American dream was about and the desirability of getting a good education. I was warmly welcomed into their fold and treated with a lot of curiosity and generosity.

I recall one occasion when I walked in around 11:30pm with $2 in my pocket, which was enough to buy four beers and play a game or two of pool. I don't recall how many beers and how many games of the pool I played that night, but when I stumbled out of the bar at the 2am closing time, I still had a dollar to my name. On another occasion, my friend, Bernie, came looking for me and he had with him a student friend, who was from Nigeria. Now a coloured person was not a welcome sight in such a neighbourhood and his appearing there created and awkward scene.

When they entered and approached me sitting at the bar, the owner, Jimmy the Greek I called him, leaned over and stared the Nigerian in the eyes and muttered, "Are you Caucasian?" Sensing trouble, Bernie and his friend immediately withdrew and I followed them outside. To my surprise, Jimmy came to the door and insisted we come back inside, then treated the three of us to a beer on the house. I had long since developed a sense of the racial intolerance of many sections of the white population towards African-Americans and this must have been a difficult thing for Jimmy to do.

I can only think that maybe he felt that he had offended me and wanted to make amends. Whatever, it was a delicate and somewhat uncomfortable situation and Bernie and his friend downed their beer and quietly departed soon after. For my part, I remained behind in the bar and had a few more beers, not wishing to display any animosity by departing prematurely.

There were other times when I ventured further afield for my social activities. A favourite destination was the bars and night clubs in Old Town on the near north side of Chicago, where the beer was cheap and places stayed open for most of the night. On many occasions, I would get back home at 3am, 4am, or even 5am in the morning, only to be up again by 8am to get to my first lecture of the day an hour later. I recall that on occasion after a late night out, I awoke with a searing headache and I had to force myself to get out of bed and go to class. I hated missing lectures, seldom did, and on this occasion, I had a mid-term exam to sit.

I got to class, the subject was statistics and I raced through the paper in thirty minutes, putting in answers that came to me for the various questions. Good exam technique suggests that if one finishes early, it is a good idea to go back over the questions and check your answers. On this occasion, I did not bother, such was the throbbing in my head. Surprisingly, I got an 'A' for that exam but I did not and would not recommend repeating the exercise as a way to pass exams.

Jenny and Philip Pay a Visit: I had not long settled into life in South Lowe Avenue when Jenny and Philip both paid a visit on their way back to New Zealand from their holiday in the UK and Europe with our mum and dad. Jenny immediately got on a Greyhound bus and rode over to Clark Lake in Michigan to meet her pen pal, Karlene, and stay with her family for several weeks. Philip stayed with us for one week and we rounded up a mattress and made a temporary bed at the street end of the huge lounge.

I had great pleasure in introducing him to my flatmates and friends and showing him around the IIT campus and other sites of interest in the city. My one strong memory of Philip's visit was the morning of his departure to catch an onward flight home from O'Hare International Airport.

I figured that Philip should allow an hour and a half to get from 3309 South Lowe to the airport and I telephoned a cab company to pick up Philip at the allotted time of 8:30am. The half hour arrived and with no taxi in sight, Philip became a little agitated and I called a second cab company to come and pick him up. Fifteen minutes late, a cab from the second company arrived and as I was ushering him into this cab, another cab arrived at our door. Philip hesitated not knowing what to do and I said, "Go, go, go, I will deal with this," and off he went, no time for hugs and teary goodbyes.

Philip on his way, I shrugged my shoulders at the driver of the second cab and retreated fast into the confines of our apartment, choosing not to wait and deal with his potential wrath.

Jenny returned to Chicago in mid-November and stayed for a week and a half before continuing her journey home to New Zealand. Again, I took great pleasure in showing her around the IIT campus and some of the city, but the one memory that has been etched in my brain was the night when Robert invited

Mike Mast, Jenny and me to join him at his parent's apartment to celebrate Thanksgiving with his family.

If memory serves me correctly, we started in the early evening by having one of the periodic clean-ups in our messy kitchen, probably inspired by Jenny's presence. Then after tidying ourselves up, we drove over to Robert's parents' home, which if memory serves me correctly occupied one entire floor of a building on the near north side of Chicago. I was struck by two things, the opulence of their home and the friendly welcome and hospitality we received from all the members of Robert's family. There to greet us were Robert's grandparents, his parents Norman and Helen his two brothers, Gilbert and Donald, and Donald's wife, the charming Carol.

After introductions, we all sat around a large table with a silver setting, gave the traditional thanks for all good things, then wined and dined and told stories about our respective lives.

It was after this evening at the Ashers that I formed the opinion that Robert seemed to be the odd one out in this family. However, initial appearances can be deceiving for as I mentioned earlier it was Robert who eventually took over running the family affairs, when his father died or perhaps even earlier. I remember Robert often spoke warmly of his grandparents of whom he was especially fond and he had a similar warm relationship with his parents, especially his mother, whom Sue Amy and I met up with three decades later on a visit to Chicago in 1995.

Over the ensuing years, Robert spoke little of his brothers, who I understand suffered ill health or other misfortune and I never pursued this subject with him.

I Run a Red Light: Early in the semester, crazy Bernie introduced me to his latest girlfriend, Carol, and her two friends, Leslie and Andrea, student nurses at a hospital near the lake on 31st Street. One evening, after partying and fooling around at 3309, I drove Leslie and Andrea back to the hospital and after safely depositing them there, I set off on my return to South Lowe and bed. It was after midnight and I slowly cruised back along 31st street through one intersection, then another, and as I turned left into South Michigan Avenue, I heard the wailing of a siren and saw the flashing lights of a police patrol car right behind me. I pulled over and an officer came up to my window and accused me of going through a red light.

At first, I challenged his observation stating that the light was on amber as I entered the intersection. However, he remained adamant that I had run a red light and it was only after a minute or so of discussion, the offence occurred at the intersection before the one I was disputing. "It smells like a brewery in here," he said. He was friendly enough and ignored my state of inebriation. However, he issued me with a ticket for running the red light and I subsequently received a notice to answer a charge of driving without a valid licence (I had an International Driving Permit but I had let my NZ licence expire).

The officer also instructed me to take a driving test at the local testing station and obtain an Illinois driver's licence.

I duly did the latter before my day in court but it was not without an amusing incident. I had to drive around a mock-up set of streets, with all the various obstacles one finds on a city street. I was two-thirds around the test course when I pulled up at a set of lights on red. The testing officer instructed me to make a right turn, which I duly did going through the light before it had turned green. "What did you do that for?" He screamed. "Now I will have to fail you." Then he went into deep thought for a few seconds and in a more relaxed tone, he stated, "What the heck, I can see you know how to drive and I will pass you now." With that, I was issued with an Illinois licence and at last, I was legal.

The court case came and went, I pleaded guilty to the red light offence but the prosecution did not press the charge of driving without a valid licence and I was free to go. Such was my one and only run-in with the US legal system.

The Egans Come to Chicago: In early December, I received news that my good friends Mike and Kath Egan were about to arrive in Chicago, where Mike was about to take up a position in the Chicago office of Dames & Moore. Mike had been a colleague at Brickell Moss and Partners in Lower Hutt and Kath had been one of the group of nurses I befriended when I was laid up in Hutt Hospital with a hematoma back in 1961. We had become very close friends and I was immensely cheered when I heard of their pending arrival.

It was the week prior to Xmas day when they arrived with their two young children, Richard, aged three, and Joanna, aged two. They were living in temporary hotel accommodation when they contacted me and I was quick to invite them around to my apartment at 3309 South Lowe. No doubt we talked about life back home in NZ and what lay ahead for both of us, I don't remember. What I do recall is that they were finding it uncomfortable cooped up in their hotel room with two active youngsters and I happened to mention that Austin's small apartment block at the rear of the property was vacant and that they might want to move in there temporarily while they looked for something more suitable for their needs.

I introduced Mike and Kath to Austin, who readily agreed to have them as his tenants and with that, they quickly moved in. From memory, the place was in a bit of a mess (Kath will tell you), but Kath set about cleaning and tidying the apartment and she soon had it spick and span and in a liveable condition. Austin was most impressed and tried to persuade them to stay on a long-term lease. It was not a place for this upwardly mobile couple and their young family but it suited their immediate plans while settling into Chicago and a new job for Mike and gave them breathing space to look for more suitable accommodation elsewhere in the city.

As for me, it was great having them next door and I was able to help them in their search for something more permanent.

One lasting memory of this search was when I was out driving around in a car they had rented for the purpose of their search. We were now well into winter with temperatures below zero and there was snow on the ground that had turned to ice. I was driving slowly along a narrow one-way street when a car ahead started reversing into a parking bay. I put on the breaks and immediately went into a skid in what seemed like a slow-motion replay plough into the side of this car. I felt bad about this, but fortunately, the damage was slight and no one was hurt. After swapping identities and contact details, we moved on.

Finally, after about a month at Austin's place, they found a neat two, or was it three, bedroom apartment in Park Ridge, a suburb some fifteen miles northwest of downtown Chicago and close to O'Hare International Airport. I was sad to see them move out and Austin even more so. However, that was not the end of our association and during the remainder of my time in Chicago, I visited often and I shared many wonderful and memorable moments in their company.

One such moment occurred the following December. Xmas was almost upon us and Mike's employer was hosting an overnight Xmas function somewhere in the city. Kath called and asked me if I would look after Richard and Joanne from Saturday afternoon through until Sunday evening. I readily agreed not really appreciating what I was in for. I turned up at their apartment around noon, we had lunch which Kath had prepared and I was briefed on what was happening and where they would be. Richard and Joanna had been told I would take them to the swings in the nearby park during the afternoon, all part of a strategy to tire them out and ready them for an early night's sleep.

Guess who was the one who was worn out at the end of the afternoon. However, this strategy must have worked, as I got them both to bed at an appropriate hour and all was well. However, I was not prepared for what came next in the very early hours of the morning.

About 2am in the morning, I was awoken from a moderately deep sleep on a sofa in the lounge area to the cries from young Joanna wailing, "I want my mummy, I want my mummy," repeated over and over again. I lay there for a short while thinking, *I can do a lot for you, young Joanna, but producing you Mummy right now is not one of them.* Then I got a little inspiration. I got up and went to her side and offered her something to eat. My presence and this suggestion settled her a little and we went into the kitchen.

I found some cereal or something, I don't remember what, and we sat at the dining table where I dreamed up little stories to tell her while she sat and nibbled away. While the tears had gone, she showed no sign of wanting to go back to sleep, something I was desperate for and slowly nodded off at the table. At some stage, I left her at the table playing with her cereal and crept back to my bed. Immediately, the cries started up again and back to the table I went. This went on for I don't know how long, but eventually, we both got tired of the game.

I got Joanna back to her bed and we all slept on until daylight when it was time to get up and have breakfast. I have no recollection of what we did on Sunday but I felt immense relief when Mike and Kath arrived in the late afternoon. By that time, I was exhausted and as I returned home to my bed at 3309, I recall thinking never underestimate the energy of two youngsters.

My other fond memory of this time was getting to know Bill Moore Jr and his wife, Sandy. Bill was a work colleague of Mike and I met them on several occasions during my visits to Park Ridge. They were an easy going and likeable couple and were to come back into my life several years later when I made my way to the UK and Europe in 1974. As for Mike and Kath, they remained good friends well beyond my time in Chicago and feature in later sections of this memoir.

Xmas Under the Stars: Xmas day was approaching and I had made no specific plans for celebrating the occasion. Robert, who was also at a loose end, came up with the bright idea that we drive north to Wisconsin where there was a park and camping ground, where we could park up for a day or two and enjoy Xmas under the stars. Always game to try new things, I said let's do it. We gathered together Robert's polar gear, persuaded two of Robert's friends to join us, and on Xmas eve, we all piled into Robert's red Pontiac and drove north to Wisconsin.

We arrived shortly before dark, ate a pre-prepared meal of what I don't remember, secured an awning between two park benches, which was to be our tent and under this a waterproof ground sheer upon which we laid out our super down sleeping bags, into which we climbed to sleep side by side through a long and freezing night.

We were in the depths of a northern winter and in the open, it was cold. However, my sleeping bag borrowed from Robert was fit for purpose and covered my body, face and head with only a small round orifice over my mouth for breathing. I was surprisingly warm, but this arrangement necessitated sleeping while lying on my back, which created a difficulty for me in that my normal sleeping position is on my side in a foetal pose. I remember waking in a panic and struggling to breathe at one stage during the night. I had rolled onto my side and lost my breathing hole, but fortunately, I recovered and am here to continue this tale.

This was also the night the Apollo 8 space mission was circling the moon and I remember thinking how lucky the three astronauts were in the comfort of their space capsule while I lay here sleepless on the hard ground.

The morning of Xmas day eventually dawned and it was cold. Robert pulled out his little thermometer to measure temperature. Minus 5 degrees Fahrenheit, it read and that is cold. So cold, in fact, that when we went to cook some eggs on a gas burner, they immediately froze solid when we took them off the heat. Robert's beard was covered in rhyme ice and my toes quickly numbed through my poorly insulated boots, and I took to kneeling on the park bench and clicking my heals together to keep circulation going.

It was at this point that all four of us quickly came to the conclusion that this winter camping was not such a good idea and we were unanimous in deciding we should pack up and head back to Chicago and the warmth of our respective homes.

We soon had all the gear packed away in Robert's car, we piled in and Robert turned the key but all we got was a sluggish turning of the engine and it would not start. However, it seems that Robert had learnt good skills in the Juneau Ice fields for he reached for his gas cooker, lit the burner and placed it under the engine sump and he said to wait a while. So we waited for ten minutes or so, he tried starting the car again, and magically and to our relief, the motor fired and we were in business and on our way home. That is my everlasting memory of my second Xmas in Chicago and I even have photos to verify it.

A Black Boy named White: For a period during the spring semester and through the summer of 1969, I became involved with a community group and was assigned the role of buddying a young black kid named Eric White. Eric was twelve years of age and lived with his mother and siblings in a tenement building in the black ghetto area twelve blocks south of the IIT campus. My task was to take Eric on occasional outings to places of interest in the city. Eric was an intelligent and lively individual, he seemed amused by my Kiwi accent and we got along well. For both of us, the Museum of Science and Industry was a favourite place to visit.

Typically, Eric would appear at an appointed time and place on the campus, we would pile into my rusty Dodge car and drive from there for the day's outing. I recall that on one occasion, Eric arrived and told me that his mother wanted to meet me and could we drive to his home on the south side. "Sure," I said, without thinking whether or not this was a good idea. Eric pointed the way and we soon arrived outside a ten-storey tenement building in which Eric and his mum lived. When I got out of the car, I recall developing this eerie sense that I did not belong in this neighbourhood.

However, not wanting to disappoint Eric and his mum, I pressed on and climbed the stairs until we reached his apartment on the fifth floor of the building and went inside. Our interaction was brief but pleasant. Eric's mum expressed her appreciation for what I was doing for Eric and we parted on good terms. I had come to no harm and Eric and I continued on our way for that day's outing, to where I do not remember.

Sometime during the summer, these outings ceased and Eric passed out of my life. For me, it had been a rewarding opportunity for direct interaction with a young man growing up in an urban area where tensions between the races abound. I think of Eric whenever I hear Elvis Presley singing his hit song *In the Ghetto*. He would be in his late fifties now and I hope he thrived. He was a good kid.

Back on the Tennis Court: My exploits on the court in Portland during the summer just gone had rejuvenated my interest in tennis and I took to the court again during the fall semester, playing a few games in the multipurpose stadium on the IIT campus. I must have been showing some good form as I was spied on by the sports director and invited onto the IIT tennis squad.

We practiced indoors during the latter half of the fall semester and I was selected to play at number 4 in the team that was entered in a Chicago area conference during the spring semester. We were a remarkably successful team winning all our matches in the team conference and performing with similar success in a knock-out tournament against players from the University of Chicago and the University of Illinois. In this tournament, I had my own personal success being runner-up in my section of the singles contest and taking out the doubles title by partnering with our team number one. The following excerpt from a letter home explains how I felt:

What a day's tennis it was, I was absolutely exhausted at the end. I was on the court for about five hours. I won my first singles 5-7, 7-5, 11-9 and fifteen minutes later, I was back on the court to play the final. I was easily beaten 6-1, 6-2 mainly because I couldn't run. After this game, I rested for half an hour and then I was back on the court to play the final of the doubles. During the hit-up, I couldn't hit a thing and it looked like I might let the team and my partner down. However, I slowly warmed to the task and getting rid of my stiffness, I rallied well and we went on to win the match 5-7, 6-4, 7-5.

Winning this match clinched the team contest for IIT. I got home at 9pm and went straight around to the corner pub with Bob, Mike Mast, and his friend, Jim Graf. We celebrated the team's victory and they all expressed amazement at my ability to stay on my feet after such a gruelling day of tennis. I guess that is due to the Kiwi in me.

As part of an effort to build up my fitness, I took to running round the track at the northwest corner of campus. Again, the director of sports spied me from a distance and track one day in the early spring of 1969, he approached me while I was out on the track.

"You run at a good pace," he said. "Would you like to join the cross-country team in the fall semester?"

"Yes," I replied and as a result, I secured a place on the team. My memory is a bit hazy about what we achieved, but I do recall the team captain was a gun runner five years my junior, who would refer to me as granddad; cheeky sod. Also, the conference in which we participated took us further afield than the Chicago area, for I recall one time piling some of my teammates into my trusty old Dodge and driving ninety miles or so to Rockford in the northwest corner of Illinois for one meeting.

We would periodically go for training runs along the lakefront on the parklands south of 31st Street and I recall that on one occasion when my sister, Vivienne, was visiting Chicago, I took her along and left her by the lake to admire the view while I took off with my teammates on our scheduled training run. Now, this was not the most sensible thing to do, leaving a young female of European extraction in such a location bordering on a black ghetto area. About a mile into my run, I woke up to the potential danger I had left her in and I turned tail at raced back at incredible speed and found her waiting patiently in the summer sunshine for my return.

Two innocents abroad, Vivienne was none the wiser and I was most relieved to find her safe and sound.

My Mayor Daley Scholarship: As I mentioned earlier, money, or lack of it, was always a concern and midway through the fall semester of 1968, my coffers began running very low. I was earning about $20 per week from my job in the chemistry laboratory and Robert was helping out by kindly lending me money to pay my share of the rent. At one point, it seemed like I would not have sufficient to meet course fees for the following semester and my fallback option was to temporarily withdraw and fly to Canada where I was confident I would find work and save money to return and pick up my studies a year later.

Fortunately, it did not come to that as I managed to obtain some financial assistance from the university and better still, I landed a position as an engineer-in-training at the waterworks department of the city of Chicago.

During the fall semester of 1968, I was taking a course in environmental engineering. My lecturer was the deputy commissioner of works for the city of Chicago and he happened to mention midway through the course that the city ran a work experience programme for students planning to pursue a career in engineer. I approached the lecturer (whose name I do not recall), informed him of my predicament and asked to be considered for a position in this programme. He told me to put in an application which I duly did, I was accepted onto the programme and started working part-time in February 1969 at the start of the spring semester.

I was soon to find that this was not only a job but also an opportunity to study and get paid for my effort at the same time. I could report for work at any time during the normal working week and my official tasks were not that onerous. I would take along my books and I seemed to spend as much if not more time on my studies as I did attending to assigned tasks. I came to refer to this as my Mayor Daley* scholarship. I ended up working fifteen to twenty hours a week, earning $3 per hour. I retained this position until I graduated one year later.

Always on the lookout for financial assistance, I applied for a Student Chapter scholarship put up by the American Society of Civil Engineers and in September 1969, I received notice that I had been awarded one of four scholarships offered nationwide. By this time, I was on the home stretch and my financial woes seemed all but behind me.

Summer of '69: I decided to stay in Chicago in the summer of '69. I had a secure and well-paid job at the water filtration plant and I took up the opportunity of enrolling in a couple of night classes to speed up my progress towards graduation and lighten my workload in the coming fall semester.

Apart from days at spent working at the filtration plant and evening classes at summer school, my memory of that summer is a bit vague. However, looking back through my letters home, they have come back. Several times I complained of the stifling heat and humidity, my boredom during long days at the filtration plant with little to do except read books and magazines, offset by the occasional field trips to observe drain laying operations of predominantly Italian contracting crews, who seemed to amuse me with their ethnic mores.

On the brighter side, I continued to enjoy an active social life with old friends and new and roommates, Paul, took me on as one of his crew in several weekend races on Lake Michigan.

I had become acquainted with Carl Kupfer, who was an engineer and colleague at the filtration plant. Carl was about my own age and he, at one stage during this time, involved me in a water pipe flow experiment he was conducting, which helped to relieve my boredom. We became very good friends and on one occasion, he invited me to his home for a meal where I met his wife, Carol, and they introduced me to a single friend of hers named Jackie. During the weeks that followed, I dated Jackie quite frequently and I spent many happy times with Carl, Carol and Jackie picnicking and going to evening concerts in Grant Park on Chicago's lake shore and more parties at the home of Carl and Carol.

Jackie and I dated on numerous other occasions and a budding romance came to a sad end when she flew off to Switzerland for two years of study abroad.

There were the coming and going of my various roommates with Robert Asher flying out to Juneau, Alaska, as part of a scientific group doing research on the glaciers north of Juneau. Paul Wurtzebach was left to hold the fort for a few weeks until Mike Mast came back to town to join us over the summer. Robert arrived back in town in early August to an unusual reception which gained the attention of the Chicago papers, which I feel is worth recording here. The following is an excerpt from my letter home dated 10 August 1969:

Saturday of last weekend, Mike (Mast) and I set about putting down the quarter-round in the kitchen, a job left over from last November, when we laid the tiles. We ended up doing a major cleaning job in the kitchen under semi-fixed objects, particularly under the stove. The grease had really piled up. I guess we should do some spring cleaning a little more often. That night, Bob Asher came round for a few beers and to spin a few yarns. He had just come back from Alaska where he had been for the past two months.

Fortunately, he had cleaned up for a while in Alaska he refrained from taking a bath, which was part of an experiment on human odours in which he participated. Apparently, no one sat next to him on any of the flights back. He made headlines in the Chicago papers as the 'stinking explorer given sniffing all for science'.

Summer school ended early in August and I obtained B passes on the two courses I had been studying with a grade point average of 3.31, tantalisingly close to the 3.5 needed to graduate with honours. There followed a four-week break before the fall semester and the boredom of work at the filtration plant intensified, with the need of study to fill in the time. However, this was countered by the knowledge that I would graduate at the end of the coming semester and I would have a relatively light work study load.

I also received the news that I had been awarded the ASCE scholarship I had applied for earlier in the year and finally, my financial struggles seemed to disappear.

Fall Semester 1969: Now I was on the home stretch and with a relatively light study workload, I had time to think and plan for life after graduation. I started making extensive inquiries about job prospects, post-graduation and the option of continuing on to do post graduate study somewhere. Vivienne, who was on a US Government sponsored trip, arrived in Chicago and stayed with us for two weeks at the end of September. I ran on the IIT cross-country team doing sufficient to become a letterman (the US equivalent of a university blue).

Study and good grades remained a top priority and the normal round of socialising and parties continued and a retinue or girl companions, old and new, featured in my life. At some stage during the semester, I formed a close relation with Juanita Mast (no relation of Mike Mast), but this relationship was doomed not to last beyond my last days in Chicago. This time, it was me that broke the bond that was developing.

Earlier in the year, I had been initiated into Chi Epsilon (civil engineering) and Tau Beta Phi Honour (Engineering General) Societies in recognition of my scholastic achievements at IIT. These are very American institutions and for the ambitious career individual, membership is a highly desirable reward as it opens the way to the best job opportunities. They operate along fraternity lines with rituals that do not have a strong appeal to me. However, I was prudent enough to recognise the potential benefits of belonging and before I knew it, I was elected to the presidency of the IIT Chapter of Chi Epsilon.

In this capacity, I was required to act as Master of Ceremonies at a banquet we hosted on campus attended by a large group of civil engineers including what I described as 'all the big shots in the fraternity'. During the course of the evening, I spoke to a Senior Vice President of Woodward Clyde & Associates, a large consulting group and the outcome was an invitation to fly to New York to be interviewed for a job. For some reason, I didn't take up this offer, but there were others and I just prior to Xmas I went east to be interviewed for two jobs, one in Boston and the other in Newark, New Jersey. More about that further on.

In October, the trial of the infamous Chicago 7(8) was got underway during November and more civil unrest descended upon Chicago coinciding with a strike by service workers on the IIT campus. This drew the attention of the activists, but apart from rubbish piling up and those living in dormitories having to fend for themselves, life on campus went on as usual. The trial of the Chicago 7 went on for many months and came to a predictable end early in 1970. In a letter home, I made the following comment:

Among all the interesting things going on in the US today, one of the most revolting episodes came to an end this week. I refer to the trial of the Chicago 7 for conspiracy to inspire a riot. Five of the seven were found guilty. No doubt news of this trial has been published in local (NZ) papers, but I wonder to what extent. In my opinion, the trial made a mockery of justice here in the US. From the start, the defendants were set on disrupting the judicial system and did a mighty successful job. In the process, they were able to provoke the judge into taking sides on the issue involved.

The fact that they have been convicted is not important (I am sure the defendants never expected any other decision), but the manner in which they were found guilty goes against the grain of justice and in this respect, I regard the convictions as a victory for the defendants and revolutionaries in the US.

I also commented in the same letter: *US newspapers are terrible when it comes to writing world news. World news consists of what Nixon decrees from the White House, i.e., Reduction of troops in Vietnam, more planes to Israel, Jacquie and Onassis's marriage on the rocks etc., etc.*

A professor of civil engineering at Cornell University came to the campus in October to interview potential candidates for admittance to the post graduate programme. I was interviewed and a few weeks later, I received notification of my application being accepted. Things now seemed to be falling into place—pending graduation this coming January, a job during the spring and summer, and back for advanced study in the fall of 1970.

Snowfalls in Vermont: In the week leading up to Xmas, I arranged to travel first to Boston and then on to Newark, New Jersey, to attend two job interviews that eventuated from my earlier enquiries. It was about this time that Hippie Sarah informed Bob that she was moving on and intended to return to her home and family in Vermont for Xmas. I jumped in and offered to drive her there on my way to Boston. My job interviews had been set up for Monday and Tuesday prior to Xmas day (Thursday).

I contacted a car delivery agency and contracted to deliver a car to Boston (the same arrangement as my Miami trip the previous year), with pick up on Friday morning and delivery on Monday evening.

I packed a travel bag and Sarah packed her few belongings, we said farewell to Robert and Paul, and we set off from Chicago in the early evening. We drove east all through the night and the next day and arrived in Sarah's hometown (whose name I never recorded) twenty-four hours later. I was given a good welcome, but I was very tired and retired early for a good night's sleep, planning to stay on until Monday morning before driving to Boston and my first job interview.

The next day, Sunday, Sarah took me for a walk in the nearby woods. I recall that it was a wonderful winter setting, with tall but well-spaced trees all around, fresh snow on the ground. As we walked deeper into the woods, fresh snow flakes started falling; it was heavenly. I also sensed that as we walked deeper into the wood, Sarah seemed to have lost her bearings and we risked being caught out in the wood when darkness fell. I pride myself on having a good sense of direction and I quietly took over, eventually steering us out of the woods onto the road into town and then a short hike back to the warmth and safety of Sarah's home.

On Monday morning, I said farewell to Sarah and her family and drove the relatively short distance to Boston, arriving there in time for my interview in the early afternoon. This seemed to go well and from there, I delivered the car to its owner, checked into a hotel for an overnight stay, and then flew to Newark the next morning. I was met at Newark Airport by one of this firm's representatives, taken to lunch, followed by an interview in the afternoon, and back at Newark Airport to catch a night flight back to Chicago.

When I took off from Newark, heavy snow was falling in all the northeastern and mid-western states of America and when we reached Chicago O'Hare Airport, outward flights had been suspended and inward flights were being held in a holding pattern, while snow ploughs worked feverously to keep runways open and allow inward flights to land. It was an interesting sight peering out the window seeing dozens of planes circling around in an ever-decreasing spiral until they landed one by one. It was more than an hour after our scheduled arrival time before my flight hit the ground and taxied to its assigned berth.

In a letter home, I mentioned that both interviews went extremely well and I expressed confidence that I would receive a job from both firms. As it turned out, this did eventuate and I was forced to make a choice, opting to take up the position with the firm Haley & Aldrich in Boston in neighbouring Cambridge, Massachusetts, on the north side of the Charles River, which separates it from Boston, Massachusetts.

Final Days at Illinois Tech: It is often said the journey is always more satisfying than actually getting there. I had been striving for almost ten years to reach this point, with all the ups and downs along the way and now I was about to graduate. Apart from the initial euphoria of stepping up on the stage of Herman Hall, it all seemed an anti-climax and just one more stepping stone in my development and my longer journey through life. My prospects were good. I was about to move on to a new job in a new location, but there was a certain sadness about leaving behind an active and enjoyable student life and the circle of friends I had made.

At this point in this memoir, I would like make mention a few of those friends, who came into my life and helped me to enjoy, what on reflection has been one of the more stimulating and exciting periods of my life. First and foremost is Jean-Michel Baryla, who along with Robert Asher has remained a lifelong friend with whom I continue to correspond to this day.

Jean-Michel was one of several French and Belgium students at IIT. If memory serves me correctly, Jean-Michel was from Lyon and he was studying for a master's degree in civil engineering. I first met Jean-Michel and his friends when they crashed a party we were hosting at 3309 South Lowe sometime during the fall semester of 1968. In a letter home to the family dated 22 February 1969, this is what I had to say about Jean-Michel.

Last Saturday night, I went out to a party with Jean-Michel and Bernie. Before I go further, perhaps I should tell you a bit about Jean-Michel. With a name like that, I guess it is not hard to guess that he is a Frenchman. Philip and Jenny, you will remember him for he was at the party we had back in October. He was the blonde-haired fellow who was stretched out all evening on one of the sofas with the beautiful Japanese girl.

It was through Bernie that I got to know Jean-Michel and his friends very well, mostly at the numerous parties we all attended. They were great, fun-loving individuals and good company, although, on occasion, I would feel some frustration when they would suddenly start talking away in French and I would struggle to understand what they were saying. However, I did learn one French phrase, 'Voulez vous couche avec moi', which they cheekily used when chatting up any female whom they confronted.

Together with Bernie, Jean-Michel features regularly in my letters home during 1969. We have remained in contact over all the years since I left Chicago and he reappears in this tale on several more occasions down through the years.

There were the four nurses: Carol Yep, Leslie, Andrea and Michelle from the hospital down the end of 31st Street. I had met them through Bernie and they would come along to a lot of the parties Robert, Mike M, Paul, and I hosted during the eighteen months of residence at 3309 South Lowe. I dated all of them except Carol (she was one of Bernie's several girlfriends) and they were good company. Andrea seemed to have a crush on me, but strangely enough, it was Carol that I developed the strongest relationship with.

We kept in loose contact by mail for several years after I left Chicago and we met up a decade later, when at a loose end back in New Zealand and unsure of what I wanted to do with myself, I flew back to the US and floated around for several months visiting friends old and new during the spring and early northern summer of 1982. I will write more about Carol later.

Next, there was English Carol, the term I used in letters home to distinguish her from Carol, the nurse. Another of Bernie's imagined conquests, Carol was good fun and joined us all at some of the parties we went to during the year. I ended up dating Carol (much to the consternation of Bernie) on one occasion when I learnt that she was about to leave Chicago to return to England. Our relationship was purely platonic. Bernie had been ignoring her and really there was nothing for him to be concerned about (refer to letter home dated 29 March 1969 for more on Carol).

I should mention Chief Petty Officer Doherty. A naval officer, Chief as I came to call him, was on the staff of the IIT Reserve Officers Training Corps (ROTC) and had responsibility for issuing textbooks to students attached to the unit, of which Bernie was one. Bernie introduced me to him at the beginning of the fall semester and when he heard my voice and learnt where I came from, he said to me, "When you know what courses you are taking and the texts you need, come and see me and I will issue them to you, no charge." He told me that he had served in the Pacific during World War 2 and had spent several wonderful months on furlough in New Zealand.

"Loved the place and loved you Kiwis," he said. From that moment on, he could not do enough for me when it came to providing me with the textbooks I needed. As any poor student will know, textbooks make a big dent in one's budget and I was forever grateful to the chief for his bending the rules and supplying me with what would have amounted to several hundred dollars' worth of books during my days at IIT.

There were many others whose names I have long since forgotten through lack of contact. Many were Americans and others were from Africa, Europe, the Middle East, Asia and South America. IIT had a very strong international contingent of students representing sixty countries from memory. I was the first and only ever student from New Zealand to enrol at that time. Some of the names I do remember; Arthakorn from Thailand, Deepak from India, Johannes from

Ethiopia, Zohair from Israel. Among the IIT staff names worth recording here include: Julian Snyder, Professor of Structural Engineering, who inspired me to an A in Structures and helped keep me in good physical shape on the squash court, the Diana Rigg come Emma Peel lookalike of the hit TV program *The Avengers*, who inspired me to an A in English Literature, a subject I always struggled with in my secondary school years, and John Root, who lectured me in in a course on the history of Western Civilisation to 1648 and rekindled my interest in history.

Finally, how could I ever forget hippie Sarah and her fresh and insightful view of the world? She was Robert's friend who accompanied him back from Juneau, Alaska, following his summer on the ice fields in 1969. Sarah spent the fall semester living with us in our untidy apartment on South Lowe and I found her quite different from anyone I had ever met before. Her home and family were in Vermont and quite what she had been doing in Alaska, I never asked. My memory of her was that she was pleasant to talk to. She was one of the flower generation who challenged the political system shouting the slogan 'Make love, not war'.

I enjoyed the many discussions I had with her and I recall her saying to me one time, "I can't believe you are studying engineering, you are not like those others I have met from IIT." Reflecting on these words and looking back at my academic record both at Wellington College and at IIT, I had achieved some of my highest grades in humanities and liberal arts subjects. Down through the years, my interest in philosophy, politics and how the world functions has come to outstrip my knowledge and interest in technical matters. Perhaps Sarah observed a side of me that was lying dormant at this stage of my life.

In the final few months leading up to my graduation, our eccentric landlord, Austin, seemed to tire of our presence, making it known he would prefer a married couple, whom he imagined would be more inclined to make the small capital improvements around the apartment we had always promised, but never quite got around to doing. It was only my diplomacy that saved the day and allowed us to stay on as long as I was there in residence.

Now the end had come. I received my degree on 23 January 1970 and a week later, I was due to move on to Boston and the next stage of my journey. Time for a party and farewell. Many of the above-mentioned turned up and what a happy and sad event it was for me. I remember very little of what was said or went on, but I had a small auction where I sold memorabilia for nominal amounts to all and sundry, including my treasured 'We Love Mayor Daley' sign which Jean-Michel took possession of. I left Chicago a week later in a not-so-new car I had bought with the proceeds of my ASCE scholarship, leaving my trusty Dodge abandoned on the streets of Chicago 1000 miles.

A notice from the city authorities was forwarded to me a few months later. This I ignored and I assume the car was eventually impounded for scrap, a sad ending for something that had served me so well and in which I had so much fun.

Homesick in Boston: I left Chicago during the last week of January and drove east in my not-so-new Pontiac direct to Boston a journey of some 1000 miles. I made no record of this journey or of when I arrived, but I am sure I must have called in on the Reynolds in Michigan en route. What I do remember is that my first port of call was the boarding house at 44 Winslow Road, Brookline, a suburb of Boston, which was to be my home during the time I was in Boston. Harlow Wheeler, a colleague at the Chicago Water Works Department and a friend of the proprietor, had kindly arranged a room for me, which I was happy to accept as interim accommodation while I settled into Boston.

As things turned out, it suited my immediate needs and I remained living there for the eight months that I lived and worked in Boston.

The boarding house was a large three-storey house on a corner section at 44 Winslow Avenue, Brookline, a relatively quiet residential area east of the city centre. It was located within a short walking distance of the metro, on which I was to make my daily commute to the office of new employer, Haley and Aldrich, on the east side of the Charles River, which separates Boston from Cambridge, Massachusetts. In close proximity were the prestigious institutions of the Massachusetts Institute of Technology and Harvard University.

The boarding house comprised seven or eight rooms on levels two and three, each occupied by a single male occupant most, probably all of us in our mid to late twenties. Much of the first floor was occupied by the proprietress, Mrs Wyman, a kindly lady in her seventies. What I do recall was her quiet efficiency in keeping a house full of male boarders in order, whose ages ranged between early twenties and late twenties. There was a basement in which there was a communal kitchen, which provided a social setting in which we could mingle and get to know one another. I became particularly friendly with Norm Scarpulla, who was a banker and grew up in the Durham, New Hampshire.

It was the depth of winter when I arrived in Boston and snow was all around. Norm was a member of the Appalachian Mountain Club and a keen hiker and skier. I spent many weekends away with Norm on the mountain slopes in New Hampshire, learning the intricacies of cross-country skiing and in the spring and summer, hiking along mountain trails in the same countryside. When spring came, we took to hiking in these same hills and I recall visiting his mother's home on more than one occasion and being warmly received.

The only other character I remember from my time at the boarding house was Alphonse. I was a light social smoker (a dreadful habit) and had been for the past several years. Alphonse also smoked and both of us wanted to kick the habit. One day, he challenged me to a contest to see who could go the longest without smoking and I took up the challenge. My pride took hold, I was determined to win and I successfully quit smoking for several years after that. As for Alphonse, I never saw him smoking again, so perhaps it was a win-win situation for both of us.

Work and Play in Boston: I commenced work with my new employer, Haley & Aldridge, during the first week of February. This was a relatively small company specialising in geotechnical and environmental engineering and had four partners and a staff of approximately thirty engineers. I was well received by these people and quickly put to work on a number of different projects including supervision of a grouting operation in some underground water storage tanks, a series of pile load tests in Providence Rhode Island and later when spring and summer came, earthworks supervision on a construction site in Buffalo New York, and days spent rowing a boat around the wharves at the Port of Boston undertaking a pile condition study.

The work was varied and for the most part different from what I had done in the past. Also, I was travelling out of Boston quite frequently, which provided me the opportunity to explore and see new territory in the northeastern states of America.

On the social scene, I slowly developed a coterie of friends and one or two romantic interests. Among the latter was Rosemary from Boston, who I dated quite frequently and a zany Brazilian girl, Virginia, who on occasion would cook me a meal and drive me around the countryside in her sporty MGB car. After my days at work, particularly on Fridays, I liked to visit various small bars and nightclubs and listen to jazz and converse with the clientele. I remember one evening going to a jazz club called Lennie's and Gerry Mulligan was playing a gig. He was a prominent saxophonist and a favourite of mine, who had topped many music polls over the previous two decades.

He features on the soundtrack of the movie *I Want to Live,* which I had in my collection of vinyls back home. The movie is based on the life of a San Francisco prostitute Barbara Graham, who was convicted of murder and eventually executed. Her life revolved around drugs and alcohol and she frequented the jazz clubs in San Francisco. My interest in jazz was stimulated after seeing that movie and to see Mulligan in person was quite a treat. In a letter back home, I mentioned, 'he's a very crude person but his music was good'.

I visited the Boston Playboy Club on a few occasions, where I used to enjoy the jazz that was featured there and one of my favourite haunts was Barney's a bar in Harvard Square where some of the students from Harvard would gather and it provided a good opportunity to get involved in political discussion about issues of the time. I made reference to this in a couple of letters home, which give an indication of my political views at this time of my life.

In the early spring, I stumbled across the Boston Community Sailing Club on the south side of the Charles River. It was a wonderful facility for learning to sail. For a small joining fee of $25, boats, equipment and tuition were provided. I used to go there often on weekends and soon learnt to master the art of helming a boat and taking it out onto the river solo or with one other as crew. A sailing yacht gains its motion by the force of the wind in the sails and the counter force on the keel (or in the case of a dinghy, the centreboard) below the waterline propelling the boat forward like a pip being squeezed out of an orange.

I remember on one occasion, I invited a friend along and we set off from the jetty and out onto the river. Ahead of us was a bridge and I went to tack out of its way, but the boat did not respond and we kept heading towards the bridge. I tried again but still no response and by now we were getting alarmingly close to it. Fortunately for me, there was a watchful eye on the shore and suddenly I heard over a megaphone, "Sail No. 329, put down your centreboard," which I duly did, we came about and disaster and embarrassment were averted.

As I gained confidence, I went on to participate in weekend races and this was the start of a sporting interest that I pursued during much of my adult life.

Also, during the spring and early summer, I had a string of compatriots call by and visit me in Boston in fairly quick succession. First came Cos Kingston, an acquaintance of Vivienne, who was on an around the world vacation seeing new sites and visiting old friends in the UK where she was originally from. She stayed with me in the Brookline boarding house for several days, using my room while I bunked down in Norm's room along the corridor. It was a highly unusual arrangement to have a female to stay at all, but I had managed to charm Mrs Wyman to bend her rules, although she did alert me to the fact that under state law, I should never be in my room with the door closed while Cos was present.

Soon after Cos departed, Vivienne's friend and colleague, Judith Cornwell, arrived. Judith worked with Vivienne at the US Information Service in Wellington and was on a similar familiarisation junket in the US. She stayed in Boston for almost a week and once again I was able to accommodate her under the same arrangement I had with Cos. I knew Judith well and it was good to share her company and get first-hand news of family back home.

On the weekend when she was not involved in business activity, Norm took us up to New Hampshire to explore the wilderness there and I recall spending a delightful Sunday afternoon canoeing on a small lake with Judith while Norm went on a vigorous hike up a nearby mountain with a group of his mountain club friends. Around the same time, Kiwi expatriate Jenny Officer, another acquaintance of Vivienne, who worked at the NZ Embassy in Washington DC paid a fleeting visit one day and called by to say hello. It was great to have this contact with fellow Kiwis and it made me nostalgic for a return home, at least for a visit.

While all this was happening, I was quietly contemplating my future plans. Although the opportunity to stay in America was there and I had taken the first step by applying for a change in my visa status shortly after I arrived in Boston, I never felt that I wanted to stay on permanently and make it my home. I had enjoyed wonderful hospitality from the many Americans I had met and I could not fault them for their warmth and generosity. However, there was something about the social and political fabric which did not gel with me. I came to refer to it as a plastic society and I never bought into the American dream that anyone can make it in America, whatever that may mean.

During the two and a half years I spent in Chicago, although I missed my family and had little contact with my fellow countrymen (apart from the Egan's and brief visits from Philip and Jenny), at no stage did I feel a tinge of homesickness. Life was too busy and exciting for me to feel otherwise. However, after settling into my new surroundings and life back in the world of work, I started to get this yearning to return home for at least a short visit to see my family and friends of old.

Compounding my dilemma were plans I had set in train to go on to undertake advanced studies at Cornell University in Ithaca in upper New York State. Also, one of the firm's partners was a former professor at the Massachusetts Institute of Technology. Knowing it was my intention to go onto graduate school later in the year, he introduced me to one of his former colleagues a MIT and encouraged me to consider enrolling in the institution's master's programme, where I was told I would be accepted with open arms.

With financial support that was offered, it was a tempting proposition, but one I did not take up, nor did I pursue taking up a placement at Cornell. Now that I was back earning a good income ($11,000pa), I had no strong desire to go back to being a struggling student once more.

As the months went by, I started planning my visit home, first in August prior to the start of the new university year in September, then changing this to Xmas time when I was informed by the US Immigration Authority that I could not leave the country until my visa application had been processed. "When would this be?" I asked early in August, to which I received a reply it could be anywhere between six to twelve months. It was shortly after this exchange that I made a somewhat impulsive decision to pack up and return home, regardless of the consequences.

Shortly thereafter, I handed in my notice to my employer, made flight bookings, said goodbye to my friends and acquaintances, and flew out during the first week of September.

Immediately prior to my departure, Norm took a week's leave and together we drove up to the State of Maine and spent a wonderful four days camping and hiking in Mt Katahdin National Park. Etched in my memory was a wonderful day hike from the valley in which we pitched our tent, up to a ridgeline on the southern side of the valley. When we reached the top we proceeded along the ridgeline to the north slopes of the valley below, then back down to camp several hundred metres below.

Norm had obviously been there several times before and was well used to the terrain. For me, it was an exhilarating and sometimes scary experience. I have never had a very good head for heights and there was one moment, when we had to make our way around a rock outcrop along a narrow ledge, barely two feet wide with a vertical drop below. Other parts of the ridge were no more than six feet wide with similar drops on both sides to the valleys below. Somehow, with Norm's calming manner and steadying hand, I made it without mishap to live and tell this tale.

We returned to Boston, I said my farewells to Norm, Alphonse, Mrs Wyman, and others at the boarding house and flew out on my journey home. Enroute, I stopped over in Chicago where I had a boozy week catching up with old friends, a quick hop over to Clark Lake to say goodbye to the Reynolds, on to Spokane in Washington, a stopover in San Francisco to enjoy the sites and nightlife of the City by the Bay, then across the Pacific, arriving home in mid-October 1970.

Chapter 4
Back Home 1970–1972

I Had Changed

I arrived home in the spring of 1970. It was wonderful to be back after three years in America and without much thought to where I would live, I just moved in with Mum and Dad at the family home in Eastbourne. Finding work was not a problem. I just went back to the same job with my former employer, albeit with a bit more seniority. I slotted back into the Eastbourne scene and pursued my sporting interests: sailing during the summer, coaching rugby during the winter and nights on the town with an old flame.

I had been away for just over three years and I was now twenty-seven years of age. It was wonderful to be back home, but after the initial euphoria of seeing family and friends, I soon became bored. I had changed, the community to which I returned had not. It became a time to reflect and decide what now. Mum and Dad seemed happy to have me move in and for the next nine months, I occupied the same bedroom in which I had slept during my youth.

I commenced work as a staff engineer with Brickell, Moss et. al. at the beginning of November 1970. The geotechnical and civil engineering section was now operating out of new premises in Daly Street, Lower Hutt. As previously, it was an easy and uncongested commute from Eastbourne; this time I did it in a sparkling new Toyota Corolla, which I purchased with my Yankee dollars. Currency controls were still in effect requiring the ownership of foreign currency to make such a purchase. With my own office space on the upper floor of this two-storey complex, during the next two years, I worked on a number of projects, most of which I have long since forgotten except for a research project for the National Roads Board.

The only reason I remember this particular project was not so much for its technical content, rather its bureaucratic gobbledy-gook and my first exposure to the workings of a highly bureaucratic government department.

On the sporting front, I slotted back into the Eastbourne scene. Keen to pursue my new sporting interest, I joined the Muritai Yacht Club and started sailing and racing an International Moth, a class of dinghy that was popular at the time and which there was a sizeable fleet at the club. During that summer, I spent many a weekend in a yacht I had purchased pitting my wits against my fellow Moth sailors, including my mate Wal, who had been sailing there since he was a small kid. I soon found that sailing in the strong wind and rough waters of Wellington Harbour was quite different from the gentler breezes I had experienced in Boston.

Launching a boat from the beach during a strong northwester was particularly hazardous and I recall my small craft being damaged on at least one occasion, as the rudder dug into the sand before I could clear the beach. I also soon learnt that there was more to sailing fast around a standard triangular racing course than just pointing in the direction one wanted to go. Still, it was all good fun and the comradie in the clubhouse at the end of an afternoon's racing made it all the more enjoyable.

When winter came, I re-joined the Eastbourne rugby club, following the fortunes of the senior team and coached an under-seventeen age-grade team. My memory of this team was that they were full of enthusiasm and a pleasure to coach. The following winter, I was made coach of an under-nineteen age-grade side, which turned out far less satisfying. All season I struggled to assemble a full team and most of those who came along, all they wanted to do was drink beer and get plastered. I found myself getting sucked into the drinking scene and I got little satisfaction from the antics that followed.

During my first year back home, I started dating Cos, who had visited and stayed with me in Boston. We had our first intimate moment during that visit and we picked up on the romance during that summer of 1970/71. I would usually see Cos on the weekend, we would go out for dinner and return to her flat on the Terrace, where we would share intimacies in the privacy of her bedroom before I returned home to Eastbourne in the early hours of the following morning. I recall on one occasion after one such romantic encounter, I had put the shirt I had been wearing out to be washed.

It must have been mid-week for when I returned home from work and went to my room, I saw a condom sitting on the pillow of my bed. When I went out to the kitchen where my mother was preparing the evening meal, she said, "And I thought you were such a good boy." There was nothing else to say and nothing else was said. Looking back, it seems a sign of the social mores of the time, where matters relating to sex were not spoken. My, how times have changed.

Later that year, I moved out of Pukatea Street and into the city and to flatting with a work colleague, Don Raisebeck. Ours was a two-bedroom flat on Clifton Terrace and only a short walking distance from where Cos lived. With greater freedom, we got more adventurous and on occasion, we would venture away from Wellington and go for an overnight tryst out of town. Though we never discussed it, I am sure I was not Cos' only lover; a situation that did not really bother me. I enjoyed her company and sex with Cos was always very satisfying for me.

She was the first female with whom I had an ongoing sexual relationship for several years whenever we were in the same location, but marriage and settling down was not something I contemplated.

In her job running the Wellington City Information Bureau, or I-Site as it is now known, she was in close contact with politicians (both local councillors and MPs) and business people, and she often,threw parties, entertained in her apartment on the Terrace. I remember one cocktail party she hosted in the early hours of the evening attended by such individuals including a few high-ranking government cabinet ministers. We were all merrily drinking champagne and other forms of liquor when the magic hour of 7:15 came and the ministerial cars appeared outside to take them back to parliament for a late night session to debate important issues of the day.

It seemed to me that all of them were by this time highly inebriated and I thought to myself 'heaven help us if this is how our leaders behave and go about debating and passing laws'. Perhaps I was a bit naïve back then.

Violet

During the spring of 1972, I had another romantic interlude which was more intense in its passion and was to cause my family, particularly Malcolm and Audrey, a certain amount of distress. Violet was her name. I met her at an office function in July and we started dating. It was not long before a passionate romance developed. I moved in with Violet and for the next several months, my life revolved almost exclusively around her. We would go to our respective jobs during the day and by night and on weekends, we would enjoy torrid sex.

One long weekend, when we spent three days in bed emerging occasionally to eat, then back to bed for more sex. The sex was great, but one cannot survive on sex alone.

Violet was a Mormon. I had a cursory understanding of Mormonism and like Socrates, I have an enquiring mind. I decided to investigate the Mormon Church in greater depth. I read a book about its founder Joseph Smith, its history from the founding days in the Midwest of America, the migration west and the establishment of the Church of Latter Day Saints in the State of Utah. I attended church meetings on Sundays, I sat through a six stage induction course given by two local missionaries and together with my sister, Catherine, and her husband, Herman (also Mormons), I spent several evenings dining and discussing Mormonism with the Stake President.

I thought I was in love and I threw myself into it with abandon. What started out as an intellectual exercise gradually became a battle of wills, as I slowly felt myself being sucked into a mystic world which seemed to defy all common logic. I had long ago abandoned a belief in an all-powerful God on high casting judgment upon his flock below, but not my belief in a spiritual side to life, a unifying force (call it God if you like) that exists beyond the physical world in which we live. Mormons are strong on the nuclear family and there is much to be admired for his trait. However, their fundamental view of the world and literal interpretation of the Bible are so at odds with what I believed.

For me, major sticking points were the creation of our world in six days, six thousand years ago and pragmatic issues such as the rejection of the practice of polygamy and the acceptance of coloured people into priesthood following revelations from God, conveniently timed to comply with new federal laws at the time. I remember having long arguments with the missionaries and church officials (including some eminent scientists) discussing these issues. The stock reply was, "Don't worry about these things, Michael, you will come to know in time."

Given my total immersion, I felt strong forces willing me to do just that, don't worry, just accept what we are telling you. I recall one Sunday session in the chapel where the flock were invited to the lectern to confirm their belief. Strangely, I also found myself up there, saying some words to the effect that I was investigating, but yet to be convinced. Shortly thereafter, Catherine went up and told the flock I was her brother and she was hoping and praying that I would see the light and join. As she spoke, I developed an uncontrollable shaking of my body, which I could not explain except it was like some strong force reverberating between me to my sister.

Sometime soon after this incident, while visiting the Stake President in a warm and seductive atmosphere, I found myself saying I would join. Before I knew it, I was going through a baptismal ceremony and being welcomed into the fold. Nothing was spoken (we Barnetts tend to hold things back), but I know my parents were deeply upset and as for siblings, Philip and Jenny, they thought I was bonkers.

I seemed to have succumbed to some hypnotic spell. Next day, I woke up and realised that being a Mormon was not for me. I also realised this action and my intense relationship with Violet was causing a rift between me and my family, not to say my friends and my newfound interest in sailing, which Violet tended to discourage. For a short while, I was a mental mess with conflicting desires and emotions.

In January 1973, I took up a work assignment in Western Samoa. This put distance between me and the religious fervour I had encountered. My feelings towards Violet remained and we stayed in contact for several months, but eventually, the passion died and we went our separate ways.

Chapter 5
Global Roaming 1973–1980

Western Samoa 1973–74

On reflection, I often wonder whether I had made a good decision to return to the fold at Brickell, Moss. I had more seniority but little had changed except a few new faces and much of the work I was assigned differed little from what I had been doing in the past. To put it bluntly, I was bored with my work and I struggled to relate to the Eastbourne community I came back to. I had changed, but the community had not. Apart from my newfound interest in sailing, there was little to hold me there. I yearned for more adventure abroad.

An opportunity to go to Samoa arose when Brickell Moss and Holmes Miller (another Wellington engineering consultancy) were jointly awarded a contract to design and supervise the reconstruction of the East Coast Road, from Apia to Falefa on the Island of Upolo. I volunteered for and was duly appointed to the role as site engineer.

In November 1972, I went on a two-week trip to Samoa with Brian Jackson the project manager, and two others to reconnoitre the road and organise accommodation and a site office. Getting to Samoa involved flying from Auckland to Fiji on a second generation jet aircraft, then an onward flight to Samoa aboard an ageing DC3 prop aircraft. Flight schedules were such that a one to two-day stopover in Fiji was necessary and this afforded an opportunity to indulge in duty-free shopping from a large selection of largely Indian merchants.

Our initial objectives were achieved, I was able to return home to spend Xmas with the family, before returning to Samoa early in the new year to commence my assignment properly.

While this assignment in Samoa gave me a certain amount of autonomy and satisfied my desire to be working in the outdoors, things moved slowly on island time and I had plenty of downtime to reflect on what I really wanted to be doing at this stage of my life. I was still lacking a certain amount of confidence and assertiveness to put my stamp on the project.

An example of this was how the design team dealt with the issue of manufacturing aggregates for the road base to be constructed and designing culverts to cope with the intense rainfall on a tropical island. At the time I was a great fan of the novels of James Michener and had just completed reading *Tales of the South Pacific*, in which he had given a fictional account of the construction of an airfield in the Guadeloupe archipelago during World War 2. On it, they used crushed coral for the base, a material that was in abundance, very cheap to mould for this purpose.

Our team called for crushed rock for this purpose, following standard practice in NZ. This proved to be a difficult and expensive exercise in Samoa given the relatively primitive crushing equipment available and accessibility to suitable quarries on the island. The American method seemed ideal, but I lacked the confidence to push it as an option even if only to be trialled.

Funding for the project was an ongoing issue which tended to cause delays in construction. The Samoan government was on a mission to upgrade its badly potholed and degraded roading system around the main island of Upolo. The first stage of this programme, the road from the airport to the capital, Apia, had just been completed. Our project consisted of upgrading the East Coast Road from Apia to Falefa at the eastern end of the island. I recall several visits by representatives of the World Bank in Washington DC where negotiations with government officials took place to obtain finance to carry out construction. At times, things seemed to move at a snail's pace.

The year and a half I spent in Samoa was far from being a highlight of my career and I won't dwell on these aspects. However, there were compensations in the social life I enjoyed with both the Samoan people and expatriates who were living there. And it was in Samoa that I found the opportunity and time to indulge in my new sporting passion, dingy sailing.

Apia is centrally located on the northern coast of Upolu with a small natural harbour capable of accommodating small ships east of the town centre. West of the town centre lies the Mulinu'u Peninsula, a narrow stretch of land which houses the Samoan Parliament, an observatory, and the Apia Sailing Club. The sailing club occupied a small slither of land on the ocean side of the peninsula directly opposite the parliament providing regular weekend sailing and racing in a shallow lagoon inside a coral reef stretching from the harbour entrance to the western end of the island.

It provided a social and sporting haven for the small contingent of expatriates living in Samoa and a few Samoans who liked to indulge in this activity, including Alan Grey, son of the island's matriarch, Aggie Grey. I joined soon after my arrival in Samoa and quickly became an active member of its sailing committee and a competitive sailor matching it with the best of them on race days.

I spent many a day at the yacht club, swimming in the warm tropical waters during weekday downtime and participating in the weekend racing and social activities. Depending on the tide, racing would be held on either a morning or afternoon Saturday or Sunday, the lagoon being too shallow around low tide. Occasionally, we would set a course which took us down to the main harbour, out beyond the reef into the ocean swell, and then back through a narrow gap in the reef almost directly opposite the clubhouse. We had no rescue boat, but this was of no concern when sailing within the reef as a yacht in strife would always drift ashore.

However, sailing outside the reef was a potential problem. On one occasion while sailing outside the reef, I happened to look back and saw that one of my fellow sailors had lost his mast and was drifting dangerously close to the reef. I turned back to assist him and using my mainsheet, I managed to fashion a tow rope and towed him through a gap in the reef and safely bring him home.

When we came ashore, the cry went out, "We don't need a rescue boat when we have got Barnett on the water," to cheers and laughter.

Over the years, my racing skills improved immensely and by the end of 1973, I was up with the best in the fleet and winning my share of races. I became particularly proficient in positioning my yacht well and getting away to a flying start. The harder it blew, the more I liked it and only big John Donoghue could catch me in such conditions.

I became involved in organising the racing programme and on one occasion, I organised a novelty event, which I modelled on the Le Mans twenty-four-hour endurance motor race. I called it the Mulinu'u 120. I created several teams of four sailors and we raced our small single-handed Bonitos around a triangular course on the lagoon. The yachts would make a pit stop at the boat ramp at defined intervals to change skippers and race on. At the end of a hundred and twenty minutes of continuous sailing, the leading team was declared the winner. My team did not win but it was a great success and fun was had by all.

Another memorable event was a visit by a group of sailors from Pago Pago in American Samoa, challenging us to a series of races over two days. Because of the tidal restrictions at Mulinu'u, we held this event in the larger lagoon opposite the western end of Upolu. The Bonitos were transported there by road, but two larger catamarans were sailed there and back. Again, it was a successful regatta, held in hot balmy weather and ending in a narrow team victory for our club. My fondest memory of this event was taking time off on Monday to retrieve one of the catamarans and sail it back to Mulinu'u—four to five hours of blissful cruising in moderate winds on a cloudless day.

Towards the end of 1973, sailing and organising the racing programme and developing my journalistic skills took up a large portion of my time. 'I am fleet captain, publicity officer and you name it, I'm it', I wrote in a letter home. I started writing a weekly column for the Samoa Times and presenting yachting reports on the sports session of the local radio station.

Samoa Times 9 November 1973

Yachting

Should we still be blessed with the presence of Somerset Maugham, he would undoubtedly be considering writing an epilogue to his famous short story, Rain. *Tremendous weather for remaining indoors writing and tremendous weather for the pastime of his immoral character Sadie Thompson.*

In that roundabout way of commenting on the weather, back to my highly-paid job of yachting correspondent.

First, a major drama occurred last weekend. One of our members and his family decided to take their yacht to Satapuala due to poor tide conditions in Apia. On arrival, he found he had brought everything except his mast (a most essential piece of equipment) and he returned at record speed to Apia to fetch it. During sailing, he struck many rocks and decided it was just not his day. The family, therefore, placed the boat once again on top of the car and proceeded back to Apia.

While passing Faleolo Airport, the boat decided to imitate an aircraft just seen taking off and rose spectacularly from the top of the vehicle and alighted softly on the grass verge on the other side of the road. The joys of yachting!

There was many a day I passed the time pottering around the yacht club and swimming in the lagoon. Evenings I would spend in one of the many bars scattered around Apia drinking far too much beer and chatting up the wahines. One day, while out swimming, I came across Peka, a pretty girl with a beaming smile. We chatted and it was not long before I fell for the charms of this island maiden.

I was living on my own in a house located in the woods off the lower slopes of the cross island road. Peka moved in and became my lover, cook and maidservant all in one. However, what seemed a good arrangement did not last forever. Occasionally, Peka would disappear for a few days on the pretext that she was visiting her family on the island of Savaii. I was happy with that until I became aware that she was in fact still in town and playing around with her friends and who knows who. My pride was severely dented, and I challenged her with my newfound knowledge when she reappeared.

I erupted in anger at her deceit and told her in no uncertain terms what I thought about her deceit. She in turn reacted in anger, pulled a carving knife from a kitchen drawer and threatened to kill me. I believe she meant business. In order to diffuse the ugly scene, I ceased my verbal attack and calmly but firmly said to Peka, "You can stay here tonight but you must sleep in the spare room and in the morning, pack your bag, go from the house and do not return."

A fragile peace descended and she withdrew into that room and I to mine. Taking with me all the kitchen knives I could find and hid them under my bed. I lay awake and a short while later, Peka appeared at my door and said, "Where is the carving knife?"

I did not respond to that question and instead invited her into my bed, reasoning that having her by my side when I fell asleep was a safer option than having her roam around not knowing what she might do.

Morning came and in spite of some pleading to forgive her and let her stay, I stood my ground and insisted she pack up and go. Fortunately, she left with little fuss and that was the last I saw of Peka.

If one gets the impression that I had a lot of downtime, you would not be wrong. By year's end, it seemed like my career was going backwards stuck here on a tropical island. I began to consider my options.

***

Hal Wagstaff was an Eastbourne resident and senior official in the New Zealand Yachting Federation. Hal was manager of the New Zealand sailing team at the 1972 Munich Olympic Games and he was also national president of the International Moth Class. During the summer of 1971, when I was learning the intricacies of sailing a Moth class dingy, he asked me to take on the role of national secretary and I was happy to oblige. A year later, just prior to my move to Samoa, he informed me he had taken on the role of world president of the class and asked me to join him as his world secretary.

Again, I was happy to assist him and it did not seem to matter that I would operate from Samoa. Hal went off to the Olympic Games and from my base in Samoa, I started corresponding with the national secretaries around the world where the class was active. Through these contacts, I became familiar with the sailing programmes in the UK, Europe, USA, Australia, and New Zealand. Given my enthusiasm for racing small dinghies and a desire to expand my horizons, I decided to quit my job, travel to Europe, and spend the northern summer sailing in a number of national contests.

I had saved plenty and could afford to take time out before seeking a new job, perhaps in Canada or back in the US where salaries were much higher.

Initially, I made my plans known to several of my contacts in the UK and Europe and this resulted in invitations to sail in contests in the UK, Denmark, Switzerland and Sweden. The Swedish Association were hosting the class world championship in Taby near Stockholm in late July 1974. By virtue of being able to get myself there, I would be one of two sailors representing New Zealand. The other Mike Calkoen also from Wellington and New Zealand champion would be the other.

I would need a base and London was the obvious choice. I wrote to my old friend and tennis buddy from Eastbourne, Mike Burke, who was sharing a house with other expatriates in the London suburb of South Ealing.

'Stay here', he wrote back. 'Let me know when you will be arriving and I will pick you up at Heathrow Airport'.

Next, I would need to buy a yacht. Here, the UK secretary was most helpful, mailing me brochures of various Moth designs sailed in Europe and craftsmen who could build one for me. I made a selection, contacted a boat builder and after telegraphing the requested deposit, he promised to have a boat ready for me upon my arrival in London. With the knowledge that my accommodation and yacht were sorted, I set about planning my travel in earnest. Finally, I would also need a vehicle to transport myself and my dinghy around Europe, but that could wait until I arrived in London.

There was little point in returning to New Zealand. I made plans to fly directly to London via the US and contacted my friends Mike and Kath Egan, now living in Palo Alto, California and crazy Bernie, still living the high life in Chicago. Both invited me to stopover and visit. Mid-March, I gave notice to my employer and made plans to fly out the first week in June. I proceeded to pack up my stuff: things I wouldn't need on my future travels I sent home; my sailing gear and clothing needed for my summer holiday I packed in a suitcase to carry with me; the rest mainly books and sundry equipment I packed in a box and freighted to the Egan's to hold in storage until I arrived back in North America.

To enter the USA, I needed a visa. My student visa had long since expired. I mailed off an application to the US Embassy in Wellington and it arrived sometime before my departure. Vivienne, who was working for the US Information Service at the time, later told me of a curious interaction she had with the consular official handling my application.

"Vivienne, I have a visa application for a Michael Barnett. Do you know him?"

"Yes, he's my brother."

"I see he was a student in Chicago and applied for a green card, but then he up and left before it was approved. Why did he do that?"

I am not sure what Vivienne said next, but I was a little shocked to discover that a record of my movements was still in their system. I shudder to think what intelligence the US government has on me in this current day and age as I write this memoir.

In the final days before my departure, I said farewell to my friends and colleagues, Samoan and expatriate, then I boarded my plane en route to the US and London. It had been an enjoyable sojourn in Samoa but I was not sad to leave. *Maybe I will return someday*, I thought to myself as my plane got airborne and I flew off into the unknown. 'Better at the twilight of my career, than staying on right now'.

European Summer of Sailing 1974

I flew into London's Heathrow Airport on a clear summer day in June. Mike Burke (Burkles) was at the airport to meet me and he took me to his flat in Windermere Ave, South Ealing, which was to become my base for the summer and during my travels in and out of London during the next five years. At this time, Burkles was working nights in the markets at Covent garden and I shared his small room on the top floor of a semi-detached house at 63 Windermere Avenue, my bed at night and his during the daylight hours.

The World Cup soccer tournament was well underway in Germany when I arrived in London and the tennis at Wimbledon was about to start. I spent much of my first two weeks in London glued to a TV set watching both, tennis being my major interest. My boyhood hero, Ken Rosewell, was still at the top of his game and made it to the men's final only to be demolished by a brash young, Jimmy Connors. Sad as I was at the defeat of my hero, I was able to console myself by admitting that the brash kid had played an amazing three sets of error-free tennis.

The contrast to the slow pace of life in Samoa was quite dramatic and I had much to do in preparation for my trip through Europe and on to regattas in Denmark, Sweden and Switzerland. When I did drag myself away from the TV, I purchased a new Volkswagen Passat (rather extravagant perhaps), took delivery of my new yacht, and enquired around for opportunities to launch my new toy, tune and sail it. I quickly discovered that apart from the River Thames and a few ponds in abandoned quarry sites, London has very few sailing venues. I would need to travel further afield for the sailing and racing opportunities I desired.

A friend of Burkles who lived in a nearby townhouse took me under his wing one day and we went to a nearby quarry pond. There I launched my Moth, hopped in and sailed out onto the pond. I got off to a shaky start, punching a hole in the thin plywood decking with my knee as I hopped into the boat. My new yacht was extremely unstable, quite unlike my Bonito in Samoa and hard chine

Moth back in New Zealand. It took a delicate balancing act to keep it upright and I felt like a novice having my first solo sail.

All I needed was to repair the relatively minor damage and lots of practice to get used to its peculiarities. The repair was easy, I took it back to the boat builder, who carried out a quick repair while I stood by. Regular practice was another matter.

Why the difference in boat designs? Like the Americas Cup yachts, the International Moth is a development class of dinghy, which means that within specified length and width dimensions and sail area, the yachts can be any shape or size. In New Zealand, they tend to build as flat-bottomed skiffs and easier to control in prevailing strong winds. Here in Europe they tend to take the shape of narrow curved hulls with no chine, making them unstable when not moving forward, super-fast in light breezes and requiring a delicate balancing act to keep them from capsizing in strong winds.

Mine was definitely light and fast and pointed high sailing upwind. All I needed to do was learn to sail the damn thing to its full potential.

Opportunities to practice and race were limited but I made the most of my time visiting a contact in Lymington, where I managed to get in some much-needed practice then on to Devon where I sailed in a one-day regatta. I have struggled to handle my boat with any degree of confidence, especially when the wind strengthened beyond ten knots. Learning to sail and race this thoroughbred to its full potential was proving no easy task. It was so tippy and getting out onto the wings for maximum leverage to drive the boat forward was proving to be a balancing act which I was yet to master.

A week later, I learnt of a one-day regatta at Gravesend at the mouth of the Thames. I decided to enter as it would be another opportunity to test my racing skills against some of the English sailors in the world championship in Sweden. Early on the day of the regatta, I loaded my Moth and beach trailer on the roof of my car, threw in my sailing gear and set off on a two-hour drive to get to Gravesend. It was a Sunday and getting there was no problem. Following registration and a briefing I set about rigging my Moth and to my despair, I found had left my rudder and centreboard behind in London.

Sadly, I had to sit out the two scheduled races but I was welcomed with enthusiasm and felt a part of this British sailing fraternity. A prize giving was held in the afternoon and in jest, I was presented with a small rubber duck as a consolation prize for turning up without an essential piece of equipment.

By now, I had made myself well known among the Moth fraternity in the UK, Europe and apparently down under. One day, during the second week in July, I received a phone call from Mike Calkoen of Wellington, who had just arrived in London with his wife, Carol, and was en route to the world champs in Sweden. As New Zealand Moth champion, Mike was New Zealand's official representative, I was entered because I could afford to get myself there. Mike asked me for assistance to pick up his Moth which he had shipped from New Zealand. I was able to oblige and I also introduced him to the London-based Moth sailors.

A week later, Australian Ian Brown, the current world champion also flew into London with his superlight racing Moth aboard. Ian had made no prior arrangement to travel on to Sweden and he called me for advice on how to get himself and his boat there.

"Could I help?"

I met up with Ian and took him in tow. First, we went to Heathrow and picked up his boat and sailing gear. It was so light, I figured travelling with two boats perched on the roof of my car should be no problem.

"Come with me and I will get you there. I will be leaving London in two weeks."

On the Saturday prior to departing for Europe, I decided to make a social call on Bill and Sandy Moore (friends of Mike and Kath Egan), whom I met on several occasions during my student days in Chicago. Bill was now managing the London office of Dames & Moore and I had been given their address in the vicinity of Wimbledon. Arriving unannounced just after noon, I knocked on the front door, Bill opened it and there was instant recognition.

"Michael, what a pleasant surprise. Come inside, see Sandy and meet Bill."

As it conspired, they were entertaining a colleague, Bill Tenny from Los Angeles, and I was invited to stay and take part in a luncheon of wine hamburgers and salad, possibly the best meal I had enjoyed in recent times. Several times during the course of the conversation, Bill Moore asked me to join the firm, offering to send me on projects in any one of Scotland, Saudi Arabia or Abu Dhabi. Much flattered, I politely declined informing him of my immediate plans to travel to Europe to participate in several sailing regattas including the World Moth Championship in Stockholm, and then travel on to Canada at the end of the summer.

Having enjoyed the fine food and companionship, I bade my departure in the late afternoon with a promise to contact Bill upon my return to London from my travels on the continent.

The end of July was approaching and with all preparations made, it was time to depart for Europe. I called Ian Brown and told him to be ready to leave at the end of the week. Somewhere, I have a photo with our two yachts atop my Volkswagen Passat. It looked a little top heavy but they were secure and that is how we travelled. On Friday, early in the morning of 26 July, we set off down the M20 to Dover, boarded a channel ferry which took us to the coastal town of Oostende, Belgium.

From there, we drove north to Arnhem, Holland, where I had arranged to spend a night with Mum and pop Berends, parents of my brother-in-law, Herman. I had met Mum and pop on at least one occasion when they came out to New Zealand. They are a delightful couple and made Ian and I feel most welcome. At the time, I did not appreciate the significance of the area in which they lived, close to the Arnhem Bridge, a scene of a vicious battle between Allied and German forces in the latter days of World War 2 and immortalised in the movie *A Bridge Too Far*.

Many years later, Herman informed me of the hardship his family and others experienced during the war and his escapades as a young boy mixing it with the German soldiers.

With no time to linger, we said goodbye and drove north to Kiel where we planned to catch a ferry and travel on to our next stop, Aarhus, Denmark. We arrived in Kiel mid-afternoon and made our way to the ferry terminal, arriving just as the ferry was about to depart. Without a ticket, we were waved aboard by a Danish seaman.

"Don't worry," he said with beaming smile. "Report to the bridge and the skipper will get you sorted."

It all seemed so casual. To the bridge, we went, where we found the ship's captain ferrying his ship out of the busy harbour. In between giving his helmsman directions, he treated us in the same friendly manner and we were duly sorted. Two hours later, we arrived in Aarhus.

We disembarked and made our way to the address of Jesper Kold, secretary of the Danish Moth Class Association, with whom I had been corresponding over the past year. Jesper and his wife, Marianne, had kindly offered to let us stay with them in their tiny apartment on the waterfront quay opposite the large shipping port. We had also been invited to participate in a two-day regatta he had organised for local and visiting sailors, who were passing through en route to the championship in Stockholm.

Mike and Carol Calkoen were there plus a number of the English sailors I had met back in London and the contingent of Danish sailors. Five races were held over two days in light to moderate wind conditions, which was a relief to me as I was still struggling in wind conditions exceeding ten knots. I finished the regatta somewhere in the middle of the fleet, which I considered not a bad effort in the circumstances. Best of all, I discovered the warmth and sincerity of my hosts, Marianne and Jesper, and their Danish friends. I was to experience more of the same over the next four weeks while in Sweden and back in Denmark.

The racing and socialising over, we all packed up and made our by ferry to Malmo in Sweden and drove north to our destination of Taby, a municipality north of Stockholm where the championship was scheduled to be sailed on a nearby inlet on the Stockholm archipelago.

A large group of Moth sailors and their supporters descended on Taby at the beginning of August, coming from the UK and Europe plus a small contingent from the US Australia and New Zealand. Many chose to camp in a temporary camping ground set up in a waterfront park adjacent to a host yacht club. Others, myself included, were billeted with friendly hosts associated with the local sailing fraternity. A week of hard racing lay ahead and my elation and disappointment are best described in a letter home I penned on the rest day midway through the contest.

Taby, Sweden
7 August 1974

Today is a rest day and man do I need it. After four hard races over two days, I am all aches and pains, but it has really been good and this kind of racing is an experience I would like to repeat. Despite a disappointing day yesterday, in which the wind blew at gale force, I have performed quite well and I only wish I had prepared myself and my boat better for these championships.

First off some results to date. In a practice race Sunday afternoon, I placed fortieth in a fleet of sixty-seven boats, first race Monday, twenty-four, sixty-first (I broke my tiller extension when placed about thirtieth). Yesterday, I was forced to retire in the early race and did not start in the afternoon. On Sunday and Monday, the wind was light and variable and I was performing much better than

Mike Calkoen, the other NZ skipper who was well back in the fleet. He came into his own in the Tuesday races and finished third in both. I also beat Ian Brown, the current world champion in race 1 on Monday. Not bad huh!

The fleet size is sixty-seven boats, which is four times the size of previous fleets I have raced against. The need to sail in clear wind is extremely important and getting a good start is essential. Unfortunately, I have not been able to start well in most races and have suffered accordingly. In the practice race on Sunday, I was slow starting. However, I was at the windward end at the start line and was able to tack away into clear air early and when I reached the first mark, I was in eleventh position, which somewhat overwhelmed me. In fact, the shock was so great, I lost concentration and slowly drifted back through the fleet finishing in fortieth place. Ironically, I made my best start in race three Tuesday morning and was right up with the leaders, but I could not hold my boat in the strong wind and quickly dropped back.

In race 1 on Monday morning, the start of serious racing, I was determined not to make the same mistakes as on Sunday. However, due to the extremely light wind, I again misjudged the start and was soon well back in the fleet. However, I was at one end of the line and was able to grind on out into clear air. We drifted around the course for two hours and I picked up many places to finish twenty-fourth. In race 2, I was in the middle of the bunch when I was surprised by a port tack boat and forced to tack quickly and in the process, I broke my tiller extension.

This made sailing to windward almost impossible as I could not hike out. On the bow of the boat I was carrying a piece of rope, a mandatory piece of equipment for towing purposes, I did a deliberate capsize so I could retrieve this rope and made a jury tiller extension and complete the race. This was a little disappointing as I think I would otherwise have finished well up in the fleet.

On Tuesday morning, the wind was up much to my dismay. However, undeterred I rigged my boat and as I had made my usual practice was among the first boats to take to the water. From the shore, the wind and waves never look as strong as they really are. One hundred yards out from the shore, I really knew I was amongst it. Wind gusting up to 30mph, choppy sea and everything. On the way to the start line, I capsized three or four times, but by now I had become an expert at righting my boat, which is no simple task.

As mentioned earlier, in this race I made my best start to date, right on the line at the gun with no boats close on my windward or leeward bow. However, from there on, it was merely survival. I could not hold my boat to drive it fast and soon dropped off the pace. For the next hour and a half, I struggled around the course, determined to finish the race if the boat could take the punishment. However, after about my twentieth capsize, I noticed one of my rudder pintles on which the rudder pivots pulling loose. I righted the boat once more, sat for a second or two, then decided to call it a day while my boat was still in one piece.

I signalled a rescue boat and was towed ashore, a fate which befell almost half the fleet. In the afternoon, the wind was still blowing as strong and I decided not to venture out from the shore. I can now only hope it will die before the next race on Thursday.

The remainder of the regatta was sailed in medium to strong winds and though I was able to start in each race I remained well back in the fleet eventually finishing sixty-first overall, which was disappointing from a racing point of view. However, the experience of sailing in such a large fleet, hospitality of the Swedes and the friendships made it all worthwhile. My host and her son, Magnus, were very welcoming and it was nice to get back to a warm house and a hot bath after a day of hard racing.

When the regatta was over, the visiting sailors quickly dispersed but I was invited to stay on by my host and during the following five days, she showed me around the sights of Stockholm. One of the most memorable sights was a visit to see the restoration of the Vasa, a Swedish Warship constructed between 1626 and 1628, which foundered and sank after sailing 1300 metres from her launching pad. Its hull was salvaged largely intact in 1961 and careful restoration has been in progress ever since.

I met and mixed with sailors from many countries and for friendliness and companionship, I could not go past the Swedes, Danes and the Swiss. The Swiss sailors invited me to visit and participate in their national championship at the end of the summer, my newfound friends from Aarhus asked me to come back and stay awhile and then of course, there was the UK championship at the beginning of September in Lymington, in which I had planned to participate. I was in for a busy time, but first, my boat needed some repairs and modifications.

Paul Oddersborg, one of the Danish sailors I met in Taby, is a boat builder from the small town of Fjellebroen on the south coast of the Odense Peninsula. Paul invited me stopover when I headed south and I gladly accepted his offer. Five days after the regatta ended, I bid farewell to my Swedish host and drove south to Malmo and on to Denmark across the magnificent Oresund Bridge that links Sweden to Denmark. I continued on and found my way to Fjellebroen, where I found Paul hard at work at his small boat yard in Fjellebroen Haven.

During the next three weeks, I spent many a happy day pottering around his workshop doing minor repairs and modifications to my Moth and sailing out on the bay. At the end of the day, I would join Paul and his small team in the loft of his workshop to swap yarns. When they departed, I stayed on, made supper and bedded down for the night. My lasting impression of Paul and his colleagues was their casual friendliness and the manner in which they accepted me into their world. They made no special fuss and welcomed me as one of their group. They had much in common with the Kiwi character.

Paul gave me free rein in his workshop; including tools and materials to fix up my boat, which was showing significant wear and tear. Many fittings had worked loose and threatened to pull out completely. I was able to fix them more securely and I made a significant modification which improved my performance and boat speed immensely. I installed two horizontal kick bars in the cockpit, which I could use to push myself out onto wings of my boat when the wind got up. This enabled me to hike out more effectively and for the first time, I was able to get my boat planning in the manner it was designed for. I felt I was back to my best and no longer feared the heavy weather conditions.

During this time, I made several day trips to Aarhus to visit Jesper and Marianne. I must admit that I had an ulterior motive. On my initial visit, Marianne had introduced me to her friend, Kirsten, and romance was in the air once again. When it finally came time to say farewell to my Danish friends and return to England, Kirsten implored me to return in mid-September and join her on a five-day camping holiday on a small island near Aarhus in mid-September. I promised to be in touch.

It was the last week in August. In haste, I drove south to Oostende and caught a channel ferry and back to Dover and on to London. There was much to do. My funds were running low and I needed to find a job. Time to go see Bill Moore. After checking in with Burkles and my other flatmates at my Windermere Avenue base, I contacted Bill. On Monday morning, I found my way to his office in a converted Tudor mansion in Barnes on the south bank of the River Thames. The interview was short and brief.

I explained my situation to Bill. I had more sailing and touring to do and I eventually wanted to find work in Canada where salaries were higher.

"Come and join us here in London," said Bill. "We have lots going on and I can arrange a transfer to one of our Canadian offices when the heat is off. When can you start?"

"I am going to regatta on the Solent next week, then back to Europe for another in Switzerland early October. I will be back in London on 10 October," I replied.

"Done," said Bill. "I will put you on the payroll, report in when the sailing is over. Good luck and enjoy the rest of your holiday."

"Don't you want to check my credentials?"

"No need. I know you well. Besides you're a Kiwi. I would employ anyone from down under. Harder workers than these Brits."

Money worries over, I left with a smile on my face. I could look forward to more exciting sailing and a return to Denmark to see Kirsten and friends. Next stop, Lymington and the UK Moth championship.

I drove down to Lymington on the weekend with the prospect of four days of exciting sailing on the Solent, home of sailing for British elite and site of historic naval battles in centuries gone by. Sadly, all official racing was cancelled due to gale force winds prevailing throughout the week of the regatta. To pass the time while hanging around, we sailors amused ourselves, playing cards, having a water polo competition in a local pool, and holding a series of impromptu races in the close vicinity of the Lymington Yacht Club. I launched my boat for the first of these races and surprised myself by staying upright and matching it with the best.

However, it was hard on gear and fearing the risk of breaking something, I decided one race was enough.

I returned to London then back to Denmark, retracing a now familiar route. En route I stopped by and stopped a night with Mum and pop Berends. They were delighted to see me. Next day, I drove on to the northern German city of Lubeck, where I called on Philip's friend, Gerhard Richter, and his charming wife, Barbara. They invited me to stay with them and I lingered two nights before continuing on. I recall their wonderful hospitality and the ancient inner city surrounded by thick masonry walls, behind which we spent two wonderful evenings soaking up the atmosphere of a typical German beer hall.

I bade farewell to Gerhard and Barbara and drove on to Denmark, first visiting Paul Odersberg in Fjellebroen. Then it was on to Aarhus to see Jesper, Marianne and Kirsten. I returned to Denmark to get in some practice sailing, but my prime motivation was to be with Kirsten once more. Like her male counterparts, she was warm and friendly and I enjoyed her company.

Marianne and Kirsten were teachers at a school for handicapped children and they had organised the holiday camp we were about to embark upon. Here is my account of the five days spent with my friends and their twenty-five pupils.

We stayed in a big house on the island and while there I was able to sail and relax as a guest of the State of Denmark, which financed the camp. Even the beer I drank was on the State. As the week went by, I developed a special rapport with the children and I helped out with organising some of the activities. Despite the language problem, we seemed to communicate and many would come up to me and talk and talk, laugh and smile. They seemed to like me and I got a special satisfaction from associating with them.

One evening, we took the children out into the woods for a barbeque. It was after dark when we returned to the house, put the children down for the night and set about relaxing over beers. One hour later, two of the children appeared and said: "Where is Fleming?"

"Isn't he in bed?" Marianne asked.

"No," came the reply.

There followed a mad panic and we went out into the woods: "Fleming, where are you?" went out the cry and we went on frantically searching. Eventually, we found Fleming sitting under a tree at the barbeque site. All was well and with a relieved teaching staff, we brought him back to base and all settled down for the night.

Camp over, I returned to Aarhus with Jesper, Marianne and Kirsten. I was enjoying their company so much, I was easily persuaded to stay on a few extra days. I delayed my departure for Switzerland until the last minute and made a mad dash across Germany arriving at the small canton Murten on the shores of Lake Murten, where the Swiss Championships were about to commence. I had cut it fine, checking in at the sailing club at nine in the morning with the first race due to start in the afternoon.

It was overcast and raining steadily and I had to rush to get my boat ready for the first race. The race committee were particularly strict on boat measurement and my boat did not conform to their standards. I made modifications to satisfy the committee and got to the start, but I was cold and damp and by now not very enthusiastic. However, after the start, I forgot my misery and was going quite well when I was involved in an incident with two other boats, capsized, broke a fitting and was forced to retire and make urgent repairs in order to start the following day.

This seemed to be a portent, for I only finished two races during the rest of the regatta. Wind conditions and gear failure conspired against me and I suffered a similar overall result as in Sweden. My disappointment at my poor effort was more than counterbalanced by the warm reception from the Swiss and German sailors and members of the Murten Sailing Club. At a prize giving at the end of the regatta, I was given a special mention and awarded a bottle of prime whiskey by the club president, for having travelled the furthest distance to sail in their contest. His comments and the cheers that followed made me feel like the contest winner.

Sometime during the regatta, I went with a group of my newfound friends to the nearby city of Neuchatel where we participated in the nighttime festivities to celebrate the start of the grape harvest in the region. Maybe that had something to do with my sailing performance, but mainly I put it down to a not so well constructed boat. Fittings were continually failing and throughout the summer, my limited repair skills were being tested to the limit. I was bitterly disappointed. When I left to return to London, I left it behind with my German friend, Christoph Meyer, to sell on my behalf. I had no regrets.

It had been a wonderful summer; I met many fine people and given a warm reception wherever I went. I could not have asked for more. Now it was time to return to the world of work.

Dames & Moore International

On a cool autumn morning in mid-October, I reported to the London office of Dames and Moore. Bill Moore was there to greet me. I was shown around, met my London colleagues and was introduced to the way the organisation functions.

Dames & Moore was a multinational geotechnical and environmental engineering consultancy, with offices scattered throughout the USA, Canada, Europe, the Middle East, Asia, Africa and Australia. Geotechnical engineering being the investigation and assessment of the engineering properties of soil and rock is at the forefront of any construction project.

The bulk of the work undertaken by the London office focused on Britain and the Middle East, but it also supported sister offices in Madrid, Beirut, Tehran and Lagos in West Africa. To make optimum use of technical expertise spread among the various offices worldwide, the company operated a system of temporary transfers (coordinated by the head office in Los Angeles) to meet an immediate need in any office lacking the particular skill resource. I was hired for my expertise in geotechnical engineering and this was a system that suited my psyche and work ethic. Being relatively young and adventurous, I was willing to go anywhere and D&M was about to oblige.

I spent my first weeks doing little except getting acquainted with my London colleagues, spending long lunch breaks at a nearby pub and waiting for my first assignment. One morning near the end of my third week, I received an instruction to pack my bags and fly to Madrid with Richard, a young geologist, to lead a foundation investigation for an aluminium smelter to be constructed at San Cyprian, a remote part of northwest Spain, near where the Bay of Biscay meets the Atlantic Ocean.

Off to Madrid I went with Richard, who was sent along to assist me with the exploratory fieldwork. On arrival, we made our way to the Madrid office of D&M at 8 Pedro Muguruza Ave., where we introduced ourselves and were made most welcome. After introductions around the small office, we were taken to the nearby Hotel Cuzco on Avenida Generalissimo, which was to be my home for the next eight months I was to be in Spain.

During the following two days, we were given a briefing on the project, its location and how to get there, then Richard and I set off in tandem in two rented Seat Bambinas and drove north, a seven-hour drive, to the small town of Viviero, where we were to stay in the only hotel in the area during our time on site. During the next four weeks, we would be up early and drive the short distance to San Ciprian and the large site to be investigated.

San Ciprian, as it was then, was a very remote town of Spain where the locals farmed very small plots of land in a manner going back centuries. It was very much subsistence living and I remember thinking they were in for a shock and their way life was about to change dramatically when a smelter came to be built. We soon got to know and became friendly with the local farmers and fishing community and although communication was a problem, we had an official from the smelter company with us during this phase of the work to help with translation.

We remained on site for four weeks, drilling many holes and gathering soil and rock samples. We worked a long day, six days a week, but the work was satisfying and I really warmed to all the Spanish people I met including a group of young chicos and chicas up from Madrid to negotiate the purchase of land.

At night, the young ones would join us at the only restaurant in the area, 'Nito's', run by Nito and his wife. Most nights, it was like a big party with wine and chatter flowing freely and Nito was a wonderful host. Seafood was the specialty of the house and the menu changed each night depending on what Nito had caught earlier in the day. I had never eaten so much seafood in my life. I recorded in one letter home—clams, crab, shrimps, percebes (an ugly but tasty shellfish), lobster, and white fish of several varieties. To this day, I have not forgotten the warmth and friendliness of the people I met here and back in Madrid.

We finished the first stage of this investigation at the beginning of December and Richard and I made our way back to Madrid. Richard flew back to England while I stayed on to analyse the data collected and write a preliminary report. My senior to whom I reported on this project seemed pleased with my work for he made it known that he wanted me to come back in the new year to carry out an expanded investigation and remain for the construction phase of the project when and if it eventuated. I was happy to oblige as I was enjoying the challenge of the work, my exposure to Spanish life and its people, and living on an expense account with little to spend my money on was proving to be a big incentive.

Apart from Christmas and New Year spent back in London, I spent the next four months in Madrid, analysing all the data, writing a report and meeting with the client organisation. Madrid is a wonderful city and I have many fond memories of the time that I spent there; its colourful and vibrant people, my frequent evening visits to the Plaza Mayor and elsewhere where I frequented the many Tapas bars where the wine flowed the food was gratis and one was entertained by passing by musicians, the magnificent Prado museum and the artworks out of this world—El Greco, several visits to the nearby Valle de los Caidos Basilica, a magnificent cathedral carved into a granite mountain and of course the wonderful variety of food.

One of my daily pleasures was breakfast at one of the many cafes on my short walk to 8 Pedro Murguruza and the wonderful Spanish omelettes which I have adapted as one of my own specialties over the years. While I was there, General Franco was still head of state, but of ill health and never seen.

Madrid
23 March 1975

Last week, one of the D&M partners from San Francisco was in Madrid. His name is Bob Darragh, said he had heard about me and called me aside for a chat so we could get personally acquainted. I gave him details of my background and why and where I wanted to go. He in turn indicated the openings that existed in various offices and I concluded from this talk that I would end up in Seattle or Portland. It was a fortuitous meeting as he is one of the most senior soil engineers in the company and is directly involved in planning manpower requirements.

By April, I had completed my report and I waited around for it to be translated into Spanish. In this I had little cooperation from my Spanish colleagues except for a young engineer Jaime from Chile, who I had befriended but whose South American Spanish needed further translation into the Spanish idiom. Manana seemed to be the catchphrase. Although the investigation was now complete, there was no indication that the construction phase of the project was about to start. I had too much idle time and I became restless to get back to London and on to something new.

Ten Days in Dhahran

London, Wednesday, 21 May 1975

I have been enjoying a leisurely three weeks in London, waiting for a new assignment. Now after a hectic few hours, I am sitting in a British Airways jumbo jet waiting to take off from Heathrow Airport.

Since I returned to London, I have spent much of my time at home in South Ealing. I've started jogging again and been out on the tennis court several times. In addition, I have become addicted to chess and spent many a morning doing battle with Mike Burke.

Yesterday afternoon, I received a call from John Rankin the Dames & Moore office administrator, requesting I call into the office first thing in the morning as I may be required to go to Dhahran in Saudi Arabia. When I arrived this was confirmed and I was already booked on an afternoon flight to Beirut, Lebanon, where I was to meet the local agent and organise immigration formalities.

"Do I have a baptismal certificate?" John asked. Apparently, one needs proof one is not of the Jewish faith to get into Saudi Arabia. Of course, I wasn't carrying anything of the sort and I spent a hectic few hours with the help of Charlie, the company cabbie, back to Ealing to pack my bags, look for an Anglican cleric and persuade him that I was a member of the faith and give me a letter to that effect. This was no easy task, but eventually, we bailed up the headmaster of a church primary school and obtained a short statement. I hope it works.

I am told this is just a short assignment, maybe three to four weeks and I will be back in London. We shall see, I have learnt that things can change quickly at Dames & Moore.

Beirut Lebanon, Wednesday, 24 May 1975 (10pm Local Time)

I arrived at Beirut Airport at 10pm and for the first time in recent years, went through a health check and of course, I no longer have a valid smallpox vaccination certificate. A medical officer took me aside and informed me I would need to be vaccinated there and then. I politely explained my medical history and showed him a letter I was carrying and on the basis of this and the reward of three cigars I produced from my pocket, he waived the requirement and allowed me to proceed.

My departure for Beirut had been very rushed. I had no accommodation organised nor was I expecting to be met at the airport. Fortunately, there was a message awaiting me at the airport informing me to proceed by taxi to the Bristol Hotel in the centre of town. An hour later, I was clear of customs, I hailed a taxi and was whisked away into the city.

As we drove along, we came to what seemed like a major intersection and the driver became very animated, gesticulating wildly with a shooting sound and pointing to the surrounding area. I thought little of it, but next morning when I had a chance to read the local English language newspaper, I learnt that the intersection had been the scene of some vicious fighting an hour before I came through. Sometimes ignorance is bliss. It was close to midnight when I reached the Bristol and there to meet me was Mal Horton, the D&M partner and man on the spot. Mal took me to his apartment where I was invited to stay until I flew on to Dhahran.

My first impression is that Beirut is not a pretty town, but it is in the early stages of a civil war and this perhaps clouds my judgment. It is in a good location being right on the Mediterranean coast and the climate at this time is very pleasant, not too hot or cold. Political trouble abounds and visible signs of conflict are to be seen everywhere. Roadblocks, tanks and the military on the city streets and militiamen scattered here and there. On Friday afternoon, I was walking around and strayed into a maze of narrow side streets. I soon became aware of groups of young men sitting on street corners and outside of shops, supporting machine guns on their laps. I bid a hasty retreat.

I have been in Beirut for three days and arrangements for my travel on to Dhahran are sort of complete. I say sort of as I have a visa, a first-class plane ticket, contact details of the client company, and a drilling contractor to be hired for the investigation. However, I will have to sort out accommodation when I arrive as none could be found. This is a common problem I am told, as there is so much business activity or kings arriving in town, that what hotels exist are perpetually full. Before leaving Beirut, I sent a message to our client hoping he could assist and meet me on arrival. However, as I soon learnt communications with the outside world are precarious at best.

It was midnight when I arrived in Dhahran, no one was there to meet me nor was there any message. I was on my own. Worse, the airport terminal was abuzz with people desperately trying to find accommodation. It seems the Saudi King is here with all his entourage and has taken over the largest hotel in the city.

While contemplating my predicament, I chanced to meet an Englishman, Andy, by name, who was a resident and working in the city. I explained my predicament and he kindly offered me a bed in his flat for the night. I gladly accepted and when he had finished his business at the airport, I went with him to his house in the nearby town of Al Khobar. I slept well and next morning, Andy drove me to the Aramco compound where he worked. I got a taxi and made my way to my client's compound where I found my contact, who was able to find me a room in a not-so-elegant hotel in Al Khobar.

I had the penthouse suite; a 12 x 12 square foot room with a window, single bed, sundry furniture and an air conditioner. In a separate room, there was a toilet and shower. Actually, it was considerably better than my $3 room in Tahiti eight years ago and was comfortable enough for a short stay. The management and staff were quite pleasant and I can honestly say I like it here. My hotel was only a couple of blocks from Andy's flat where I had dinner with Andy and his flatmates. I have been invited to move in for the duration of my stay and I have accepted this offer. I moved in tomorrow.

I made contact with my driller and I was waiting for him to arrive from Riyadh. Meantime, I have had a quiet day, sunning myself and loafing around.

I was in Saudi Arabia for ten days in all. My driller eventually turned up and turned out to be a fellow from Greece. He was very pleasant, spoke good English and was a good driller to boot. We worked steadily commencing last Wednesday and finishing yesterday afternoon (2 June). We worked from 6:30am to 2pm then finished for the day. Man, it was hot and I am now sporting a healthy tan. One day, it was over 110 degrees Fahrenheit. On Friday (Islamic Sabbath), we did not work and I went for a swim with some of my Aramco friends. I got a bit burnt, but fortunately, not badly.

To get to the beach, we drove about 30 kilometres from Al Khobar and then about 2 kilometres off the main road across the desert. I can now say with authority mirages are real. It was fascinating to see sand hills perched up in the air, apparently separated from the surrounding ground.

Little else to tell you about Saudi. I drank a lot of Pepsi and cider, alcohol was not available. Many expatriates brew, their own in the seclusion of their compound, but penalties are very severe if caught in possession of the stuff. The Saudi's attitude towards alcohol is similar to Western attitudes towards hard drugs.

Beirut, Tuesday, 3 June 1975

I finished my work in Dhahran yesterday and flew out earlier today, arriving in Beirut in the late afternoon. After the recent shooting, the city seemed relatively quiet and I hope it stays that way. At the moment, I am not sure how long I will be here, but hopefully, it will only be for a couple of days.

My impression of Beirut was not very favourable, perhaps I was influenced in this by the civil war going on around me. It was not a pretty town. The political situation tended to influence my attitude and worst of all, the locals did their utmost to cheat you out of your money. The taxi drivers were the worst. There seemed to be a standard fare of 3 Lebanese pounds for trips around the city. If you have the right change, things are fine, but if you have only large notes, seldom do you get any change. I have paid as much as 10 pounds for one trip.

On my trip from the airport today the driver asked for 15 pounds, I gave him 10, told him that's enough and walked off. In the airport, porters tell you they want more if you are light on a tip. I now tell them all they are robbers and that they have got enough. In Saudi, it was similar though not quite as bad. Taxi drivers would at least stand by their standard fare. Can't say I feel particularly endeared to the Arab based on these experiences.

Inflight Beirut to London, 9 June 1975

At 1pm, I was in the air on my way back to London. For a while, I thought I would be flying in the other direction and on to Tehran. When I arrived back in Beirut last Tuesday, a message was waiting for me instructing me to go directly to Tehran, where I would be required to work for several months. I put in a call to Vancouver to check on the situation there. Later, I received counter instructions to return to London and make plans to get to Vancouver as soon as possible. For me, this was good news as I find this preferable to a stint in Iran.

There was one problem, however, a visa. The process of getting a work permit was taking a long time. Canada seemed to be as bad as the US those days when it came to admitting permanent immigrants. D&M were working on it for me and hopefully, my case will be resolved shortly. If not, Tehran may become a reality.

Not much to report from Beirut. I spent six days there doing very little. On my return from Saudi, the city was much calmer, with very little fighting going on. One thing I did like about Beirut was the weather, wonderfully fine and temperate. Yesterday, I was sunning myself on the patio of my room at the Holiday Inn overlooking the bay. I was most envious of the small sailboats I observed bobbing about on the water. This is another reason why I am keen to get to Vancouver. Jumping around Europe and the Middle East like this, I am not getting any chance to go sailing.

While in Beirut, one thing of note that I did was take a drive north along the coast to the old town of Byblos, which has a history stretching back seven thousand years I am told. While there, I spent an hour wandering around excavated ruins of Phoenician, Roman, and Crusader towns. It was very interesting and picturesque. A pleasant outing was marred only by my driver trying to take me places I did not want to see and hence up his fare. He did not seem too happy with the 50 Lebanese pounds I gave him when we returned to Beirut, but then he was probably skimming me at that.

In spite of the negative impression I may have given, not all Arabs were bad. I sat next to a very pleasant man from Saudi, who was on his way to the US to study civil engineering at Purdue University. We talked a bit and I liked him. I am sure there are plenty of others like him.

Now we are descending and soon the wheels touched the ground at Heathrow Airport.

Lagos, Nigeria 1975–1976

In July 1975, I was a day away from flying out to the US and Canada en route to Vancouver, which was to be my home and base for the foreseeable future. As I strolled into the office to say farewell to my London colleagues, I was once again called aside by Bill Moore Jr and asked to delay my departure and go on another short assignment, six weeks I was told, this time to Lagos, Nigeria. After all he had done for me, I could hardly say no and reluctantly agreed to take on the assignment.

Dames & Moore had a small office in Lagos, which had been run by its local partner, Joe Folayan. Joe was a native of Nigeria and after studying in the US and gaining several years of work experience with the company, he was sent back home to establish a presence and develop business in West Africa. Two problems had developed that were causing the company management great concern. The first was that Folayan had recently broken away from D&M and set up his own geotechnical consultancy in opposition to the company.

Secondly, it had experienced great difficulty in getting American engineers to go and work there. Those who did soon packed up and flew home, the latest being an Australian, who had enough and returned to London the previous week. My task was to go there and tidy up some existing projects while senior management considered their options for continuing operations out of Lagos.

Once again, I packed a suitcase and two days later, on 25 July 1975, I boarded a plane bound for Lagos. With me was an American, Bruce Martini, an administrator sent out from Los Angeles to assist in dealing with the problems being experienced in Lagos. On arrival, we were met by the local office administrator, Remi Oyewo, who escorted us to the nearby airport hotel, which was to be our base for the next few weeks. Four days later, on the morning of 29 July, I woke up and turned on my radio to learn that a military coup had taken place in the early hours of the morning and an army general, Murtala Mohammed, had seized power.

On this occasion, it was a bloodless coup as the existing head of state, Yakabu Gowan, was out of the country at a Commonwealth head of state conference. Needless to say, he did not return.

Murtala quickly seized control by taking over the radio and television networks and closing the airports, a standard procedure during such events. My reaction was one of curiosity rather than fear and I soon noticed that life seemed to carry on as normal.

Sometime either before or shortly after the coup, Bruce and I were joined by New Zealand expatriate David MacGregor and Charlie Newlin, a D&M partner from Phoenix Arizona. David was a civil engineer and was recently hired by D&M to establish and develop the general civil engineering capability of the organisation and take advantage of the burgeoning opportunities in West Africa. David had come out ahead of me and established a small office in the town of Ilorin approximately 100 kilometres north of Lagos. I don't recall why Charlie was there. Perhaps, it was to assess the situation in light of the difficulties the firm had experienced with the local partner, Folayan.

Lagos airport remained closed for about six days and during this time, I became friendly with a number of stranded expatriates including flight crews from various European airlines and others like Charlie, all quite anxious to leave. Confined to the local environs of the airport hotel, we amused ourselves as best we could while life outside returned to some form of normality.

Curiosity got the better of some of us and one night we ventured out to experience the delights of the New Can in downtown Lagos. A restaurant became a nightclub with dancing girls of African and Lebanese extraction it was a popular hangout for the expatriate community. Open twenty-three hours a day seven days a week, it only closed for one hour at 7am in the morning, presumably to clean up before starting over once again. It became one of my favourite haunts and I spent many a night there enjoying the food, entertainment and the company of the girls, who were not backward in coming forward.

On one memorable occasion, an attractive Nigerian lass attached herself to me and we sat together cuddling in a corner while listening to the music. Several times she jumped up saying, "I'm coming, I'm coming," and ran off. *My god*, I thought, *am I that hot?* It was only after the third "I'm coming" that I realised her true meaning being I am coming back.

Another favourite haunt that I was to return to on many occasions was the Africa Shrine in the Empire Hotel, where I discovered Fella Ransome Kute and his band, Afika 70. I was fascinated by his sound a combination of African rhythms mixed with jazz and disco. Later, I returned home with several of his recordings and those of other similar Nigerian bands. His fame eventually spread beyond Nigeria and several decades later, he became fashionable with Amy and her friends.

It was soon apparent that it would take more than six weeks to tidy up affairs and there existed an opportunity to significantly advance my career within the firm if I was to stay on. Young Bruce was of a like mind and together we made it known to our respective bosses in London and Los Angeles that we may be prepared to stay if agreeable conditions of employment could be agreed. I sensed a certain adventure and excitement attached to being there and an added attraction was the Lagos Yacht Club, which offered the opportunity to go sailing all year round, something I had not done since joining D&M almost a year earlier.

Two months later, Bruce and I were still in Lagos, David was toiling away in Ilorin, and senior management back in London and Los Angeles were still debating whether or not to close up shop. In the knowledge that he now had an enthusiastic team in Nigeria, Don Roberts, the London-based partner in charge of operations in Africa, was pushing for continuance, while many in Los Angeles were arguing for closure. In the end, a compromise decision was made to keep the operation going for twelve months.

I was elevated to the role of Acting Principle in Charge of the Lagos office, Bruce was appointed office manager and David continued in his role out of his small office in Ilorin. Together, our combined role was to generate new business. I negotiated a 100% increase in salary that included a hardship allowance, two weeks rest and recreation back in London every quarter and three weeks leave back in New Zealand at Xmas and New Year. I had to be happy with that.

Lagos is the major port city in Nigeria and is situated on five islands which are separated by rivers and creeks fringing the southwest mouth of Lagos Lagoon. The two principal islands are Lagos Island containing the central business district and Ikoyi Island, home of the military and police barracks and an infamous federal prison. The metropolitan area spreads out beyond these islands and during the 1970s, boasted a population of six million and possibly more. It would have to be the most chaotic place I have ever been, before or since, and I could understand why my American colleagues were reluctant to stay there.

To me, there was something fascinating about the place, its people and its booming economy based around the oil industry. Staying on appealed to my sense of adventure.

During the first three months, I operated out of my base at the airport hotel in Ikeja. Doing business proved to be a nightmare. To make a telephone call, I had to rely on the hotel switchboard and it would take an age to get a local call through. Calling London was even worse, but my non-aggressive Kiwi manner seemed to appeal to the operators and I soon learnt a little bit of *dash* (financial inducement) speeded things up. Much of my business and trips to the yacht club required driving into Lagos along the Ikorodu Road, a 5-kilometre ride that could take up five hours.

The locals had a term for it; *go-slow* they called it. The fastest I ever did that trip was forty-five minutes and that was in the very early hours of the morning. Two to three hours was the norm.

American and British construction companies were here in force and I observed a massive ring road highway system being constructed around the perimeter of the urban area—a six-lane divided highway with an additional two service lanes on each side. I drove down this highway on a few occasions and it was scary. Based on American designs, access was limited to access at distant on and off points. It was not unusual to encounter cars and trucks speeding down the fast lane towards you a frightening experience when you are not expecting it.

Many a burnt-out vehicle was to be seen pushed off to the side. Mostly, I chose the go-slow route along the Ikorodu Road.

I flew back to London during the first week of October for my first quarterly break. This presented an opportunity to see my old friends in Ealing and discuss the details of the extended contract in Lagos. I picked up all my limited possessions including new hi-fi equipment and returned to Lagos two weeks later. Bruce and Remi were there to meet me and a good thing too. Two crates were missing from baggage pick up and customs wanted to charge me the earth for the hi-fi equipment.

A little dash from Bruce solved the latter issue and following two weeks of persistent inquiry, Remi was able to find one of my missing crates; the other containing some souvenirs from French wine country was lost forever.

Upon my return, Bruce had managed to secure an apartment on Victoria Island for himself and his partner Maggie, who had joined him from Los Angeles. He had also found premises in Ikeja to serve as a combined office and accommodation which was to become my place of residence for the duration of my stay in Lagos.

My role had changed from a technical one to that of generating new business, something for which I had no experience, but to which I applied myself with energy and enthusiasm. Our collective enthusiasm for the job in hand was tempered by the knowledge that the operation might be shut down and the sheer difficulty in conducting business in the local environment. We tried hard. David made several trips to Sierra Leone and I travelled extensively around Nigeria, visiting many of the major centres, including Kano, Kaduna, Jos and Maiduguri in the far north of the country.

Much of this travel involved chasing prospective work, writing proposals and tendering for jobs. It was a big ask and time and economic circumstances were against us. America was undergoing a recession, the company was laying off staff in some of its offices, and senior management was reluctant to pour more funds into keeping us going. Along the way, we managed to secure some small projects and I made several useful contacts. One in particular comes to mind, an American earthmoving and road construction group based in Jos, with whom we jointly tendered some work.

I must have impressed them for a year later when home in New Zealand, New York made several calls offering me a job back in Nigeria. I was tempted but ultimately declined the offer.

In August 1976, a decision was made to close the operation. Ironically, we secured a major contract around this time, but it was not sufficient to save the operation. David MacGregor was the first to leave under somewhat distressing circumstances for him. David had a forthright manner and was prone to criticise the deficiencies of the local administrative staff in our Lagos office. Unknown to us, Remi had reported David to the immigration authorities and on a visit to Lagos, he spent a long session being interrogated about his visa status.

When he reappeared, he was deeply distressed and it was obvious he had undergone some difficult interrogation. He was almost a broken man, far from the ebullient friend I had come to know. He couldn't leave fast enough and I assisted in his rapid departure as best I could. Bruce and Maggie Martini departed soon after and it was left to me to wind down the operation that disposed of assets. This I accomplished with little enthusiasm. I negotiated the sale of all the company assets to a Nigerian businessman, then flew back in London at the beginning of December and was in a state of limbo.

The recession in the Americas meant there was no work for me in Vancouver and my transfer there was put on hold. However, I seemed to have established quite a reputation in the firm and it was clear they did not want to lose me. "Go home to New Zealand and have a good break," I was told. "We will call you when we have a new assignment." Three weeks leave turned into two months and I remained on full pay. I could not complain.

During the eighteen months I spent in Nigeria, the yacht club was the centre for much of my social life and there I made numerous friends and contacts. I lived for the sailing and racing and as much as I could, I planned my travel around sailing activity, ensuring I was in Lagos on weekends and as much as possible on Wednesday evenings. Life for an expatriate sailor had its privileges and one such was being assigned a boat boy to take care of my yacht. I would arrive at the club, deposit my gear in the boat, then go into the clubhouse to socialise.

Come time to go racing, my crew and I would go out to the boat storage area to find the yacht rigged and ready to sail. To the boat boy, I was Mister Mike. He would assist us launch and was there to assist when we came in. An hour or so later when it was time to go home, I would find the yacht de-rigged, sails neatly folded and ready to take home. Looking back, it seems like such an indulgent lifestyle.

There were a number of different classes of dinghy to be sailed. I opted to join the Osprey class and initially, I sailed as crew for a Brit, Martin Foster, then later teamed up with another Brit, Malcolm, a fellow engineer with whom I developed quite a close friendship. Eventually, I got a yacht of my own and headed off to the UK Osprey championships in Penzance, during one of my quarterly breaks from the rigours of Nigeria.

Sailing in Nigeria was a year-round activity. The racing was competitive and I learnt new skills in a fast yacht that came complete with spinnaker and trapeze. However, the newest skill was to read and take advantage of the fast-flowing currents in Lagos harbour and keep clear of the large freighters coming in and out of the harbour all the time. I never fully mastered the tidal currents and one didn't mess with the freighters. I made good friends and acquaintances, including the American Ambassador who liked to play tennis and found me a worthy opponent and best of all, I enjoyed the competitive racing.

A snapshot of life in Nigeria, October to December 1975

For a short period, I kept a day-by-day record of my experiences in Nigeria, which best described the life I was living and how I felt at the time.

Wednesday, 27 October 1975

I arrived in Lagos, Nigeria, early this morning to commence my new assignment as principal-in-charge of the Dames and Moore Lagos office. This represents an exciting prospect both for me individually and the firm in general and with it, I have been given considerable elevation in status and salary. What is most important to me is that I am now in a position to exercise my judgment 100 per cent in relation to my work and it will be my decisions that will influence the success or failure of projects undertaken.

There is also the added incentive/reward that I will be responsible for building up a successful operation the success of which will be largely dependent on my technical and administrative abilities.

I flew into Lagos Airport at 6:45am. Remi Oyewo, the firm's accountant was there to meet me and his presence was most welcome. Entering Nigeria can sometimes be a traumatic experience and I had been anticipating problems with customs officials, because of the large quantity of personal and business effects I was carrying with me. My passage through health, passport and customs control was swift and uneventful, no doubt due to Remi's presence and ability in dealing with these officials.

Outside, Kareem and Soji, our other Lagos employees, were there to greet me enthusiastically and it was like a great homecoming. There is no doubt about it, these Nigerians respond to humane treatment. It was as if I was an old friend returning home after a long absence, not the boss returning after two weeks' leave. It is my opinion that it is a mistake to think that these people respond only to dash (i.e., reward of money, a Western failing). They are much more basic and have an understanding of human nature that many of us in the Western world have lost. Establish rapport and secure the trust of these people and they will do anything for you.

We drove to the airport hotel and similar greetings were awaiting from the people at reception, porters, room service boys, and others whom I had come to know during my earlier stay. Unfortunately, a mix-up over my arrival found me without a room. However, my friend the hotel accountant worked hard and with ingenuity known only to him, he came up with a room in the annex at the back of the hotel. It was a bit crummy but will suffice until tomorrow when I hope to be accommodated in more comfortable quarters.

I slept for most of the day, then arose, showered and shaved, and went to the grill for dinner. Adia was there to give me the impeccable service I had come to expect from him. His pleasure at my presence was obvious and genuine. Again, it is the rapport I have established with him that gets me what I want in a reasonable time, without delays and ill will often complained about by others.

There can be little doubt I like Nigeria and the opportunities open to me here. The people are OK and generally, I feel secure and positive towards them.

Thursday, 24 October 1975
Ikeja, Lagos

Up at 6:45am and breakfast in the Hungry Man Restaurant. Today has been a quiet and unspectacular day, though I do seem to have achieved quite a bit. Having reoriented myself at the office during the morning, I proceeded to Lagos about noon to make several business calls. Traffic was light and I was in Lagos in good time. Called on Babs Williams, then lunched at the Quo Vadis with friends Joan and Ian. In the afternoon, I called at Mertz & McLellan to discuss the project at Maiduguri for transmission line tower foundations and further investigation.

M&M not keen to undertake detailed investigation due to the time factor, but requested further consultation to help identify problem soils and assess planned raft foundations. Call on Sokoloff re house for D&M, but S not in. To call tomorrow.

Return to Ikeja, drinks with West African Survey personnel and friends then to hotel at 7pm. No swim today must do so on rising next morning. Dined at Mandarin Restaurant solo.

Friday, 24 to Tuesday 28 October 1975
Lagos

Friday was a quiet day, with some work in the office in the morning then some minor business activity in Lagos in the afternoon. In the late afternoon, I went to the yacht club, there were few people around and after having a couple of beers and a reminder that my temporary membership had expired, I returned to the airport hotel.

Saturday morning, I went to a travel agent in Ikeja to make reservations for my trip to New Zealand. The agency seems to be managed by an English girl and I was attended by a pleasant and reasonably efficient Nigerian. We worked out a schedule, which takes me via Paris then east to Sydney then Wellington. This is reasonably quick, but in hindsight seems a bit odd. Maybe a connection to Bahrain or Nairobi might be better. I will check with the agent later. On this schedule, I will leave Lagos on December 16 and be in Wellington on 19 December.

At noon, I drove into Lagos and to the yacht club. Lunch is spaghetti bolognese and I ate with Ian, Heinz, Ken Kent and Phillip Schiller, whose Osprey I will soon be buying. A message arrives from Malcolm Frost telling me he will not be racing that afternoon. Malcolm is 'skipper' described in my recent essay 'Boat Race to Badagri'.

This did not upset me and I was quite happy to volunteer for duty on the rescue boat. However, no sooner had I done so than another Osprey skipper, Norman Talbot snapped me up to crew for him. It was a fine afternoon with a moderate Force 1-2 wind blowing and I enjoyed it out with Norman. Not as proficient as Malcolm and we raced towards the rear of the fleet, but more relaxed and easygoing.

After racing and a beer at the club, I was off to join Malcolm and Barbara for dinner at their home. Fine hosts they are too. Drinks, dinner, coffee, liqueurs, cigars, everything. Well-prepared and well-trained servants. By the end, I was pleasantly satiated.

The drive home to Ikeja was fast. In fact, too fast for my own good, but I arrived safely and in one piece and was soon asleep in my bed at the hotel. Sunday, I was tired, up at 9am for breakfast but back to sleep and dozing until noon. A lazy afternoon doing nothing special, then dinner in the evening at the Mogambo.

Monday and Tuesday were two uneventful days working. Difficult to get myself motivated and except for some administrative matters, little was achieved. Expecting David MacGregor to arrive, but as of Tuesday night, David was not here.

Wednesday, 29 October 1975

Ikeja

The early part of Wednesday saw me tending to more administrative tasks, which are the duties of my absent colleague, Bruce Martini, who is still in the US awaiting receipt of a work permit. This could be ages and I have called Bruce to come immediately on a visitor's visa as I have done and collect his work permit from within Nigeria. Doing Bruce's work, I am neglecting my own, which is not all to the good. However, I must admit I could be doing my own, but I am having a little trouble getting motivated. I must get stuck into the Kaduna report and get it drafted and complete by the weekend.

I have actually postponed a trip to Maiduguri to carry out further consultation on the transmission line project in the Northeast state. This is as well as I should be here when David MacGregor arrives.

In the afternoon, I go to Lagos to check with Bruce's friend, Sokolof re, housing. Despite the previous weeks assertion, no house is available yet and it may take several weeks before one does eventuate. Perhaps I should follow up Oceaneering again. The longer I stay here, the more it seems to make sense that we establish in the Ikeja area.

Late afternoon, I go to the yacht club but there is no race due to the lack of wind and troublesome tide. A couple of beers with colleagues and skipper arrives to invite me to his house for dinner once more. Again, a top-class dinner and we carry on until after 11pm, when I set off to Ikeja. I arrive at the hotel at midnight to find David MacGregor waiting in the lobby. No room for him of course, but we rustle up an extra bed for my room and David moves in. Before we retire, we waltz to the poolside bar for a beer and a chat.

The usual mob of prostitutes are there and a new face plops herself beside us, Florence from the Cameroon. A bit chubby but with a pretty face. A friend of Comfort she says, Comfort being a regular, who has sat with me in the past. In between business talk and talk of love, we sip our beer and let Florence amuse us. In no time, an hour has passed and we retire to bed (to sleep).

Thursday, 30 October 1975

Ikeja

I wake and rise early (7am) but David sleeps on till after 8am. I do not disturb him and amuse myself by reading the latest issue of Newsweek. Several pages of the documentary on Generalissimo Francisco Franco. They had already written him off for dead, but even on this day, a week after the first of a series of heart attacks, the tough old devil is still confounding all and hanging on to life.

Franco is a much maligned and hated leader by those representing the so-called democratic countries. However, he has endured a long time and brought order and stability to a highly volatile people. Some would say was the loss of freedom worth it? What loss of freedom? During the five months I was in Spain during 1974/75, I observed that in some respects people had a lot more freedom than we do in a sophisticated democracy.

The freedoms I speak of are the freedom to walk in the streets without harassment from unlawful elements of the public, non-restrictive licensing laws and a law abiding citizenry, who are not unhappy and oppressed. The restrictions on free speech and the press and the extremely harsh and often brutal measures condoned by Franco to achieve this order leave much to be desired and I do not wish to champion his cause. However, the point I wish to make is that the current Western style of leadership is not much better.

Our leaders in general have abdicated their responsibilities and a relatively lawless public minority are free to run loose and restrict the freedom of the masses. Which is better?

From that small digression, back to the present. Actually, it is not the present for as I write this it is now Tuesday. I can't remember all that we did yesterday. Into Lagos and visits to Mertz & McLellan and Nepa, then shopping for a bicycle for David. This will be his main transport in Ilorin. A bicycle in Lagos? I wouldn't feel safe. A motorcycle maybe, but even that is dubious.

That evening, we dined at the Casa Pepe, the best restaurant I have tried so far in Lagos. Over a leisurely dinner, we talked about many things with emphasis on New Zealand. We are men of similar outlooks on life and perhaps not surprising as we are both engineers and choose to accept the challenges in a place like Nigeria. Dependence on the state is not for me nor I suspect for David. By this I mean NZ and likewise the UK does not offer the challenge and excitement can find in Nigeria and places like it.

Welfare has dulled the public spirit as people demand more and more from the state while giving less. I hope there is a reversal in this trend before both countries are led irreversibly down the path to that extreme form of socialism that is the communist state.

Another day on the town with David and more business calls and shopping. We also stop by at Alliance Francaise, where I enrol in class to take French lessons. The purpose of this is to help me in communication with clients when we visit the French-speaking regions of West Africa.

We drove to Apapa in the early afternoon to see a potential client, a Mr White of Holt Engineering. He is out and we return to Lagos. I am driving the Peugeot 404, which has seen better days and just as we are leaving Apapa a red warning light on the dashboard starts to glow. I don't know what it is but David refers to the auto manual and discovers it is a temperature warning light. By this time, we are almost on the overpass and must continue on till we come to the first exit where I branch off only to find a stalled truck blocking the way ahead. I slow down to top and then the motor stalls. Would it start again? You guessed it, no.

After trying the starter for several minutes, I reverted to the tried and true standby in this underdeveloped country, human muscle power. David rounded up a few boys and together they pushed me along the off-ramp. After a few kicks and shudders, the motor turned over and was running again. I picked up David and we continued on in search of a gas station. These were all on the wrong side of a divided roadway to make things more difficult. However, we finally got to one and luckily it had water, a factor not to be assumed in Nigeria. With water in the radiator, we were on our way again.

First, a call to Babs Williams, then to NET to send a telex, then to NEP for a business call and after this, around to Alliance Francais to enrol in a course of French lessons as we propose doing business in French West Africa. This seemed a logical and necessary step.

Finally, we drove to Kingsway to pick up David's bike. While David was inside, I stayed in the car and almost negotiated its sale to a streetside merchant. This started with some friendly banter with some small boys and ended up with big brother coming along with chequebook in hand. Unfortunately, we couldn't agree to a price (mine was too high) and no deal was cemented.

At 6pm, it was back to Ikeja, a shower, then off to the Mandarin for dinner. After dinner, a drink at the poolside bar of the airport hotel in the company of my favourite prostitute Annie and her friend, Christine. It seems I was out of favour this night as we had been spied sitting with Florence the other night. Well, I guess I needn't worry about that.

The temperatures are getting up now and it is noticeably warmer than when I was here from July through September. At the time, I seldom felt uncomfortably hot. Now, I perspire easily.

David and Remi went to the airport to pick up David's unaccompanied baggage. Mine, though shipped at the same time, has yet to arrive. Clearing things through customs can be a daunting task. Finding things is often impossible I am told. Actually, on first appearances, the cargo shed is not the complete shambles I had been led to believe. Only a small shambles really. David and Remi found his gear quite quickly, but clearing customs took time, all morning in fact.

While waiting, I fill in time with a visit to Transcap Travel to rebook my schedule to NZ and rebook David's flight to London at Xmas. David was rather upset a I had sent Soji to the agent the previous day to obtain a booking for him from Lagos to Freetown (Sierra Leone). David already had a confirmed booking Freetown to London, but when Soji returned, this booking was no longer there. The agent had booked him on another flight. Anyway, I straightened this out though I have still got to get reconfirmation for David.

Poor Soji! He is a nice enough fellow but quite timid (unusual for a Nigerian I find) and not too bright. He cannot read my writing too well even after a month of trying. But not only mine, David's he cannot decipher at all. As a message boy, he fares a little better, but I am sure we can find better and I will have to replace him soon. Fortunately, he is only with us for a three-month trial period. I do not relish putting him off but he is not suitable and it must be done.

While all this activity at the airport is going on, I dash back to the hotel to call our lawyer about a document (Business Registration Certificate) David needs with him in Ilorin. I had picked up what I had thought was this document on Thursday, but on closer reading found it to be a copy of the application for a certificate. Babs Wilson was not in his office, but fortunately, his secretary was there. However, getting him to understand what I wanted was a problem.

Easiest thing was for me stop by, thumb through our file and find the correct document. However, I was not expecting to get into Lagos until 2pm, what with go-slow at the airport and on the road and the boy would not stay in the office until then. I did manage to elicit a promise to stay there till 1pm and now the pressure is on to get there in time.

Fortunately, customs came through upon my return to the airport and we left from there at 11:30am, enough time to call by the office, swap the Landrover for the Peugeot and on into town. This we did and shortly after noon, I was at the wheel weaving my way down the Ikorodu Road once again matching my wits with the mad/crazy Nigerian drivers. Passing through Yabathe, a red light on the dashboard started glowing again. A quick pit stop at the nearest petrol station, top up with water and on our way again.

Crossing the Eko bridge, the traffic was not moving and once off the bridge on the marina, it was backed up to go-slow proportions. The clock was running and we were only just moving. At 12:50pm, we cleared the bottleneck and five minutes later, we pulled up outside Western House. Another five minutes to the eighth floor and William's office. The boy was still there but only just. We got our document and David was happy. From there, I went on to the yacht club and David went his separate way to catch a taxi back to Ikeja.

Saturday afternoon was racing as usual. I had lunch and sat with Philip Schiller and a pretty blonde Dutch girl, Ineka, who I had seen at the club recently. It seemed we were both wanting to buy Philip's Osprey dingy, but fortunately, Philip had given me the first option to buy. Perhaps Ineka could crew for me. A bit light perhaps, but with the prevailing light winds from here on this may not be a problem.

This afternoon's race was another bad one for skipper and I. We lost out from the start. Opting for a port tack start (as did most of the fleet), Skipper was up to the line but in a poor position and we wallowed in bad wind for the first three minutes. Malcolm needs to be bolder. Nothing much more to tell of that race except that we finished sixth.

At the end of the day, with a Chapmans (sprite, orange crush/soda with ice and a twist of lemon and some bitters) and a beer, I troop back to the hotel in Ikeja, arriving at 8pm. Dinner at the Mogambo with David then home to bed at 10pm. I was dog-tired.

Sunday 2 November 1975
Ikeja

Up early today. David is off to Ilorin and is keen to get away as soon as possible. Kareem is to drive him in the Landrover KWB17 which will stay with David in Ilorin.

Actually, we are not as early as all that. We get to Navigator House to pick up the L/r and David's gear at 9a. Kareem is not there. He was supposed to report at 8am. David curses and I am annoyed also. Kareem is generally reliable, but he has a tendency to roam free if you give him the chance. Sometimes he disappears for days on end when not given specific instructions. I must curb this tendency.

For one hour, we ponder the situation until Kareem finally appears. It turns out that our admonishing him had been unjust. He had arrived on time and when we had not appeared he went looking for us. We all cooled down, David proceeded to lead the L/R and finally got underway at 11:30am.

After saying farewell to David, I make my way to the Lagos Yacht Club for lunch. A race has been scheduled for the ospreys but is cancelled due to lack of wind. I go out sailing anyway with Norman Talbot and we cruise up to the harbour entrance, the back to the yacht club taking three hours to complete the journey. By the time we got back, I was quite exhausted.

The drive back to Ikeja is uneventful, though the car Is only limping along. Maybe I have cracked the block as it only seems to be running on two cylinders. Still, I make it just.

Today, I moved out of the hotel and into Navigator House. It is quite a pleasant change though ultimately I must get my own flat. I don't mind living in Ikeja and it is more logical to have the office there. However, socially I would probably be better off in Ikoya or Victoria. After dinner to bed. I am exhausted.

Monday, 3 November 1975

Today, I am due to fly to Maiduguri. Actually, I can only go as far as Kano, then I must wait until Tuesday morning to fly on to Maiduguri. This does not suit very well as the chances of hotel accommodation in Kano are remote. I refuse to spend the night in the airport.

I guess I have talked myself out of going. I drive over to Transcap and rebook for Wednesday morning. Nigerian Airways has changed the schedule again and now it is possible to get to Maiduguri in one day.

Among many other things I have done today, some of which I can't remember, I rescheduled my booking to Maiduguri. Now I will go on Wednesday morning, which means I will be able to attend my first French lesson on Tuesday evening.

Monday has been a busy day but I cannot recall much of what I did. No matter, an early evening I think.

Tuesday, 4 November 1975

It comes back to me now. The Peugeot was out of action and I could not get around as I wanted. My time was spent chasing alternative transport and then making trips back and forth to Oceaneering trying to locate Tony Parker re our hiring/renting one of his company's flats in Ikeja.

Kareem arrives back from Ilorin and I get him on to fixing the Peugeot. Fortunately, it does not appear to be in a serious condition, just water in the carburettor and elsewhere. Replace a broken hose and a good cleanout is what is required.

Try to locate Tony Parker once more but to no avail. In the afternoon, I go to Lagos and attend 1ˢᵗ Lecon Francais. All in French, no English spoken and I must admit to being a bit lost. The class is made up of mainly Nigerians plus a couple of Indian girls, two European ladies and myself. The lecturer is a bouncy madam, probably in her fifties, bright and pleasant. Let's hope I do learn to speak French.

I arrive home (home is now Navigator House) to find a message from Tony Parker. He wants to see me and will be calling by tomorrow morning. It is about the flat no doubt and is important enough to postpone yet again my trip to Maiduguri. So I decided to stay in Lagos another day.

Wednesday to Friday, 5/7 November 1975

This period was a continuation of my on-again off-again trip to Maiduguri. Wednesday I did not catch my flight so that I could see Tony Parker. Thursday morning, I was up at 5am, and off to the airport at six, but I could not get on the plane. I had sent Soji to the agent the previous day to get me a booking. Foolishly I did not check the ticket and as it turned out, I only had a requested booking, which is about as good as no booking here in Lagos.

When I could not get myself on the plane, I looked around for Kareem who had brought me to the airport to hassle with the desk clerk. Of course, Kareem was not to be found. This made me angry. Kareem has a habit of not being around when wanted. Actually, to be fair, he is reliable and quite good at his job, but he does wander. Like most Nigerians, he requires precise instructions on what is required. I finally did find him standing out in the departure lounge waiting to see me go, after I had given up all chance of catching the plane. My anger soon subsided.

The rest of the morning I settle into analysing the settlement of the Federal Secretariat, Kaduna. The analytical work bores me a little and I find it a lot of effort to do. Consequently, it takes me more time than it should. More French lessons in the afternoon Thursday and to the yacht club afterwards. I stay longer than I intended and drink more than I should. The drive home is fast and in hindsight, I drove more aggressively than I think I have ever done before in my life. This is unusual for generally after drinking my driving is subdued.

Friday, I have a headache, which is not surprising and it lingers all day. Perhaps I have a touch of malaria.

Saturday, 8 November 1975

Up early in the morning and George Ogston drives me to the airport and this time, I get on the plane. My headache is still with me and slight chills and perspiration seem to indicate that I do have a mild dose of malaria. I certainly don't feel like travelling.

I have to change planes at Kano, which is a mission. When I came north to Maiduguri previously, the one plane went all the way and I was there by 10am. This time, I must wait at Kano Airport for three hours and I do not arrive at Maiduguri until 2pm. Even then, I am not sure of catching the second plane as my ticket has only a request booking. However, I do get on the plane much to my relief. Being stranded in Kano with little prospect of finding accommodation is not an appealing thought. Hotel accommodation is very hard to find in Nigeria, if not previously booked, it's generally impossible.

It is also indecently expensive. Often as not one has to rely on the goodwill of business contacts and friends for accommodation. In its rush to spend its newfound oil wealth, Nigeria just does not have the accommodation to cope with the influx of businessmen. The same can be said of the Middle East, where I travelled earlier this year.

I arrive in Maiduguri and am quickly approached by a cabbie, who wants to take me into town. I agree and wait while he finds my travel bag.

"Where you wanna go, Master?" He said as I piled in the cab.

"To Mafoni Ward," I reply. "You know where that is?"

"Where?" He asks.

"M-a-f-o-n-I w-a-r-d," I repeat and I get out Mani's card to show him the address.

"Oh," he says and we drive off.

As we approach the town, he calls over his shoulder, "You waning go to Nigeria Airways, Master?"

"No," I said, "I want to go to Mafoni Ward. Do you know it?"

"No, Master."

"But you told me you did. I know you lied to me to get my custom. You cabbies are all the same. Take me past the Lake Chad Hotel, I will show you the way. I think I remember."

When we approached the hotel, this time he asked me if I want to go to the hotel, but I tell him to go straight. My memory serves me well and we soon find ourselves at Mani's office and house.

I find Mani and pay the cabbie. Mani's colleague, Bala Khrishnan, was also there (I had met him before) and beer and biscuits were offered around. About 3pm, Mani takes me to meet the Mertz & McLellan field engineer, Ian Fair, but he is not at his house nor at the Maiduguri Club. We leave a message and Mani takes me to the hotel, where I manage to get a room in the VIP suite, the only room available. Mani leaves and I put my feet up for the afternoon for a thankful rest. My headache is still with me, though by now it is fading.

Ian Fair calls by at 7:30pm and after a drink at the hotel, we proceed to his house for dinner, then later to his club. He is from Newcastle, single and about my age. Pleasant enough, stocky in build and likes his beer. It is quite a pleasant evening we have. I return to my hotel and bed about midnight.

Sunday, 9 November 1975

Maiduguri

Awake at 7am and rise at 8:30am. Feeling much better this morning. Go to the dining room for breakfast. It is filthy and the service is slow, typically Nigerian. Take forty-five minutes over breakfast and have to fight/argue for the fruit juice I want.

I finish breakfast and get back to my suite just as Mani comes to call. Pack my bag and go to reception to check out of the hotel. I must admit to being disgusted with the bill. N60 (US$10) for the suite, on top of that, a 10 per cent service charge. What service? Still, not much I can do but pay.

Mani takes me to Ian Fair's house then later to his own. At 1:30pm, we join Ian again at the Maiduguri Club for a drink and curry lunch. This club is typical of many to be found in the towns and cities of Nigeria and probably in other former British colonies. They are merely a drinking facility mainly for the expatriate community, where one can go and socialise. In many towns, the club may be the only such facility. Lunch was a bit of a joke. They sell a countless number of tickets for a limited amount of food and when the food runs out as it invariably does I am told; well, bad luck chum. We manage to get some dregs, enough to fill the void in the stomach.

At 3pm, we leave the club and start off on our drive to Bui. We have planned to go there so that we can get an early start the following day. It is the start of Hamadam season, the big dust storms that blow down from the Sahara. At the moment, visibility is good but I am told that at the height of the season, visibility gets down to almost zero.

We followed the same route I had driven back in August and arrived at Biu shortly after dark at 6:45pm. We go straight to a new guest house where arrangements have been made for us to stay. It is very clean which is unusual; the Nigerians generally don't run a clean establishment, not by European standards. However, this place was and except for the fact that there was no running water it was a comfortable establishment. Water was supplied in buckets from a central source. After dinner consisting of an English-style roast, I retired for the night at 9pm.

Monday, 10 November 1975

Rise early and breakfast at 7:15am with Ian at the guesthouse. Breakfast consists of cereal, kidneys eggs and chips, and is quite appetising.

Join Mani and Compton people all eight and set of for inspection of the excavations on the Bi/Damba section of the transmission line. Access is along a rough track cut by a bulldozer and it is a long and tiring ride. We are away all morning and part of the afternoon and return to Biu at 2pm in the afternoon. Mani's colleague, Mammen, has lunch prepared for us and a fine meal it is too. Spiced chicken and vegetables Indian style; very tasty.

After lunch, I only feel like sleeping and I return to my chalet and do just that, rising at 7:15pm to join Ian and Mani at the guesthouse bar for a drink and dinner. Dinner is simple fare of mince and vegetables but edible. The bar contains a group of boisterous Nigerians, one of whom is stoned out of his mind. Retire at 10pm.

Tuesday, 11 November 1975

Rise and breakfast the same time as yesterday then to work at 8am. Today, I inspected the Biu/Dadinkowa section of the proposed transmission line. We complete this in the morning, then drive to Gombe to rendezvous with David Lyons, the Mertz & McLellan engineer from Jos. David is an Irishman in his mid-fifties, six foot tall with thin greying hair. He has a slow but precise manner of talking with little hint of an Irish accent.

We arrive at the Gombe club shortly after noon. David is not there so we have a drink and some lunch. Come 2pm, David has still not arrived. Mani heads off to Kaltunga to make arrangements for our inspection of the Gombe/Nama transmission line. Finally, David radios through from Bauchi explaining that he has car problems and is delayed. We arrange a new rendezvous and he finally turns up in Gombe at 3:30pm.

We inspect the sites on the Gombe/Dadinkawa section of the line then return to Gombe shortly before 6pm. Hot and thirsty, we head straight to the Gombe club for a nice cool ale. Also, eat dinner there and retire to the catering guest house for sleep at 10pm. We have a VIP suite once again but cost is reasonable this time; N4.50 for the night for one person.

Wednesday, 12 November 1975

Today has been a long day and we have covered many miles, about 350 to be exact. After a not so appetising breakfast, David and I drive south from Gombe to meet Mani and his compatriot. The morning is spent inspecting three tower sites on the Gombe/Numan section of the proposed transmission line. Two of the sites are threatened by erosion and require special consideration. We have to trek over several kilometres of bush-covered terrain, where there is no vehicle access at present. It was 11:30am by the time we finished this inspection and arrived at Kaltunga for refreshments.

Again, we enjoy another fine Indian meal of spiced chicken and other well-prepared food. I must admit to feeling quite partial to the way the Indians prepare food.

At 2pm, we set off to complete our inspection of tower sites on the Gombe/Numan section. This takes most of the afternoon and it is 5pm when we return to Kaltunga, where David and I leave Mani and Co. and drive north on our way to Jos. It was our intention to stop overnight in Bauchi, but we decided to continue on to Jos where we arrived at 11:30pm. We go straight to David's house where I stay for the night. I am tired and after a cup of tea and a light snack, I retire for a well-earned sleet.

Thursday, 13 Nov 1975

Today, I flew back to Lagos and what a hassle that was. I had travelled north with an open return ticket from Jos. This was a mistake and I should have known. Getting on a plane in Nigeria without a confirmed booking is almost as difficult as getting into a hotel.

After breakfast, David Lyons took me to Nigerian Airways to reserve a seat on a flight to Lagos. We had tried two days previous when I was in Biu, but David did not have my ticket, which they (Nigerian Airways) insisted on seeing before they would make me a reservation. This morning, all they would give me was a request booking on the morning flight to Kaduna and a request booking on a connecting flight to Lagos in the early afternoon.

From the booking office, we returned to David's house to pick up my luggage and proceeded to the airport. It seems that yesterday's flight never arrived and today was uncertain. At first, the desk clerk would not give me a seat, but after a while, a plane arrived and most of the waiting passengers were checked in. Fortunately, I was among them. We piled aboard and the plane took off for Kaduna almost on time.

Arrived at Kaduna at 12:15pm and I was immediately faced with the daunting task of getting myself on the plane to Lagos. As it turned out, there were many others like me waiting with request bookings to Lagos. There was a mad scramble for the ticket counter with masses of bodies pushing and shoving trying to get to the head of the non-existent queue. For most it was to no avail as the plane was almost full with confirmed bookings. After standing amongst this rabble for almost an hour, I finally resigned myself to not getting on the plane. Fortunately, there was another flight in the early evening and I was able to get my name on the passenger list.

After a four-hour wait in Kaduna airport, which has the usual minimal facilities, I was on the plane to Lagos. Arrived as night was falling and proceeded by taxi to Navigator House. It was 7:30pm when I arrived and there to greet me was Bruce Martini, who had arrived from the US earlier that day. It was good to see Bruce as he will relieve me of a lot of the work I am doing.

Friday, 14 November 1975

Workwise, I did not manage to achieve much today. The morning and the early part of the afternoon were spent discussing business matters with Bruce Martini and attending to routine office matters. At 3pm, set off first to Apapa to make a business call to Holt Engineering, following up a business contact established by David MacGregor. This was fruitful but time-consuming and other business planned in Lagos had to be abandoned for the day.

Instead, Bruce and I proceeded to the yacht club for a late afternoon drink. There we met up with Ian and Henry and eventually Malcolm Frost who called by for a quick one. Malcolm invited us to his place to discuss the logistics for tomorrow's race to Agaja and by the time we got there, had a few more drinks and dinner, it was past 11pm and time to go home. It was a quick but safe trip back to Ikeja and I was cooped up in bed by midnight.

Saturday, 15 November 1975

This weekend witnessed another yacht race up the Badagri Creek, this time a race to the village of Agaja, an overnight stopover on the beach at Agaja, then a second race back to the yacht club in Lagos on Sunday afternoon. These races were sponsored by Heineken Breweries and several trophies were up for grabs including cups, glasses and beer.

After having breakfast I hurriedly put together supplies for the overnight stop in Agaja. I must admit my planning for this event had been almost nil, due to being out of Lagos for most of the week. However, Barbara and Malcolm were well organised and as I had guessed/ hoped, catered for me on the food line. After picking up my gear, Bruce drove me to the yacht club and we arrived in good time for the race up the creek which was due to start at 1pm. Ordered a salad lunch at the club and washed this down with a cold Chapmans. The salad was delicious, consisting of potato salad, tomatoes, onions, cucumber and tender cold beef. Food at the yacht club is always very good.

Following lunch, I helped Malcolm rig the boat and we were soon on the water preparing for the start. Twenty-five boats were entered including ospreys, a fireball, catamarans, HP14s, tarpons, in fact, most of the classes in the club. From a bad position on the line, we managed to get away to a good start and soon worked our way into second place behind another sailed by Tony Clare. However, with our boat pointing much higher than his and the rest of the fleet, we soon took over the lead.

This was a position we held until 200 metres from the finish when we suffered the extreme disappointment of being passed and beaten into second place. At times, our lead was as much as 500 metres, but during the final stages, the wind dropped and Schiller's Osprey closed on us and taking full advantage of a wind shift close to the line, he glided by as we were slow to react.

After crossing the finish line, we went straight ashore where a large group who had travelled upriver in motor boats were gathered. I did not feel like talking for a while, so strongly did I feel disappointed at losing like that. However, I quickly got over that and into the spirit of things. Beer was flowing freely and as the rest of the fleet came in, I rested on the adjacent ocean beach. This beach which stretches from Lagos to Badagri and beyond consists of fine golden sand of the type found on many of the beaches in the north of NZ.

The sea comes in with short high dumping waves of a type which are not particularly good for surfing. At first, I was hesitant about going in but there was little or no undertow and only a strong lateral current. Finally, Schiller and I took the plunge and others followed. The water was wonderfully warm and I enjoyed being in it and the raging surf.

Evening crept upon us and preparations for a barbeque dinner were started. After washing off the salt water and changing clothes I joined Schiller and the Dutch girl, Ineka, whom I had met a couple of weeks ago. We spent the early part of the evening sipping wine and talking then about 8:30pm joined the main group for a chat. This consisted of barbequed beef, salad and tomatoes, etc. Again, the meat was deliciously tender.

After dinner, some of the local villagers came by with their drums and we danced on the beach. There were young children from four and five to adults and the dancing was fast and furious. Some of the Europeans joined in including myself and at one stage, I had a group of about eight children dancing with me in a circle and then we all sat down and they started mimicking me as I made odd sounds and spoke different words. Finally, they all asked me for a coke. I went to the bar and bought six cokes and before I knew what had happened, they were whipped off me in a flash. It was a lot of fun.

Eventually, the villagers left and the party broke up as most bedded down for the night. I grabbed my lava-lava, spread it on the sand then dozed off; a little while later I woke and recovered my sleeping bag. It was cold under the stars and I was thankful for having brought it with me. The sand was hard and lumpy but I was tired and slept well.

Sunday, 16 November 1975

I awoke very early about 6am. Not surprising considering the hard ground I was sleeping on. Not feeling inclined to remain sleeping on that hard ground, I got up and watched the sea pounding on the shore. Others soon rose and an early breakfast was prepared by the ladies.

After eating breakfast and waiting a short while to let it settle, I hit the surf. During the next three hours, I spent two long sessions battling the surf trying to body surf in the tumbling water. The waves were really too short for this activity and I only got the odd good ride but it was fun trying.

An early lunch was prepared by some of the ladies and preparations were made for the race back. About 11am, a short storm blew over bringing cascades of rain and followed by sunshine and no wind. This more or less cast the fate on the race home.

The race was started at 12:35pm after some confusion as to the actual start time. It was a slow drift down the creek with four of the ospreys creeping out ahead and leaving the rest of the fleet far behind. After some initial swapping of positions, Scheller gradually took the ascendency and the race developed into a boring slow procession. Malcolm and I drifting along in second place finally made it to the finish line at the yacht club at about 6pm. By this time, many of the slower boats had withdrawn and were being towed home. In the end, only eight of the twenty-five boat fleet made it to the finish under their own wind.

The contest augured well for Malcolm and I. Beaten into second place overall, we collected the winner's prize for the race home (won only on a technicality). Among the booty was a cup, six beer glasses, twenty-four cans of Heineken and a silver astray. Malcolm was kind in not forgetting his crew and presented me with the Heineken.

We celebrated for a while then Bruce, who had come down to the yacht club took me to Antonio's for dinner. By this time, I was fading fast and gulped down what was really a very fine steak meal. We made our way home soon after and I immediately crashed on my bed.

Monday, 17 November–Saturday, 22 November 1975

This week, Monday through Friday was another busy week, made all the more difficult by the need to move from my quarters at Navigator House and recurring breakdown of our vehicles. Monday was spent moving the office to the flat at the Oceaneering compound which we had leased for this purpose.

Tuesday, David MacGregor arrived from Ilorin for the purpose of meeting his wife, Joy, who arrived from the UK. Tuesday was the day of my first drama with the Peugeot 404. After completing my activities, report and reporting on my visit to Madugaric during the previous week, I set off for Lagos and made a business call on Malcolm Frost at Hay Barry Odrense & Associates. Proceeding along Marina Ave after my visit to Malcolm, the engine of the Peugeot died on me. My small knowledge of auto mechanics told me it was an electrical fault.

In the middle of the go-slow traffic, I hailed a boy in a truck immediately behind me and before long he and others who appeared from nowhere were pushing me off to the side of the road. Naturally, one of them was a mechanic and within seconds, the problem was diagnosed—a burnt-out coil. Almost as quick as the diagnoses, was the appearance of a replacement coil which was connected in no time at all and voila, the motor she ticked over. The next shock came when the price was quoted; 80 which I managed to bargain down to 30.

From there, the mechanic would not budge and he even went as far as taking the replacement coil out again. I had little choice but to pay up or abandon the car. I did the former.

All this made me late for my French lesson once again. Up to this day, I had either missed my class completely or arrived up to an hour late. This day, it was 5pm when I arrived, 1 hour late.

After the lesson, I returned direct to Iheja. David MacGregor had arrived and settled into Navigator House. Now there were three of us there, stretching the hospitality a bit I fear.

Wednesday, we got our marching orders. We must move out of Navigator House. Fortunately, Mrs MacGregor was not due until Thursday and we got an extension of one day at Navigator House. I spent Wednesday getting some supplies in at the new flat so that at least we would have made up beds to sleep on and some basic foodstuffs. Wednesday evening, I went sailing and joined David and Bruce at the Mogamba for dinner.

I was so hungry that after soup and a nice tender steak with chips and onions, I ordered a second steak. It seems I started something as first Bruce and then David followed me and ordered a second meal themselves.

Thursday morning, David's wife, Joy, arrived from London. David and Bruce were up very early to meet her plane. Joy, also a New Zealander, was a very pleasant person and during much of the next two days, I had a very enjoyable time showing David and Joy more of Lagos in between attending to business matters.

Thursday was a day of moving once again. This time, I moved all my personal belongings out of Navigator House into the office/flat, which I will live in during the next few months. Bruce moved his things to a house on Victoria Island which we have managed to obtain at reasonable rental, through the good graces of the Bechtel man, Al Sokoloff. David and Joy moved into the office/flat for the short time they were here.

Thursday afternoon, I went to my French lesson, arriving on time for the first time ever. Not surprisingly, I followed the lesson better than ever before. At 6pm, immediately after my lesson, Joy and David were waiting to pick me up and we all drove to the yacht club to meet Bruce and have an early evening drink. David and Joy left us at 6:45pm to visit Joe Folayan, D&M's ex-principal in Lagos. Folayan is a devious and dishonest character whom by choice I have nothing to do with. In my opinion, he has bled D&M during the time he was in charge in Lagos but that is history.

For ourselves, Bruce and I dined at Antonio's once again. Both of us were a little high by the time we left Antonio's at 10pm having drunk wine and several rounds of liqueur. Bruce was really wiped out and I remember thinking as we left Antonio's that he shouldn't really be driving. We both had vehicles, however, and we didn't give a thought to leaving one behind.

We roared off along Broad St, across Edo Bridge and out along Western Ave. All of a sudden, as we came off the elevated portion of the expressway, I observed the headlights of numerous vehicles coming towards me along the wrong side (my side) of the expressway. Bruce got caught up in the confusion and was forced to stop, but I was able to duck off to the right and avoid the chaos that was developing. As I passed by the overpass ahead, I noticed two vehicles stalled on the bridge completely blocking off traffic on the outbound lanes. Vehicles trapped behind were therefore turning around and coming back to detour the way I had gone. Crazy!

From there, I made it home in quick time. Bruce arrived safely shortly after, though completely bombed.

Friday saw Bruce rather sick, a combination of rather too much booze the night before and a bit of a fever. David and I spent a leisurely morning discussing general business matters, then in the afternoon, set off for Lagos to attend to several matters there. First, we stopped off at the Neg. Railway Corporation at Ebeie Melta Station to obtain additional details of a construction project advertised in the Daily Times. This station is an old colonial-type structure of the type I have often seen in movies in India.

The meeting with the NRC project engineer was successful and we left with an invitation to submit credentials. Now we need to get a group together to handle the work that cannot be undertaken by D & M. From there to Lagos to buy food supplies for me and drawing and other equipment for David. By the time we were through, it was about 6pm. We set off for Ikeja, not arriving to the flat until 7:30pm. Several times the L/R stalled and threatened not to start. However, we managed to make it home safely.

On reaching home, I found a letter awaiting me from Jim Rutherford of Ore. It was an invitation to attend a film evening in his flat on Lagos Island. Jim is a fellow NZer of David MacGregors vintage, who has been working in Lagos for the past fifteen-odd years. I met him once back in September when I was making enquiries about consultants' scale of fees in Nigeria.

I was hot and dusty and didn't feel much like going out, but the movies promised sounded interesting and the prospect of meeting new people persuaded me to go. David and Joy decided to come too. After a shower and freshen up, we set off for Lagos in the Peugeot 404. Despite the possibility of it breaking down, I decided to risk this and have the relative comfort of the car.

First, we stopped at the airport hotel for a quick meal in the Hungry Man Restaurant. Fortunately, Friday was on duty, which ensured us of relatively quick service. We were soon on our way again and made good time to Lagos arriving at Rutherford's flat at 9:45pm. A big crowd had already gathered and movies were just starting.

The movies themselves were quite good but the gathering was rather dull. Both David and I were nodding off at various stages. The movies were homemade travel logs; one of a trip across the Sahara and one of a trip to New Zealand via Kenya and the Seychelle Islands. They were well-edited and contained dialogue and music, but scenes tended to be too repetitive in format and after a while, interest was lost. At about midnight, we gracefully made our departure.

From there, we went to the new Can club and I introduced Joy and David to the charms of a Nigerian nightclub. I was propositioned immediately and later another girl made a play for David much to Joy's amusement. We sat through the floor show and again it was the African dancers who provided the excitement. This time the show included a stripper.

We left the show at about 2am and set off for home along Western Ave. While still on the elevated portion of the expressway, the motor died and we cruised to a halt. There was no way I was going to get it going again with my limited knowledge of the workings of an engine, David likewise. The decision was quickly made to push it off the expressway and abandon it. With Joy at the wheel, David and I got behind and pushed for about a quarter mile until we found an exit and got it off the expressway. We pushed it into a vacant lot, purposely left it unlocked, then thumbed a ride for home where we arrived at about 7am, hot, tired and ready for bed. In all, it had been an exciting day.

Saturday, Joy and David went on their way to Iloria; I went sailing in the afternoon and returned for an early night at home.

Sunday, 23 November–Saturday, 29 November 1975

Sunday, I stayed in Ikeja all day intending to spend the whole day working. Morning was productive, but come noon, I got to be very hungry so Bruce and I went to the Mogambo where I scoffed down a curry lunch. Instead of working in the afternoon, I slept.

The working week was an extremely busy one in which I purchased a new car, established a cable address and attended to numerous other tasks pertaining to setting up the office. Unfortunately, I have not had the time or inclination to tackle the few technical matters still outstanding. The problem is a little accentuated by Bruce's current disorganisation, which is possibly a result of the settling-in process. I seem to get through twelve times the amount of work he can manage at the moment and to get things done I have to do them myself. Maybe I have more energy. Maybe? I think I do.

I guess I get a little annoyed that Bruce seems to get through so little. For instance, we need to get office furniture for which we are getting quotations from several cabinet makers. This far we have one quote only and that I arranged through Remi. Bruce was to have sent an urgent telex message for me Wednesday but come Friday, it still hadn't gone. No doubt he will get more efficient. I hope it's soon so that I can divert my attention to technical matters and business development.

Besides work, sailed Wednesday evening and again Saturday and attended French lessons Tuesday and Thursday. The French learnt in college is really coming back. With a bit more effort on my part, I should be able to speak the language at least a little in a few months. I note that at times I come up with Spanish phrases or words. I guess I did partially learn Spanish while in Spain earlier this week.

Saturday morning, I passed a body lying stiff and unattended on the Ikorodu Road near Ebetu Metta. Life has little value here.

Sunday, 30 November 1975

A day of work to get documents together for sending to London by courier tomorrow. Included is one of the jobs from the old partnership which I am sending to London for completion. I just don't have the time.

Lunch at the yacht club, but back to Ikeja and work at 3pm. Nothing else special about today.

Rest and Recreation July 1976

At the end of June 1976, I flew out on my quarterly R&R to combine a little business with sailing; my first stop the US and the and the International Moth Class World Championship in Yorktown, Virginia. On route to Virginia, I stopped off in New York and Washington DC to conduct a little business including a short visit to the World Bank for what purpose I never recorded. On 4 July, I arrived in Yorktown where I met up with Bruce Johnson (my ex-hometown Eastbourne, NZ) and three Swiss sailors I had met during the 1974 event in Sweden.

Hal Wagstaff was also there for one day before travelling on to the Olympic Games in Montreal. What follows is my account of this regatta and the UK National Osprey Championship in Penzance in the UK.

It (the Moth Champs) was largely forgettable. The organisation was very bad and for me personally, my results were even more disastrous than in 1974 in Stockholm. During the first race, I capsized among a school of jellyfish and got stung in my left eye. It was very painful and I could not see properly for several days. I missed most of the races after that and finished third from last overall. The eye has since cleared up and my vision is back to normal.

Although the sailing was disappointing, I enjoyed the holiday and the US. The countryside in Virginia is very attractive and the weather was very good. I shared a motel with an American, Harry Hood, He was a good companion and we had a lot of fun together. He spent a lot of time helping me when my eyes were closed up.

The people of Yorktown were friendly, if not a little odd. It is a deeply religious community and there were no pubs for miles around. After racing they disappeared and us sailors were left to our own devices. Harry and I took to stocking up with beers from a local supermarket and we became the centre of social activity at the end of a day's racing.

From Yorktown, I made the short hop to Washington and boarded a plane to London and made my way to Penzance. In contrast to the event in Yorktown, the Osprey Championship sailed in Mounts Bay was a huge success. I excelled my expectations and was extremely pleased with my performance.

Pirate of Penzance

I arrived in Penzance several days before the regatta and this gave me time to pick up and familiarise myself with the new dingy. My crew, Robert, was already there and so too were the four other crews from Lagos. I was raring to go.

Penzance is a town on the south coast of Cornwall and situated in the shelter of Mounts Bay which is a large sweeping bay and looks out the English Channel. At the northern end of the bay is St Michael's Mount on which is situated a castle and the current occupant was an aristocrat who also happened to be patron of the host club of this year's National Osprey Championship. A fleet of 123 yachts, their crews and supporters had gathered to participate in this year's event and what a memorable occasion it was for me, both in terms of the hospitality extended and my performance on the water which far exceeded my expectations.

To kick off proceedings, our patron hosted a grand party in his castle atop the Mount for competitors and their families prior to the start of the regatta. Then followed a week of sailing out on the bay, one race each day. I had sailed in many contests before this one, but the spectacle and the size of the fleet exceeded anything I had experienced before and was not without some personal dramas out on the water.

Competitors would gather in on the beach where our boats were parked under moderate security which was all that was needed at the time. We would rig our boats and head out onto the water, with the first boats leaving the shore about 9:30am. With a prevailing offshore wind throughout the regatta, it would take up to an hour to get out to the coarse for the start of each race. I was usually among the first boats off the shore and when well into the bay and looking back, what a spectacular sight it was looking back seeing all these boats with spinnakers set. Start time was 11am each day and there followed one and a half to two hours of racing then another one hour back to the shore. It made for a long day.

Given the size of the fleet the organisers had opted to adopt a gate start, designed to spread out the fleet and avoid the jostling at close quarters of a standard race start a starting technique foreign to me, but one I adjusted to quickly and found myself getting away to good starts in almost every race. In each of the first three races, I found myself up among the first ten boats around the first mark, but poor spinnaker work usually found me dropping back on the offwind legs of the course. However, I was improving with each race and results of thirty-seven, twenty-four and sixteen put me in twenty-three place overall going into race 4.

Sadly, disaster struck when midway through race 4, as young Robert injured his knee and I had to retire from the race with a did not finish. I still had hopes of a top-20 finish at the end of the regatta with one race to go, but it was not to be. In the fifth and final race, I sailed badly with a substitute crew, finishing the race in the fiftieth position, but still good enough to finish the regatta in thirtieth place overall and top boat of the Lagos contingent. In spite of the disappointing end, I was exhilarated, knowing I had competed with some of the best in the class.

Last Days in Lagos

Contest over I returned to London where I was informed that a decision had been made to shut down the Nigerian operation. I was instructed to return to Lagos and assist David MacGregor, our man in Ilorin in winding up the company's affairs. By this time my American colleague, Bruce Martini and his wife, Maggie, had returned to the US and the task of winding up and disposing of the company's assets was left to me and David Macgregor in the Ilorin office to carry out.

Within weeks of my return to Lagos, an unsettling incident occurred involving David. I enjoyed David's company. We worked well together and would socialise together whenever he came to Lagos. Being senior in years and a lot more experienced than I, I often sought his advice on various issues. David was personable and friendly, but he did have a sharp tongue and at times could be highly critical of the indigenous people and their ways. At some point on a visit to Lagos, he had obviously said words that upset my office administrator, Remi, who had unknown to me made a complaint to the Nigerian authorities regarding David's visa status.

Apparently, David had two passports, one New Zealand and one British. Nothing unusual in that but Remi had framed the issue in such a manner as to present David in an unfavourable light. There followed a short investigation and David was interrogated by immigration officials. Normally, a confident individual, I recall David was visibly shaken by this interrogation, his fate uncertain and the possibility of an unspecified spell in jail. At the time, the Nigerian government was cracking down on visa fraud and it seemed that David had become an innocent victim.

Seen in the light of the political climate of the time, New Zealand was a political pariah due to its sporting contact with South Africa, David was fortunate that his fate was deportation. In September, he was on a plane to London leaving me in sole charge of winding up the company affairs.

Ironically, the next three months turned out to be the happiest and most carefree time I experienced in Nigeria and my social life blossomed. The task of winding up and selling off assets was simplified by an offer from a Nigerian contact to buy all these assets at a price that was subsequently approved by London office. My days of travel around Nigeria over, I had ample time to participate in sailing and social activities. My social life blossomed.

Earlier in the year, I had become friendly with Gordon, who was attached to the American Embassy. Gordon was an engaging character who had a penchant for drawing attention to himself. I remember one occasion that he recounted to me after the fact, being locked up in a military prison over the US anniversary weekend of 4 July. According to his story, he had been caught up in 'go-slow' traffic early on the Friday afternoon and rather than carrying on to his destination, he turned off into the entrance of a military establishment intending to back out and drive off in the other direction.

Unfortunately, before completing this manoeuvre, a military vehicle pulled up behind Gordon, and those inside impatiently waved him on. The gate to the establishment was open so he drove on in to clear the way. Next minute, he was challenged for being unlawfully on a military base and thrown in a cell on the base. There he languished for four days before he managed to get word out to alert the embassy of his predicament. What Gordon's role was at the embassy I never knew. Maybe he was attached to the CIA?

What I do remember, he was an engaging character and he introduced me to the diplomatic circle, where for the remaining time of my stay in Lagos I became an intimate friend of the US Ambassador, Dennis Essum.

How did this come about? The ambassador was a keen tennis player and Gordon must have mentioned my prowess on the court to his boss, for one day early in September, I received an invitation to join the ambassador for a game on the court at the ambassadorial residence. He was a better player than I, but I must have acquitted myself well for I was invited back for several more and the diplomatic functions that he hosted. It was a one of these functions that I met Petra from the Netherlands, who was attached to the United Nations Development Programme (UNDP) in Lagos. For a while, Petra became my romantic interest and my racing crew at the Lagos Yacht Club.

Sadly, all good things come to an end. By the end of November, I had completed my task of winding up affairs in Nigeria and after saying farewell to my many friends, I was on a plane to London. During the weeks leading up to Xmas, I was in a state of limbo as Dames & Moore spent time deciding what was in store for me. London office made it clear that they were keen to retain my services and suggested I go to Vancouver, take some time to settle in then come back to the UK on another temporary transfer. For some reason which I cannot recall, I had cooled on my plan to settle in Canada and I made it known that I was not keen on this option.

In the end, my London boss told me to fly home to New Zealand and have a good holiday there with my family. "We will call you when you are needed for your next assignment." I couldn't complain as I remained on the payroll and it would be a good chance to catch up with family and friends and consider my future. On New Year's Eve, I was on a plane bound for New Zealand and home.

While in London, I was contacted by the management of an American civil engineering firm with business interests in West Africa with an offer of employment back in Nigeria on several earthwork and road-building contracts they had secured. I informed them that I would consider it while at home in New Zealand. The job offer was very tempting and within the range of my technical competency. However, I was not so keen to return to Nigeria given the political climate of the time, I made my misgivings known to these people and stalled on deciding in spite of several calls they made to me during January.

I recall receiving one of these calls mid-afternoon at the Nelson Yacht Club, where I was sailing in the New Zealand Laser Championships. All good for the ego, but in the end, I declined the offer, feeling a certain loyalty to Dames & Moore and the flexible terms of employment with the latter.

My holiday in New Zealand lasted until the end of January 1977, when I received a call from Carol Dolan, the temporary transfer coordinator in Los Angeles, that I was wanted for an assignment in Indonesia and would I accept. By this time, I was ready to get going again and willingly agreed. Arrangements were made for my travel to Jakarta for a briefing on the job requirement from the D&M partner in charge of the local office and once more I was on my way to the Asian continent, a part of the world I had yet to experience.

Padang, Indonesia, 1977

It was about this time I was starting to tire of the nomadic life I had been living during the past ten years. It had certainly been an exciting period of my life; I had seen a big chunk of the world, which had satisfied my yearning for travel and given me exposure to various nationalities and ethnic groups and how they function. I was now thirty-four years of age and although my career had trajected in my chosen direction, I was no nearer satisfying an urge to settle down, marry and raise a family. In this frame of mind, I started thinking about returning home and settling down in New Zealand. First, I had this assignment in Indonesia to which I was committed.

Indonesia, 1977: From February to September 1977, I was stationed in Padang, West Sumatra, supervising earthworks and road construction for the expansion of a large cement factory, P T Semen Indonesia. It was not one of my more memorable assignments, but even so, perhaps it is worth recording a few details here.

Padang is located on the West Coast of Sumatra, the northernmost Island of Indonesia. In recent decades, it has grown significantly with a population approaching one million, but when I was there, it was a much smaller city, in a remote location and social activity was limited. The climate was hot and humid and extremely wet site conditions led to protracted periods of downtime. That said I developed good relationships with the project management personnel of F L Smidth & Co., a Danish engineering company and the local Indonesians working at the plant. I will spare you all the details but suffice to say, I was bored and unsettled and of a mind to return home and make a go of things there.

I was eyeing some property developments in Auckland with Ian Creighton, a cousin of mine. Meantime, in Indonesia, my services have been in demand for several quarters. First, my employer, Dames & Moore, went to great lengths to persuade me to stay with them when I made it known I intended to resign. They offered me the carrot of working out of Hawaii and running an office in Guam of all places. It was tempting but I said no. The F L Smidth, a Danish company that was managing the cement plant project asked me to join them.

I had developed a good working and social relationship with the Danes, but I did not take it up. Then the earthwork contractor made an approach and asked me to stay and join them. I was led to believe they were in line for several large government contracts and they wanted me as part of their team. The offer was tempting as I would be closer to NZ and I saw an opportunity to retain my international connection and would be closer to home. Against the advice of my Danish friends, I accepted the Indonesian company's offer, but things did not eventuate and I was back home by the end of September.

I spent the next year drifting between Auckland and Wellington working on a property development business venture with my cousin, Ian Creighton. That came to nothing when for reasons of his own, he pulled the plug. I was struggling to settle back home, I set about looking for work abroad and in January 1979, I was on a flight bound for Dubai in the United Arab Emirates to take on the role of a project manager for the contracting firm McConnell Dowell, NZ.

Dubai/Abu Dhabi 1979–1980

I first came across McConnell Dowell when working at the Marsden Point Power Station in 1966, where that company had a contract to construct undersea water discharge tunnels. It had grown in size and gone on to establish a presence in Australia and the Middle East. The Dubai operation was managed by a dynamic engineer, Marshall Hudson, only three years older than I and a small team of technical people. Hudson, an entrepreneurial type, had established good relations with the ruler of Dubai and had secured contracts to drill for water supplies in the barren mountains inland from the coast and a contract to manufacture and lay interlocking paving stones on the wharf structures of a new shipping port of Jebel Ali some 30 kilometres south of Dubai.

My appointment was as project manager to oversee the work on the block paving contract. There was a lot of learning to do, both for me and my employer.

When I look back on my engineering career, my involvement on this project would have to be the highlight. The port construction was well-advanced when I arrived in Dubai. Under the engineering direction of British conglomerate, Balfour Beatty. It comprised the excavation and progressive flooding of the desert landscape a giant port facility in the shape of an inverted F when completed. Now forty years later as I write this section of my memoir, Jebel Ali is reputed to be the world's ninth busiest port, the largest man-made harbour in the world, and the biggest and by far the busiest port in the Middle East.

The work was challenging and I was personally pleased with my effort, but I slowly became disgruntled with the McConnell Dowell; the way it operated and the way some staff were treated. The hours were long; ten-hour days six days a week with a rest day on Fridays, the Islamic holy day. These long hours did not bother me unduly, the work was absorbing and I learnt heaps about myself, my management abilities and perhaps most interestingly the culture and conditions of employment of our labour force, predominantly Indians and Pakistanis.

I had an enjoyable social life, which largely revolved around the Dubai Offshore Sailing Club where I spent most Fridays sailing and racing 470's Lasers all year. I became active in developing the racing programme and made many friends, including a Scottish couple, Ian and Marie Brodie, who invited me to join them at their home in Glasgow over the 1979 Xmas and New Year period. Hogmanay on New Year's Eve was a wonderful experience.

My disillusion with the company grew as the months passed and maybe it showed, when one day in August, one of the other project managers was put in charge of the paving contract and I was sent to assist on another project in nearby Bahrain. When I returned to Dubai a month later, I was put to work on managing the water drilling project in the mountains.

My situation became too much to bear and rather than complaining, in my quiet way, I started looking for work elsewhere in the Emirates. This was not hard and before long, I had resigned from work and joined an Arab earthwork and pavement contracting company Gulf Syndicate Contractors, in Abu Dhabi on a government contract. Not long after joining GSC, I received a message from my friend, Jean-Michel, offering me an opportunity with a major American company in the Sudan. I was only a couple of months into my new job, I felt some loyalty and turned the offer down.

Six months later, it was obvious GSC were in financial difficulty and they were struggling to pay me and at Xmas, I was on my way home.

A Bulging Briefcase

I am rushing down Khalidiya Street in downtown Abu Dhabi, suitcase in hand with US$15,000 notes inside, desperate to get it banked before I am accosted. No, I have not been dealing with cocaine. I have just been paid long overdue salary and expenses by my employer, Gulf Syndicate Contractors, a local construction company.

My contract has been terminated by mutual agreement and I had been sitting in the company office all morning, while company directors, George and Hosni, made a series of calls to their bank for funds to cover their current commitments including my overdue salary and that of fellow employees. All very worrying, for they owe me three months' salary, which to me is a small fortune. With me is an Englishman who is my direct report and who has been with George and Hosni for several years.

"Don't worry, Michael," he says several times. "I have seen it all before and they never fail to deliver." Soothing words, but they do not allay my concern. I am soon to leave for New Zealand and $15,000 is a lot of money to write off.

At midday, George finally presents me with a cheque and I rush to their Arab bank to cash it in. I have long since become wary of their promises and want to see cash in my hand. I am in luck. After another long wait, I find myself at a teller's grill and present my cheque. He lazily gazes at it, fills out some paper forms, and then hands over a wad of US dollar notes. These I hastily pile into an empty suitcase I have with me.

Now I am on my way to the Standard Bank to deposit my cash in the safety of its vault. When I get there, I will breathe a sigh of relief. As make my way along the street I ponder: how did it come to this?

Xmas 1980 was approaching and I had been in the United Arab Emirates for just on two years. Dubai and Abu Dhabi were exploiting their newfound oil wealth and developing rapidly. I had been sent there by McConnell Dowell, a New Zealand construction company which had a small team of engineers based in Dubai, manufacturing interlocking paving stones for installation on the wharves of a massive shipping port under construction at Jebel Ali, some 30 kilometres south of the emerging city. I had been appointed to manage the manufacture, supply, and laying of these paving stones.

The Dubai governing authorities were led by charismatic Sheik Rashid bin Saeed Al Maktoum, who was responsible for the early transformation of Dubai from a small cluster of settlements near the Dubai Creek into a modern port city and commercial centre. The port of Jebel Ali was to serve as a base for the large supercontainer ships and oil carriers traversing the region. Construction involved the excavation of a gigantic hole in the coastal shores of the Persian Gulf and flooding it with seawater to provide these huge vessels. Taking the shape of an F, the port stretched inland some 4 kilometres, with the protruding fingers occupying a similar distance.

It seemed that money was no object time and performance were. Ours was a small subcontract in the overall scheme of things, but the port project itself was huge and on a scale that I have not experienced before or since.

McConnell Dowell (Dubai) was led by a young engineer, Marshall Hudson, not much older than myself. Marshall, or Marsh as we called him, had an entrepreneurial streak and when I arrived on the scene, he had established a cordial relationship with the Sheik and had also established close links with the head contractor, British firm Balfour Beatty, and convinced them to award his small team this work. No one on our team had any experience in the manufacture and laying of Euro stones, myself included, but Marsh was able to find the necessary skills when he needed them: a machine technician from Germany and an experienced block layer from England. The rest of our team learnt fast.

When I arrived on the scene, the machine to manufacture the Euro stones was being assembled and my first task was to establish a testing regime to measure the quality of the paving stones. I quickly moved on to the logistics of transporting them to the wharf areas where they were to be laid, checking the quality of the aggregates used in the pavers, and the quality of the laying. It was challenging work and I thrived on it. However, for some reason, I seemed to fall foul of the culture of McConnell Dowell and its method of operating. In January 1980, we had a parting of the ways and I went searching for another contract.

My enquiries led me to Abu Dhabi and an interview with George and Hosni who hired me on the spot promising good things ahead. And so, I moved south to manage the earthworks and pavement construction on a new military compound then under construction.

During the next four months, things went smoothly. I was paid on time and my accommodation in a studio apartment overlooking the city was adequate and paid for by the company. However, as the months went by, they were slower at paying my salary, then one evening in July, or was it August, I found myself denied entry to my apartment. It seemed that George and Hosni had got too far behind in paying the rent and I was being used as a pawn to extract payment from them. From then on, I started experiencing delays in being paid and the uncertainty had me wondering, was this the Arab way or were George and Hosni on a slippery slope to insolvency? I never did find the answer to that question.

Chapter 6
Home Again 1981–1984

I arrived home just before Xmas, relieved to have that drama behind me, but still unsettled and a little unsure what I wanted to do next. Perhaps seek out another assignment back in the Middle East after spending the current summer home with family. Summer came and went and as I drifted into autumn, I dropped the urge to go back for another foreign assignment and decided to seek employment here in New Zealand. This was the era of the Muldoon Government's thinking big projects and opportunities were abounding.

I applied for a position on the oil refinery expansion project at the entrance to Whangarei Harbour and I was appointed civil project manager for Badger Chiyoda, the international conglomerate managing the project.

I moved north, bought a house and started on the job in early May. I soon came to regret my decision to be there. I was working a sixty-hour week, for half the salary I had previously been earning, the operation was highly bureaucratic. On the positive side, I rekindled my friendship with Kevin Bradley and his wife, Judy, and family, and made new friends including Karl Schwinn from Germany, my immediate boss and others working on the project. Given the hours worked and commuting time to and from the construction site, my social life was very limited.

I lasted six months, finally handed in my notice and returned to Wellington with no idea of what I wanted to do next. On arriving home, all I said, "The worst job I've ever had." I suspect Audrey and Malcolm were a little perplexed.

Out into The Pacific, February 1982

In December 1981, I headed home to spend Xmas with Mum and Dad. I had been working as a project engineer on the Marsden Point Refinery expansion near Whangarei for the past nine months and I was far from happy. A six-day week, long hours, a frustratingly bureaucratic environment and relatively low recompense, it was not providing me with the life I wanted.

I packed my few possessions into my shiny new Toyota, said farewell to Karl, my German boss, and other friends and colleagues and drove the five hundred miles south to Wellington and home. When I arrived, I announced to Mum and Dad: "I have quit at Marsden Point, the worst job I ever had."

I don't recall their reaction. They were obviously pleased to see me but I suspect they sensed my mood and uncertainty as to what I would do next. The festive season came and went and I was far from certain myself. Adjusting back to life in New Zealand was proving difficult.

My dream of going sailing on the ocean blue was still in the back of my mind and one Saturday afternoon in mid-January, I spied an advertisement in the local paper for a crew that wanted an ocean-going yacht for an adventure cruise out into the Pacific and on to the South America. I contacted the advertiser, Bill, who gave me brief details of the proposed voyage and invited me to Auckland for an interview. I flew up or did I drive, I don't remember and spent a morning with Bill on his newly fitted out yacht, a fifty-one-foot motor sailor.

Bill was putting together a crew of six including himself and he was planning to set out mid-February bound for Tonga, then eastbound to the Easter Islands and on to Chile, then make his way up the South American coast as far as Panama, the sail back to New Zealand on a more direct route via the Pacific. All very exciting it seemed to this novice ocean sailor.

I returned to Wellington and waited to hear from Bill. He called a week later and told me he had selected his crew and I was not on the team. Oh well, what next, I thought, but I didn't have to wait long, for a week later, I received another call from Bill who told me one of his original selections had pulled out and would I come along. I said yes, readied myself with some sailing kit and a few days before departure, I drove north and Mum came along to see me off. Again, I have no recollection of what she thought about me going off into the unknown on a small boat with a group of people I did not know. Perhaps some trepidation, I don't think we discussed it.

Bill had his yacht moored in the Viaduct basin on Auckland's waterfront, where years later the Americas Cup was sailed when NZ held the auld mug. I reported aboard and was introduced to the rest of the crew. Two females and two males whose names I have long since forgotten, all four in their mid-twenties. Then there was me approaching forty and Bill the senior in years at fifty. We spent the next two days getting familiar with the boat and getting to know each other.

It turned out that none of the four had any sailing experience, which made me wonder what Bill's selection criteria had been. Perhaps it should have rung a few alarm bells but I was itching for adventure and to get going. I gave it little thought.

The boat was well provisioned and on the third day aboard, we set sail, or rather motored out of Auckland Harbour and steered a course north up the east coast as far as Whangarei. From there, Bill set a course which would take us out into the Pacific and towards our first destination, Tonga. All day, the wind had been blowing a steady 20 to 25 knots from the north and we punched directly into it as we motored up the coast. As we steered our course northeast out into the Pacific, Bill continued to proceed under motor, which was a disappointment to me, for with the wind on our beam was ideal for putting up some canvas and proceeding under sail.

To me, the motion of a boat is much more pleasant under sail, but Bill was the skipper and there can only be one in charge at sea. I had a special interest in keeping me amused during the coming days and weeks, of navigation.

I had developed an interest in navigation and with some basic tutoring from Dad and self-tuition from a book I had acquired, I set out as an exercise to test my skills and chart our course. I am a self-taught navigator. Bill did not have any modern navigation aids on board. Instead, he had a sextant, navigation tables and charts. He also had a radio direction finder which could be used when we were closing on land. Obtaining latitude, and position north and south is relatively easy. Take a noon-time sighting of the sun and measure the angle to the horizon, then it is a simple calculation to determine latitude.

At night, you can use the stars, but one has to be able to identify them. Calculating longitude is more complex and again requires a sextant reading and using a set of tables to work out one's longitude.

During the next three days and nights, both Bill and I independently took sextant readings of the sun (identifying stars was too difficult for both of us). At the end of the second day out of site land, I noticed that Bill's course was diverging from mine which was starting to cause me some quiet concern. Both of us can't be right. Who was in error? The answer came towards the end of the third day, when we sighted the Kermadec Islands which lay on my charted course. After that, Bill seemed happy for me to take over the navigation completely.

It was about this time that I started having misgivings about the entire venture. A novice crew, a skipper who didn't want to put up sail and now apparently quite happy for me to take over the navigation. I am not prone to panic and as I pondered the situation and how to react, Bill was soon to come up with the answer.

During the night of our fourth day at sea, I was off watch and sleeping in a bunk up forward. When I awoke at daybreak, I noticed the motion of the boat had changed from a constant thud as it punched into the waves and now there was a gentle pitching motion to and fro and side to side. What was going on? When I went up on deck, the wind was blowing over our stern and we were heading south back towards New Zealand. Sometime during the night, Bill had decided to turn tail and head back towards New Zealand. I was quietly relieved and so I suspect were the rest of the crew. We had been getting along fine, but Bill and his eccentricities were proving somewhat disconcerting.

With the wind easing a bit and off our starboard beam, Bill raised some sail and cut the motor for the first time. It was good to be cruising comfortably along with only the sound of the sea and the wind and some of the tension that had been growing started to subside as we headed back home. I remained in charge of navigating and I was supremely conscious of the narrow spit of land that was the top of the North Island. The last thing I wanted was to find us on the wrong side and heading down the west coast of the island.

I took to using the radio direction finder as my main aid to navigation. Scattered around the coast are lighthouses and other stations emitting a series of pulses, each with its own distinctive code. I was able to pick up the signal from the light at North Cape and I figured that if I kept the direction of the signal on the starboard (right-hand side) of the boat all would be well. And so, it was and shortly before noon on day six, we sighted land on the starboard quarter, adjusted our heading and made our way towards the Bay of Islands.

It was late in the afternoon when we arrived at the entrance to this haven. I was keen for us to find a sheltered spot off one of the outer islands where we could moor overnight and rest. However, Bill had other ideas and he wanted to continue south and head for Whangarei where he intended to take up a permanent mooring and send us, his crew, on our separate ways. There was no objection raised, I think like me the rest of the crew were keen to abort. My only concern at this stage of the voyage was cruising through the night close to a rocky coast we could not see in the dark.

Midway between the Bay of Islands and the entrance to Whangarei Harbour lie the Poor Knights Islands, a collection of rock outcrops some three to four miles off the coast east of Tutukaka. Keen to stay well clear of land in the dark, I suggested to Bill that we steer a course well to the seaward side of these islands, then in the morning alter course towards Whangarei his desired destination. Bill had his own idea and instructed me to steer a course directly towards the lighthouse on the northernmost island. I had some reservations about this directive, but he was the skipper and I felt compelled to obey his instruction.

If I did not appreciate it before, I soon came to realise that there is no perception of distance when one is journeying at night. Darkness came and we continued on this heading towards the flashing light. It never appeared to be getting closer and several times I suggested to Bill we change course and head out to sea. He would have none of it and insisted we hold our course. I was on the helm, frequently raising my head over the bulkhead to observe what was up ahead. Suddenly, I was shocked to see the dark outline of a rugged cliff face looming directly in front of our passage. We were almost upon it.

My survival instinct cracked into gear and without consulting Bill, I spun the wheel hard to starboard and steered a course to take us clear of the cliff face. The immediate hazard was dispelled, we were not yet out of danger. I was reasonably familiar with the layout of these islands, having cruised there four years prior, when as a guest on a friend's launch I spent a week participating in a big game fishing contest, but that is another story. I was conscious the southernmost island was somewhere close but I could not see it and ordered one of the crew to go forward and keep an eye out for it while we sailed clear of the main island.

I had now taken charge, Bill was standing speechless and the crew responded to my commands. Time seemed to stand still and for a while, the tension was immense, but finally, the southern island was sighted and we sailed on past it. When I was satisfied, we were well clear of all the islands, I handed the helm over to Bill and went below deck.

One of the girls followed me below to check out how I was. I was mentally, if not physically, exhausted. She brewed a coffee, gave me a cuddle, and thanked me for getting them out of a dangerous situation. There followed a moment of intimacy before I crashed into a deep sleep and remained in that state until morning.

It was daylight when I went up on deck. I had expected to see us well along the coast and near Whangarei Heads, but to my surprise, we were still in the vicinity of and to the east of the Poor Knights Islands. One of the crew later explained they had spent the rest of the night sailing round and round in ever-increasing circles to end up where we were.

That was not the end of the drama for it was as if Bill had lost his nerve and reasoning. It was now daytime and though we were not in any danger and making way under our own steam, he put out a Pan call on the radio to seek assistance. This is a distress signal, one down from the ultimate SOS. We didn't need assistance, we didn't get it, and he/we were admonished for making the distress call when we finally berthed at the wharf at the entrance to Whangarei Harbour.

So, came to the end of my first venture into sailing offshore. I came away thinking if I was going to fulfil that dream, it would have to be in my own yacht with a group of people I knew. Another lesson I learnt post-voyage voyage, it was the cyclone season in the Pacific and we had been heading into a tropical cyclone of the shores of Tonga. Maybe this was the reason Bill turned back and if it was, he did us all a favour. I am not sure we would have survived had we sailed on.

Drifting 1982–1984

Following the aborted trip out into the Pacific, I bought a plane ticket and flew to the USA with no great plan in mind except to visit places old and new and catch up with friends from the past. At this time, the major US airlines were offering foreign visitors (aliens they term us) unlimited travel within the US on each airline's network. For the sum of US$400, I purchased a first-class ticket with Northwest Air and over the next few months, I bummed around visiting places old and new—Los Angele, San Fransisco, Spokane, Chicago, Phoenix Arizona, Grand Canyon, Tombstone site of the legendary *Gunfight at OK Corral,* ending up in Nashville Tennessee where I found myself in a romantic liaison with Carol, a southern gal for several months.

There is more to this story and another Carol that I could expand on, including what drew me to Nashville, and what enticed me back there following my return home in August. There is also my nurse friend Carol, back in Chicago of whom I have mentioned earlier and a story to tell there is a story to tell, but I will let it pass for now.

Passing Time with Mum and Dad

I arrived back home in New Zealand in December and moved in with Mum and Dad in my boyhood bedroom at the family home in Pukatea Street, where I lived for the next fifteen months until I met and moved in with Sue in May 1984. I set about looking for work and was interviewed for a job as a project engineer with the Hurunui District Council in north Canterbury. However, the prospect of living and working in rural New Zealand did not appeal, but so keen was the council to hire me, I negotiated a contract assignment to peer review an irrigation scheme that had been designed and managed by a Christchurch-based consultancy.

The scheme itself was basically sound in concept—the construction of a series of large ponds on fifteen farms designed to syphon off river flows during high rainfall of the winter months to provide water during the arid spring and summer. Unfortunately, there was a problem, for none had been lined with impervious material and all of them leaked like sieves in the alluvial soils of the area. To me, it was common sense but when I brought this to the attention of the consultant, he took offence and vigorously defended his design.

This work gave me part-time employment over the next fifteen months. Typically, I would travel to Amberley and stay for two to three days, then return back to Wellington and write up my reports. It brought in a little coin and I learnt a lot about the politics of the situation. However, the leaks continued until long after my departure, another case of the big fish outmanoeuvring the small fry.

Much of the rest of this time, I spent in Eastbourne amusing myself by carrying out much-needed maintenance on the house and keeping myself in physical shape running along the coast road to Pencarrow and up and over the many Butterfly Creek tracks. This period was not a particularly happy time for me, marking time not knowing what I wanted to do workwise and otherwise. One positive thing I determined to do was buy an ocean-going yacht and satisfy my dream of adventure on the ocean blue.

Around North Cape, November 1983

One of my early heroes was aviator, sailor and adventurer, Sir Francis Chichester. Born in Devon, England, he migrated to New Zealand in his late teens, founded a number of successful businesses, then lost everything in the crash of 1929 and returned to England. For many that would be the end of a promising life. Not Chichester.

It was the pioneer days of aviation. He took up flying, purchased a de Havilland Gypsy Moth bi-plane and set off on a solo flight back to New Zealand. He got as far as Australia but mechanical troubles took hold, forcing him to disassemble the plane and ship it the rest of the way by sea.

Back in familiar territory, he set about preparing his plane for a solo flight back across the Tasman Sea. Knowing he could not carry enough fuel to complete a non-stop flight, he fitted his plane with floats and set off on a three-stage hop to Norfolk Island, Lord Howe Island, and on to Sydney. This was no easy proposition given the navigational aids of the day: a sextant, some charts, the sun and the stars. Using a concept of 'off course navigation', he purposely set a course to one side of his target islands, then zeroed in at a pre-determined time to minimise navigational error.

He successfully completed the crossing and using the same technique, he spent much of the decade hopping from island to island in the Pacific until World War 2 broke out.

Two decades later, he turned his interest to long-distance ocean sailing. Instigator and winner of the first trans-Atlantic single-handed yacht race in 1960, he almost repeated the feat in 1964, then in 1966/67, he made the first non-stop, solo circumnavigation of the world in a yawl he named Gypsy Moth IV. Sailing from Portsmouth to the South Atlantic and east to west on the southern oceans then back to England, he completed this voyage in two hundred and twenty-six days, an amazing feat of endurance, which truly captured my imagination.

During my globe-trotting days of the 1970s, I dreamed of taking part in the trans-Atlantic race, which had become a quadrennial event. Inertia, perhaps some inner sense, cautioned me against undertaking such a challenge, but the idea of going on an ocean cruise never left my mind. Back home in New Zealand and bored with my work, in 1982, I answered an advertisement in the NZ Herald and joined a motley crew on a voyage that promised to take us to Tonga and on to South America.

Three days out at sea approaching the Kermadic Islands, skipper Bill decided to abort the cruise and we turned back. I decided then that if I was ever to fulfil this dream, better in my own ship with a crew of my own choosing.

In February 1983, I contacted a yacht broker in Whangarei, then travelled north in search of a yacht I could take sailing on the ocean blue. He took me aboard several yachts and I soon singled in on Aegean, a 39-foot ferro-cement, Hartley design sloop. It was up for sale by its owner who had spent the past five years cruising around the Pacific with his wife and young daughter. Save an emergency life raft, it came fully equipped with all the gear I would need to fulfil my dream.

Smelling a potential deal, my friendly broker happened to mention his recent sale of a similar but slightly larger yacht of the same material. He went on to tell me that the owner had set off on an ocean cruise the previous year, but he abandoned the voyage and turned back, when one of his crew went crazy, claiming we were running onto rocks in the middle of the night.

"That's interesting," I said. "Was the skipper's name Bill?"

"Yes. Do you know him?"

"I certainly do. I was that crazy crewman. Would you like to hear my story?"

I left it there and returned to business. Aegean fitted all my requirements for an ocean cruising vessel, it fitted my budget and passed a mandatory condition survey. I made an offer and a deal was done.

Aegean was sitting safe and secure at a berth in the Quayside Marina, near the centre of town. I decided to leave there over the winter, return in the spring and sail it south. I returned to Wellington and made inquiries about a berth in one of Wellington's marinas. Nothing was available, so I directed my inquiries to Picton where I was able to secure a berth at a new marina in Waikawa Bay, recently opened and still under construction. I now had my yacht and a place to moor it. Now to bring it south.

I returned to Whangarei in August to go cruising in the Bay of Islands with my brother, Philip, and nephews, John and Robert, in tow. I wanted to get familiar with Aegean's intricacies before bringing it south. None had any sailing experience but this did not unduly concern me as I was confident in my own ability. Philip who worked as a meter reader was extremely fit and my nephews were talented sportsmen; John, a rock climber and mountaineer, and Robert excelled in football and badminton. They all quickly adjusted to life on the ocean wave.

As well as checking out Aegean's capabilities, this cruise proved a good opportunity to bond with my nephews. Both had grown up during my years abroad and I soon discovered their personalities were quite different. John, an extrovert, was extremely confident and took to sailing like a duck to water. Robert, five years younger, was more introverted and showed a reluctance to express himself. When circumstances demanded, both proved competent and good sailing companions.

After three weeks exploring the Bay of Islands, we returned to Whangarei, left Aegean secure at its mooring, and then drove back to Wellington.

Two months later, I returned to Whangarei and prepared for the voyage south. I needed a crew. Long-time friend Brian had expressed a desire to come along and flew up to join me. Together, we provisioned Aegean and I made it known through the local boating community that I was looking for two experienced crew to come along for the ride. Before long, Canadian Norm and English John, appeared and I signed them on.

I originally planned to go south down the east coast of the North Island, but every local I spoke to counselled against this. "Safer to go north and sail down the west coast," they all said. I decided to heed this advice and after three weeks of provisioning and making ready, it was time to set sail.

Day 1

The marina is located a short distance up the Hatea River which wends its way down to Whangarei Harbour through mangrove mud flats on both sides. The river channel is quite narrow and is subject to strong tidal flows on either side of high and low tides. To reach the harbour in a keelboat such as Aegean, it would be necessary to depart near full tide. When it came to setting sail, the favourable daytime tide was not due until the early afternoon and anxious to get moving, I opted for a nighttime departure at 2am in the morning.

This turned out to be not such a wise decision. While the channel is well marked with red and green navigation lights, my nighttime sailing experience was very limited and disaster soon struck.

The tide had turned and was ebbing strongly when we finally left the marina. A short way down the channel and in the darkness of the night, I inadvertently motored off course to port and we came to a sudden halt as the keel dug into the mud. I quickly put the engine in reverse and tried to back up, but to no avail. The tide was running too strong, we were stuck fast and would be going nowhere for the next twelve hours. My immediate instinct was to have Aegean settle on its port side and I got the crew to lean it over this way as it slowly settled on its side.

Now nothing to do but sit and wait. It was an embarrassing start and I felt a little sheepish as the morning came and I saw other vessels coming and going up and down the channel. However, I convinced myself it could have been a lot worse. By late morning, the tide was in full flood, Aegean slowly righted itself, I fired up the motor and we floated off back into the main channel. My crew seemed unperturbed by this incident and the rest of the afternoon, we motored on clearing Whangarei Heads in the late afternoon. With a steady wind blowing from the southeast, I set the sails, killed the motor, and set a course north along the coast towards the Bay of Islands and beyond.

Midway between Whangarei lies the Poor Knights Islands, some four miles off the coast. We passed them by as darkness fell. With memories of the misadventure of my previous passage in the area sharply on my mind, I wanted to stay well clear of land during the night hours. At this point, I split us into pairs and set up a four-hour watch routine for the remainder of the voyage, with English John and I taking the first watch from 8pm to midnight and rotating every four hours thereafter. A routine we maintained for the rest of the voyage.

At midnight, I called Brian and Norm on deck to take over for the next four hours. We were now passing by the Cavalli Islands and in the distance, I could clearly see the flashing light at North Cape. I altered course to a new setting to clear the Cape and was satisfied we would remain well clear of land; John and I went below for a well-earned rest.

I must have slept soundly for in no time at all it was 4am and John and I were back on deck to resume watch. When daylight arrived, there to the west was Great Exhibition Bay, where the French saboteurs were to creep ashore one year later and some ten miles in the distance lay North Cape.

Day 2

Mid-morning, we were sailing on a heading, which would take us just clear of the Cape. There was still a fresh wind blowing from the south-east and we were running before the wind in a lumpy sea. His caused Aegean to roll side to side, a natural motion in such conditions and the risk of an unintended gybe was ever-present. I was on the helm and it finally occurred. I saw it coming.

"Watch your head," I yelled, and those of us on deck immediately ducked as the heavy mainsail boom of the mainsail swung violently across from starboard to port. Fortunately, there was no damage to the yacht and I quickly brought it under control. However, at this very moment, Brian who had been down below was climbing the companionway and the sudden motion flung him onto the edge of the companionway door and hit it hard on his rib cage. He was in severe pain and went back below to rest, insisting that we carry on, he would be alright. My limited knowledge of rib injuries is that they are self-healing and after a conference with all the crew, we did just that, we sailed on.

At 11am, we reached the North Cape and changed course to sail across the top of the island. The wind strength had been decreasing during the past two hours and shortly after rounding the Cape it died completely, our sails were left flapping and we started to drift slowly with the current. Impatient to be clear of land at nightfall, I fired up the motor once again and we cruised across the top of the island on a calm sea. Soon, we were passing Spirits Bay, rounding Cape Reinga and in the early afternoon, I set a course 275 degrees on the compass, which would take us well clear of land.

Miraculously, and as if on cue, the wind started to fill in from the northwest and for the next thirty-six hours the sun shone during the daylight hours and the wind blew at a steady rate of 20 to 25 knots. These were ideal conditions for a heavy displacement yacht such as Aegean. Sailing on a broad reach, she ploughed through the waves with a graceful pitching motion getting up to speeds of 7 to 8 knots at times. It was an exhilarating feeling to be sailing out of sight of land in testing but not perilous conditions.

For a day and a half, I maintained this course and we sailed on and on out into the Tasman Sea, until the morning of the fourth day, I changed course and headed back towards the coast and with luck New Plymouth.

I am a self-taught navigator. I had none of the modern navigational aids and instead relied on a compass and sextant, ready reckoning and my instincts. Obtaining latitude positions north and south is easy. Take a noon-time sighting of the sun and measure the angle to the horizon, then it is a simple calculation to determine latitude. Calculating longitude is more complex and again requires a sextant reading and using a set of tables to work out one's longitude. I never really got to master the latter, but figured that I had fifteen hundred miles of coast to find and I was confident I would find it somewhere.

Days 3, 4 and 5

We were now some two hundred miles off the coast and I decided it was time the time to head back towards land. During the previous forty-eight hours sailing out to sea, I noticed my position as calculated from sextant readings was diverging from my ready reckoning position and though this caused me some confusion and doubts about my navigation, I did not let on with my crew. Instead, I cheerfully informed them that it was time to change course and head back to land.

Confident I had the correct latitude, we did a controlled gibe and I set a new course towards New Plymouth. It was a clear sunny day and during the morning, the wind died away and we started drifting once again. I soon got bored with going nowhere and fired up the motor once again so we could continue to make progress. Brian, who was recovering from his injury, put out a lure and before long he had hooked a large tuna, which he successfully landed. For the next two days, it provided a welcome change of diet from the canned meats we had been eating up until now.

There is something magical at sea out of sight of land watching the sun go down in the west. It is even more exciting watching it rise above the horizon the next morning. At noon, I had taken my sextant readings and calculated our position. As evening approached, I casually announced that we may see the top of Mount Egmont before the sun goes down. If not, in the morning it must certainly be there for us to see. When morning came, I was off watch and was woken by a stern call from Brian: "I think you should come up."

Up I went and I saw Brian was looking east with a smile on his face. I followed his gaze and sure enough, there was a tip of the mountain poking over the horizon. Uncertainty gone, I felt relief and satisfaction. My navigation had got us to where I wanted to be. During the morning, the wind filled in from the northwest. I killed the motor and we continued on under sail. More of the mountain came into view and by late afternoon, we were abreast New Plymouth and sailing down the south Taranaki Coast.

With night approaching and following my maxim of sailing clear of land in the darkness, it was time to change course and head back out to sea. I tacked around and set a new course in the direction of Farewell Spit.

Day 7

As darkness fell, I could see the flashing light at Farewell Spit in the distance. Four hours sailing at our present speed would take us halfway there, then a change of course at midnight in towards the Kapiti Coast would ensure we remained well clear of land during the night. And so, we sailed on. I remained on deck after midnight, we tacked about and I set a new course on a heading directly towards Kapiti Island. Satisfied that all was well, I went below for a much-needed rest. During the voyage, I came to consider this period from midnight to four in the morning the worst of the off-watch schedule.

One goes off watch in darkness and it still dark, when one returns back on deck. Insufficient time to get a good sleep, being woken prematurely, the chill of the night air and nothing to see, all of which I found a bit disconcerting.

Daylight came and there in the distance loomed Kapiti Island and to the south, Queen Charlotte Sound, our ultimate destination. With a steady 15-knot wind driving us forward, I altered course and headed directly towards for the latter. With identifiable landmarks in view, navigation became a lot simpler. At our current rate of progress, we would reach the entrance to Queen Charlotte Sound in the late afternoon.

At 6pm, we came abreast Cape Jackson the northernmost point at the entrance to Queen Charlotte Sound. It would take another five hours to reach the destination, the marina at Waikawa Bay. We cruised past Resolution Bay and Endeavour Inlet, favoured havens of Captain Cook, and on up the Sound. With the light fading and still two hours from our destination, I turned into the Bay of Many Coves, hooked onto a mooring and there we stayed overnight.

I was exhausted, both physically and mentally. I headed straight to my bunk and into a deep sleep for the next twelve hours.

Day 8

Morning came and my crew left me undisturbed for some time. Finally, Brian came with a cup of coffee and I stirred. Still tired, I managed to drag myself on deck and prepare for the short haul up the channel and into Waikawa Bay. We motored this last stretch and arrived at the marina shortly after midday. We were all tired and it seemed the easier option.

I found my marina berth, we made Aegean secure and there followed a mad scramble to gather our gear, lock up, and get to Picton in time to catch the afternoon ferry to Wellington. As we cruised home in the comfort of a much larger vessel, I had time to reflect on the voyage I had just completed. We had been seven days at sea and the responsibility for getting my yacht and crew safely home had been immense. The sailing had been second nature, my greatest satisfaction came from navigating and getting us to where I intended us to be.

We had survived some mishaps and overcome adversity. In the process had formed a bond among a small group of disparate individuals. On arrival in Wellington, we parted company. John I never heard from again, but Norm continued to correspond for several years after his return to Canada. As for Brian, he became a regular, often joining me cruising in Queen Charlotte Sound and on several trips across Cook Strait. Sadly, I have lost contact with Brian and the last I heard, he had retired to the Bay of Islands and living somewhere on a houseboat.

Postscript

My dad, Malcolm, had an interest in navigation and the sea. A few months later, I was discussing the voyage with him and the error that seemed to be creeping into my navigation when heading out to sea after rounding Cape Reinga. He pointed out to me that there is a strong current running from southeast to northwest which I had not accounted for and would explain the divergence from my sextant and ready reckoning calculations. Not too bad after all.

Chapter 7
Courting Sue

I met Sue in February 1984. We were introduced by our mutual friends, Tony and Cos. It wasn't so much a formal introduction, rather we were part of a small group of people most of whom I did not know who gathered on Friday evenings at the Royal Port Nicholson Yacht Club in Oriental Bay for an early evening drink and chat.

Tony was an old salt and sea dog, happily retired after a career as a merchant seaman and latterly an engineer with the Shell Oil Company. He built his own 34-foot yacht Archates and when he retired from the paid workforce, he passed many a day cruising on Wellington Harbour and in the Marlborough Sounds. Sue was a friend of Tony and on occasion would join him on some of these cruises as a part-time crew. Cos was my friend. We had been lovers back in the early 1970s and we had continued to see each other, whenever I was back in the New Zealand during my globe-trotting years.

I had my own yacht, a 39-foot ferro-cement cruising yacht Aegean, which I found in Whangarei and bought with the intention of cruising the Pacific to fulfil a long-held dream of sailing on the ocean blue. However, apart from a delivery voyage to Picton via North Cape, this dream never came to fruition. Sue became my centre of attention and I was soon to learn that ocean cruising was not on her agenda.

Initially, I took little notice of Sue. I was too wrapped up in my own world; bored with what I was doing in my life, seeking a change of direction but unsure of what that direction should take. Sue it seems had noticed me for it was she who took the initiative.

"I have met this interesting man at the yacht club but he has made no advances," she confided to her friend, Flo. "What should I do? Maybe I should talk to Tony and Cos and we can all go out to dinner somewhere."

"Forget Tony and Cos," said Flo. "You are a good cook, call him up, invite him for dinner, feed him and see what happens."

Sue phoned me the next week and the rest is history. Sue had not long moved into the house at 299 Karaka Bay Road, purchased with a low-interest loan under the government of the day first home buyer scheme. Right on the waterfront, seashore across the road, it was not unlike my family home in Eastbourne, where I was back living with my mum and dad, experiencing a mid-life crisis and trying to sort myself out.

The following Saturday, I arrived on her doorstep with a bunch of flowers and two bottles of wine. Sue welcomed me into her little bach by the sea; a single-story weatherboard house, tastefully decorated with some fine artwork and brimming with flowers. We drank two gins to break the ice, then Sue served up a delicious three-course meal. She had obviously gone to a lot of trouble and I quickly discovered that she was indeed a fine cook. It was apparent that the presentation of the food to be eaten was most important to her.

I have no recollection of the full menu but I do have an indelible memory of the entrée, a picturesque platter of raw oysters in their shells on a bed of ice. While I like most seafood, oysters raw or cooked do not appeal. Being our first date, I did not want to disappoint or make an issue of it and I devoured my share of the oysters. It took two more dinner dates and two more servings of the same fare, before I finally admitted that I did not like them.

During the following weeks, we continued to meet at the yacht club on Friday evenings, go out on dinner dates and to an occasional movie. I was enjoying her company and slowly coming out of my shell. Meantime, Aegean was sitting at its marina berth in Waikawa Bay, Picton. I had already planned an Easter cruise in Queen Charlotte Sound with Mum, Dad and Sister Jenny on board, and our romance flourishing, I invited Sue to join us. During the week prior to Easter, I gathered together provisions and on Thursday, we all boarded the interisland ferry to Picton.

From the ferry terminal, it was a short ride by taxi to Waikawa Bay, where we found Aegean sitting safely at its berth. We went aboard and everyone claimed a bunk; Mum and Dad up forward, Sue and I in the after bunk and Jenny was left to bed down in the main cabin. After drinks and a leisurely cooked meal, we retired for the night, each with his/her own individual thoughts on what lay ahead in the coming days.

Over the next three days, we cruised around Queen Charlotte Sound; visiting several small islands in the outer sound, fishing for blue cod still in abundance and anchoring up at night in one of the many bays that provide sheltered anchorage. Much as I enjoyed having my family aboard, I was looking to the end of Easter when they would go ashore and return to Wellington leaving Sue and I to continue cruising on our own. Monday came, we returned to Picton, and Sue and I waved them aboard the afternoon ferry bound for Wellington.

As the ferry pulled away from its berth, we gave them a final wave, jumped back aboard Aegean and followed the ferry, outward bound and on its way to Wellington. We followed the until it disappeared into Tory Channel. Sue and I continued on our way to the Bay of Many Coves where we moored for the night. At last, we're on our own.

When it comes to important decisions in life, I am usually very cautious in my approach. However, on this occasion, caution was thrown to the wind and suddenly, the other Michael appeared, the one I kept hidden deep down inside.

"Let's not mess around, let's get married," he cried out.

There followed a long silence, then:

"I will think about it."

For the next ten days, we continued sailing around Queen Charlotte Sound visiting many bays and coves, going ashore to gather muscles from exposed rocks, fishing for cod, and socialising with other boaties including Tony and Cos, who were cruising around in Archates. The weather was fair and we could find a secluded spot in a beautiful setting whenever we wished to be alone together. What could be more romantic? We did a lot of messing around.

It was as if a magic spell had been cast and sometime towards the end of the cruise and with no prompting from me, Sue quietly announced, "It's my dad, Jack's, seventieth birthday in May, come with me to Dunedin and I will give you my answer then."

We caught the ferry back to Wellington. Sue returned to her work at Radio New Zealand, I returned home to be with Mum and Dad earning my keep doing repairs and maintenance around their house and making occasional visits to Amberley, north of Christchurch where I was undertaking a technical audit for the Hurunui District Council on an irrigation project in the area.

It soon became apparent that Sue had melted and was ready to say yes to my proposal of marriage, but there were strings attached.

"I would have to get a proper job," she intimated. I soon discovered that for Sue, a proper job was one in the public service. When I mentioned that I was thinking of going back to university to study History or something, she gave me no encouragement. In her forthright manner, it was a job or nothing.

I was smitten and did not make an immediate issue of this demand. Instead, we continued to socialise with close friends, Sue would serve me scallops instead of oysters and we started making plans for our trip south to meet my potential in-laws.

Jack and Sue's mum, Ruby, had been visiting Wellington when Sue and I first met. I had already met Jack when out cruising on Wellington Harbour with Tony, Cos, and Sue. Ruby was an unknown quantity and for reasons known only to Sue, she kept me a secret from her mother. I was about to take a leap into the unknown.

The day of Jack's birthday celebration was approaching and together with Sue's sister, Deb, we piled into the red Cortina I was driving at the time, crossed to Picton on the Interislander and set off on the long drive south to Dunedin. As we drove south along the Kaikoura Coast and through north Canterbury, all I could hear was this non-stop chatter of these sisters about this tyrannical/bossy person I was soon to meet. It was enough to make me think; perhaps I should drop the sisters in Christchurch and head back to Wellington, but love won over and together we carried on to Dunedin.

It was early Saturday afternoon when we arrived at the Hannan homestead in Burkes, midway between Dunedin and Port Chalmers. I followed Deb and Sue through an open door and into the main lounge when I spied this larger-than-life woman sitting in a lazy boy chair, cane in hand, barking orders to a large throng of mingling guests. On hearing Sue's voice, she swivelled around and immediately set her eyes on me.

"Who are you?" She shouted over the noise all around.

"I'm Michael," I replied.

Then, Sue chimed in, "And we are getting married."

Sue claims she had never before seen her mother so speechless. Me, I was a little overwhelmed by all the activity that was going on as preparations for Jack's birthday were well underway and people, young and old, were roaming all around. I was introduced to several of the closer family friends, the most instantly memorable being Shirley La Hood and Mary Troop. Together with Ruby, they formed a larger-than-life trio dressed up in flowing gowns and costume jewellery. At some stage during the afternoon, I found myself sitting on a sofa beside Kay, wife of Sue's brother, Terry. She noticed my bemusement as I sat watching all the activity.

"Don't worry, Michael," she said. "Everyone talks around here, nobody listens. Just let it pass over and go with the flow."

So I sat there watching, until the place thinned out and only the immediate family remained. Jack seemed delighted that one of his daughters was at last about to wed. I was not so sure about Ruby.

Jack made his pleasure known the next day when he announced to his party guests, "You all think you are celebrating my birthday but I have a surprise for you. The real celebration is for Sue and Michael, who are getting married in the spring."

I remember little else of this visit except that I was warmly welcomed by all whom I met and was amused by the eccentricity of many. As for Ruby, she didn't seem quite the ogre I had expected. When we left for Wellington, I sensed she was warming to me and the idea of a wedding.

Back in Wellington, we went shopping for a ring for Sue and she selected a deep blue opal stone mounted on a rather delicate crown of white gold. I moved into Karaka Bay, we set about making plans for a spring wedding at Old St Paul Cathedral in Murphy Street, followed by a reception at Bowen House opposite parliament.

We were now into winter and apart from the occasional visit to Amberley, I had time on my hands. I set about reshaping the bank at the back of the house and laboriously constructing the terraced stone walls which have stood until this day. I set about making the wedding arrangements—booking old St Pauls for the ceremony and securing Bowen House for the reception to follow. A guest list was compiled, invitations sent out and liquor was ordered with strict instructions for delivery to precede the arrival of guests on our wedding day. Sue made her own arrangements for a wedding dress.

Together, we compiled a guest list of family and friends and I purchased a wedding ring for Sue. I had to wait ten years for one of my own.

As the day approached, Sue remained adamant that I should get a proper job, my meagre consulting work not being enough. I acquiesced and interviewed for a job at the Ministry of Works in its Water and Soil Division. An offer was made, I accepted the offer and agreed to start in November after returning from our honeymoon.

About a month out from the wedding, Sue and I had our first big argument over what radio station we listened to. Sue liked the classical music on concert FM, I preferred the pop music on commercial radio. It was a trivial matter, which I lost, but it did open my eyes to the differences in our make-up. She liked Beethoven, I liked Johnny Mathis. She liked theatre and the arts, I preferred my sporting interests. Sue was an avid socialist (her dad Jack was once a communist), I was a political conservative. Her mother Ruby described me as a capitalist with a conscience. Loquacious, Sue could walk into a room and attract people to her. She was generous to those she encountered and liked but could be curt in her comments about those she didn't. Forceful and forthright, she knew what she liked and what she didn't. I was quiet and reserved, tending to keep my opinions of others to myself. In spite of this, I sensed in Sue a certain vulnerability below the surface an anxious disposition she openly admitted. Could I cope and how would I survive in this relationship and not be swamped? I thought about calling the whole thing off.

Was it inertia or something else, I can't be sure. I had made a commitment and I was determined to see it through.